Miroslav Hroch
Anna Skýbová

ECCLESIA MILITANS

The Inquisition

ECCLESIA MILITANS

The Inquisition

Miroslav Hroch / Anna Skýbová

Dorset Press

Translated from the German by Janet Fraser

© 1988 Edition Leipzig
Second English–language printing
published 1990 by Dorset Press,
a division of Marboro Books Corp.,
1990 Dorset Press

Design Walter Schiller

ISBN 0–880 29–129–X

Printed in the German Democratic Republic

Table of Contents

Preface

The stakes at which the Inquisition's victims burned no longer smolder, but debate still rages about the Inquisition itself. For more than two hundred years, journalists and politicians have focused attention on the bloody and daunting institution, while scientific and pseudo-scientific controversy has continued as to the true moral responsibility for the unpardonable excesses. Modern historians researching its history reveal the underlying interplay of social and psychological forces, enabling them to propose more precise and detailed accounts of the political backdrop to the Inquisition.

It is not easy to compile a sober account of such an institution. Contemporary readers are both repelled and fascinated by the events of a time when their predecessors were fighting a losing battle for the right of freedom of belief. If we succeed in setting aside all our prejudices, there remains the problem of selecting from among the welter of historical data the essential and most significant elements. Even a book aimed at a broad general readership will find it difficult to present a balanced and even-handed picture of the history of the Inquisition.

For these reasons, then, we decided at the outset to forego a systematic historical account of the Inquisition. Our attention focuses instead on its activities at a time when persecution of unorthodox thought and belief was seen as a means of achieving unity of religious belief. This was the period when the people of Europe began to confront the problem of transition from the feudal order to capitalism. They were on the threshold of a new era in history.

The focus of this book, then, is the counter-offensive of the papal Church against encroachment by Reformation movements. This counter-offensive brought together what we now refer to as the Counter-Reformation and the Catholic revival. Starting from the Council of Trent, it continued until the final victory of absolutism in the second half of the 17th century. We intend to assess the significance of the Inquisition compared with the other means used by the Counter-Reformation movement from our basic premise that moral condemnation of the feared and hated institution by contemporary observers and historians has obstructed any objective account of its real impact.

The relationship between the Inquisition and the Counter-Reformation is an illuminating, though by no means exclusive, approach by which to examine the Inquisition itself. We also intend to shed light on its historical roots and on its success. An understanding of the underlying principles of the Inquisition, which crystallized during the Middle Ages, is essential for an understanding of its significance. The brief account given in this book should make it possible to draw a clear distinction between the old Inquisition and the new Inquisition of the Counter-Reformation.

IF A MAN DOES NOT ABIDE IN ME, HE IS CAST FORTH AS A BRANCH AND WITHERS; AND THE BRANCHES ARE GATHERED AND THROWN INTO THE FIRE AND BURNED.

John 15, v. 6

THE ROOTS
OF THE MEDIEVAL INQUISITION

On 11 November 1215, Pope Innocent III opened the Fourth Lateran Council; the unprecedented number of prelates who gathered in Rome lent it a special and solemn character. Even the kingdoms of Poland, Bohemia and Hungary and other, more distant states which had never previously been represented on councils had sent prelates. Unlike other, later major ecclesiastical gatherings in the 15th and 16th centuries, which sometimes met for several years, the Fourth Lateran Council met only three times and on each occasion completed its work within a month. The major rulings it issued were to influence the role of the Church for years to come, and represented a major intervention in the relationship between the Curia and the secular powers. The content of the council's decisions followed a specific pattern in most cases. Its work had been well prepared. Two years of preliminary negotiations had been distilled into a carefully formulated summary of basic positions adopted subsequently by the council. Moreover, Innocent III was able to use his theological and legal training, his political experience, his knowledge of contemporary Europe and his ambition in the field of Church interests to influence the council's decisions. His successors in the Holy See extended, consolidated and built on his foundations.

The council began its deliberations by considering the state of the Church at the beginning of the 13th century and the need to confront the growing threat of heresy. The proposals for reform focused mainly on the duties of the bishops, the need to fill diocesan vacancies within three months, the urgency of regular diocesan visits, the monitoring of the content of sermons in national languages and the supervision of preachers. The council also turned its attention to how the training of the clergy was organized and to the composition of diocesan synods and chapters-general of the individual monastic Orders. It further clarified ecclesiastical teachings and dogma, examined the content of the sacraments, and considered the duties of individual believ-

ers. It ruled that believers should attend confession and communion at least once each year, at Easter. Confession began to assume greater importance and became an increasingly significant instrument of control of religious orthodoxy. The fundamental principles of the distribution of holy relics and the supervision and organization of pilgrimages, along with other rulings, were revised, especially those aimed at stemming the spread of heresy. These measures were taken not only with the southern French Cathari and the increasingly popular Waldenses in view, but also with an eye to the heresy emerging in northern Italy. Thus the Lateran Council established the principles on which the subsequent activities of the Inquisition were to be based.

The church statutes initially introduced against heresy and in use until the 13th century had proved largely ineffective. Their shortcomings were discovered mainly by bishops in the front line of the struggle in southern France and in other parts of Europe. Practical experience showed that the persecution of heretics had to be stepped up and that new courts had to be set up for the purpose. The courts were to be administered by qualified churchmen instead of local bishops who were often unsuited to the task of delivering the harsh sentences dictated by the newly reorganized church legislature. The close dependency of the bishops on the local rulers also proved to be an obstacle; experience gained in southern France showed that feudal lords could not be relied on when it came to the harsh and uncompromising action needed against heretics, for not only had they failed adequately to persecute the Cathari, they had actually given them support. The placing of the courts of Inquisition outside the legislative powers of the local bishops and beyond the reach of secular powers was in later years to prove a shrewd move by the Curia. The sole instruction given to the bishops and secular rulers was to give all possible support to the Inquisition and to do everything in their power to carry out the penalties meted out by it.

Although the Roman Church engaged in the persecution and burning of heretics before the 13th century, a clear distinction should be made between what went on before this date and the beginning of the operation of the courts. Since the decline of the Western Roman Empire, any heretic had been subject only to church

law and church penalties, the severest of which was excommunication. But between the 11th and early 13th centuries, heresy was viewed increasingly as a capital crime.

The northern regions—the empire, Flanders, Lorraine, Burgundy and northern and central France

The Persecution of Heretics before the Papal Inquisition

—proceeded quite differently from southern Europe. In the north, heretics were subjected not only to ecclesiastical jurisdiction but also to the jurisdiction of secular rulers who began, albeit infrequently, to impose the death sentence in some heresy trials. Heretics were thus sentenced to be burned or hanged or to have all their property confiscated or to other penalties. In 1022, for example, King Robert of France had thirteen heretics burned at the stake in Orléans. This was the first case in France of the secular powers intervening against heretics. The sentence of burning had no prior basis in French law and the fact that the judgment is mentioned in contemporary sources indicates that secular rulers were intervening in heresy cases and were willing to implement the harshest penalty possible. Subsequently, seven women were condemned to be burned in Orléans.

In Goslar, too, around Christmas 1051, the State publicly condemned heretics to death. Unlike the French heretics, however, they were hanged in the presence of Emperor Henry III. Then, around the middle of the 11th century, a trend emerged for heretics condemned by the Church to be turned over to the secular arm for sentencing. During that time it was still unusual for the stiffest sentence to be imposed, but the frequency of the death penalty increased slowly during the latter half of the 12th century.

The development of events in the southern European regions, the Appenine Peninsula, the Iberian Peninsula and southern France was different in some respects. The heretics there were persecuted and in a number of cases condemned to death, even in the latter half of the 11th century. Contemporary sources give the example of an execution by burning in Milan in about 1030. The first heretic to be burned—Vilgard of Ravenna—came from the Appenine Peninsula. Between the late 11th and late 12th centuries, heretics were usually tolerated in these regions and only infrequently put to death. Excommunication and the confiscation of goods continued in the south because heresy was basically regarded as a grave church crime but a minor secular one. It may be that this "immunity" contributed to the spread of heresy in southern France and northern Italy up to the end of the 12th century. From the beginning of the 13th century, however, a consistent policy of persecution was implemented there, too, with penalties mostly of seizure of property, excommunication and exile. These proved entirely inadequate either to stamp out heresy or to prevent its spread. The first crusade in southern France against the heretics—the so-called Albigensian Crusade—took place in 1209. But subsequent developments gave church law the clout of secular law. Pope Innocent III had established the foundation for a strict persecution of heretics.

Dominicans and Minorites

The situation at the beginning of the 13th century may have taken the Church somewhat by surprise, but the dangerous criticism of the clergy was still at an early stage and the feudal system had become so strong that the Church was able to overcome the threats posed to it. It succeeded in glossing over all the growing contradictions and paradoxes, managing to adapt its own organization to the new circumstances. To do this it had, however, to find new, appropriate means of coming to grips with heresy. The solutions were in fact to be found within itself, and the Church was strong enough to use its power to its own advantage. Innocent III had already laid the foundations and the Fourth Lateran Council, in whose deliberations he did not take a full part, was to prove of monumental importance in the history of western Christianity. Among other rulings, it laid down the principles of the crusade against heresy.

On the question of church life and the struggle against heresy, there are parallels to be drawn between the 13th and 16th centuries. The outcome of the deliberations of the Fourth Lateran Council are reminiscent of those of the Council of Trent. In other respects, however, the Church's position was more favourable in the 13th century, especially as the Great Schism in western Christianity had not yet assumed its full significance. In the 13th century, too, the Church's basic principles against heresy were firmly established.

Innocent III's protégé, Cardinal Ugolino—later to become Pope Gregory IX—continued and completed the work started by Innocent. His clarification of the procedures to be followed against heretics was to become a reference point for all popes of the Counter-Reformation, and the extent of common ground shared by the Church in the 13th and 16th centuries is astonishing—councils, consciousness control, sermons, pilgrimages, canonization, new orders and, most especially, the emergence of the courts of the Inquisition.

After 1200, two Spanish priests—Diego, bishop of Osma, and Domingo de Guzmán—began to travel throughout southern France, fired by a calling to devote their energies to reforming the life of the Church. Both were dissatisfied not only with the behavior of the clergy but also with the level of awareness and understanding among the common people. Diego, a Castilian bishop who had been exemplary in the way he had administered his own diocese, longed to see other dioceses run in the same way, and so on his return from an unsuccessful diplomatic tour conducted in the service of the king of Spain, he altered his route. What he saw prevented his return to the king or his diocese. Together with the sub-prior of his chapter in Osma, the young and equally determined priest Domingo de Guzmán, Diego resolved to offer his services to Pope Innocent III. The two men were willing to give their lives in the service of the Church and offered to take the Word of God to the Kumans who inhabited the most easterly parts of the kingdom of Hungary. Innocent did not turn down their offer, but he did express surprise at their missionary zeal—he knew about the Kumans but did not at that time regard them as posing any danger to the Church. The pope's primary concern was, in fact, the threatening situation in southern France, in particular the fact that the Church had suffered one defeat after another in its struggle there against heresy. And so he directed Diego and Domingo toward Languedoc instead, on a journey that was to assure them a place in history.

Since Innocent III had taken office in 1198, several papal legates had been at work in Languedoc where they had undoubtedly made great efforts to counter and undermine the work of the heretics by means of sermons and public debate. Their efforts went largely unrewarded, however, and the heresy continued to spread, apparently in reaction to the legates' efforts. Innocent III knew that the lack of enthusiasm of local clerics—who were at odds with the Church's popular teachings—was a major factor in this loss of ground to the heretics. He exhorted the clergy and stepped up the sentences for heresy in the region, but nothing seemed to be effective—not the replacement of the clergymen, not the dispatching of additional legates, not even appeals for help to the secular rulers.

At the beginning of the 13th century, the count of Toulouse ruled large parts of southern France but the whole region was riddled with foreign enclaves. Until the 13th century, the region was characterized by the presence of fortifications and by its towns whose traditions reached back to antiquity. It was the home not only of the troubadours but also of the first translations of the Bible into the national language, which signified the special turn taken here by the development of Christianity.

Heresy was known to exist in the areas around Toulouse as early as the first part of the 11th century, probably as a relic of antiquity or resulting from the influence of Islam or heretical ideas from Byzantium. By the latter half of the 12th century, it was clear that there was something seriously wrong with church dogma in the southern regions. In Lombez, near Albi, a public debate was held in 1165 between the bishops and the Roman Church on the one hand and some Cathari *perfecti* on the other—it was primarily the Cathari against whom the two Spanish priests had been instructed by Innocent III to direct their efforts.

Not much is known of the nature and teachings of the Cathari. Their *perfecti* or "perfect ones" formed the clergy; they were dualists and drew a clear distinction between the material world, the domain of Satan, and the spiritual world, God's domain. They also drew a distinction between good and evil forces, preached a concept of God radically different from that currently taught, propagated a different understanding of the sacraments, and preached other ideas that make it rather difficult to classify them as a simple heretical movement. The roots of these teachings almost certainly go back deep into the development of thought not only in European antiquity (for example, the Gnosis) but also in Eastern teachings, such as those of the Paulicians and the Bogomils. The position of the *credentes*—the "believers"—was quite different. They formed the bulk of those who adhered to heretical ideas and revered the *perfecti*, whose perfection elevated them to the apostleship of the Old Church and whose way of life contrasted sharply with the feudal clergy and, indeed, the Church as a whole. Their impact among the common poor people was linked to their desire to return to the life-style and ideals of the Early Church. The Albigensians—who, like the Cathari, had taken their name from their center, the town of Albi—posed a threat to the Church in Europe at the beginning of the 13th century insofar as the feudal lords did not oppose or persecute them. In fact, some of them were themselves Cathari and they used Cathari teachings to seize the property of the Church. This finally brought together secular and spiritual powers in the first crusade against Christians whose aim was to bring the movement down. Along with the Cathari, the Waldenses were also active in southern France; they were the schismatics and, as it turned out later, they posed an even greater threat to the Church than the Cathari.

Peter Waldo was a wealthy merchant from Lyons. Waldo took the injunction in St. Matthew's gospel seriously: "If you would be perfect, go, sell what you possess, and give it to the poor, and you will have treasure in Heaven; and come, follow me" (St. Matthew, 19, 20). He sold all his possessions, put on the clothes of the poor and set out to preach. Unfortunately, he made an enemy of the Archbishop of Lyons who promptly excommunicated him, but Waldo refused to keep silent. He traveled as far as Rome, to explain his mission to Pope Alexander III, who welcomed him and had kind things to say about the "Poor of Lyons," a group of Waldo's followers which had formed in 1179. He would even have allowed Waldo to preach in public, but set one impossible condition—the consent of the archbishop. There was clearly no hope of the rich Catholic prelate allowing preaching that called for a return to the poverty of the Early Church, and persecution of Waldo and his followers began shortly afterwards when the next pope, Lucius III, had the "Poor of Lyons" excommunicated in 1184. The teachings of the group remained unaffected by these sanctions and in fact they became even more radical and critical. Waldo preached not only against the extravagance of priests and monks but also against church dogmas and their efficacy, of which he was highly critical. The "Poor of

Lyons," better known as the Waldenses after their founder, had to preach clandestinely but managed very effectively to spread their teachings throughout Europe. Soon the Lombardy section, which had come into being on the coattails of the northern Italian heretical tradition, became even more radical than its French counterpart. By the end of the 13th century, Waldenses were to be found not only in the inaccessible mountain regions but also in all the major towns of central Europe. The Cathari were wiped out and the Church believed it had thus swept away the last vestiges of the old, dissident European thinking. It did not realize the resilience of the Waldenses, whose monks had swelled through criticism of the Church, which they saw as a representative of the entire feudal system. Thus the Waldenses became the first heralds of the European Reformation in which the Church of Rome was to suffer a serious loss of standing and authority. The teachings of the two groups, Cathari and Waldenses, diverged but they shared a common enemy in the Church and were united in their self-defense against persecution.

When Diego and Domingo de Guzmán met the papal legates in southern France, they were dissatisfied with the modest success of their preaching. The retinue of priests with ostentatious wealth sat uneasily alongside the poverty of the Cathari *perfecti* and so the two priests followed Peter Waldo in foregoing material comfort and set off as beggar-priests dressed in white linen. Even so, they had limited success, and so in 1207 Diego returned to Osma to find others who shared his sense of calling. He died in Osma, however, and never returned. Domingo continued to preach alone in the dangerous and hostile surroundings, fired by a longing for martyrdom. His wish was never to be fulfilled, nor was he successful in his mission of conversion. The frustration of both these aims undoubtedly prompted his condemnation of the Languedoc region. Unfortunately, his real motivation lay more in a selfish desire for "eternal life and reward from God" than in true love for the people. At the same time, he began to found the first bases of his new preaching Order, whose adherents, like himself, took part in the crusade. The papal legates were, however, also far from idle. When, after warnings from the Church, the feudal lord and count of Toulouse, Raymond VI, was excommunicated on the consent of Legate Peter of Castelnau, the legate was murdered, probably on the orders of the count himself. This was on 14 January 1208 and sparked immediate papal action. Innocent III called for a crusade against the count of Toulouse and, knowing that unscrupulous men from all over Europe would want more than a mere promise of reward to win them for his cause, he promised a number of very specific benefits over and above the customary indulgences to those willing to join him. One was an amnesty on all outstanding debts. The French king, who at that time had his forces tied up elsewhere, handed over the running of the crusade to Simon de Montfort, a nobleman and an adventurer whose qualifications included a range of contemporary virtues such as cruelty, lack of discernment, greed and orthodox belief. The presence of a papal legate to head the crusade was suggested by Innocent III.

What followed—and continued until 1229 in this and other crusades against heretics—was in fact nothing much out of the ordinary. Europe had already seen and experienced cities defeated and destroyed, villages and fortresses razed, and women and children murdered, and this mayhem was to continue in increasingly sophisticated and horrible intensity. The crusaders made no distinction between Catholic believers and heretics. Events in the crusades were paralleled by the annexation of the entire area by France, which managed to benefit itself by incorporating regions in southern France. What was unusual for the time indeed was the vast number of burnings of those convicted of heresy. The main force behind the burnings, not only in Languedoc but also across Christian Europe, were the crusaders headed by the papal legates. The Church was adept at using theological arguments to defend its gruesome practices and for a long time employed them as the ultimate proof of its power; yet it became increasingly clear that this power was in fact very precarious.

Domingo de Guzmán had realized that if the Church was to be given lasting help, the activity of preachers had to be founded on deeper principles. Scholarship, knowledge of dogma, understanding and faith, zest for preaching and missionary zeal, together with a striving for martyrdom, could serve only one end—the elimination of heresy and thus the strengthening of the Church's authority. He also understood that the power of individuals was limited, so he soon transformed his group of zealous followers into a new Order.

The Dominicans, as they became known, actually had another title, the Black Friars or Order of Preachers (*Ordo Fratrum Praedicatorum*), which better expressed the mission with which they were entrusted by their founders. The rules of the Order had been approved by Innocent III. His successor, Cardinal Ugolino, who later became Pope Gregory IX, acknowledged the new Order's importance when he was able to use to the full its services and abilities. The Dominicans were none too popular in European society—a play on words was made with their name in the Appenine Peninsula and in central Europe, and they were mockingly referred to as *domini canes*, "the Lord's dogs." The small dog which formed part of the Order's insignia compounded this scorn. The dog was, in fact, part of the legend surrounding the life of St. Dominic whose mother was said to have dreamed shortly before his birth that she bore a dog instead of a child.

From the outset the Order, which was run along strict military lines, concerned itself primarily with preaching along with theological scholarship, knowledge of dogma and knowledge of the Bible. The main weapon against any doubters was a sharp, uncompromising intellectual rigor. Even in its early days it was successful in crushing heretics. It attracted outstanding preachers, primarily from among religious scholars who had successfully reconciled the apparently irreconcilable—faith and reason. The philosopher and scholar Thomas Aquinas, whose teachings were to support the Church for centuries, was a member of the Order. He died only fifty years after the Order's founder, in 1274.

The Dominicans' influence spread rapidly throughout Europe. When Dominic founded the Order in 1216, he had only a few followers; in 1221 on his death in Bologna (where he is buried) he left dozens of convents in eight provinces. Barely twenty years later, virtually every major town in Europe had its own Dominican convent, and the Dominicans rapidly established their own educational hierarchy, staffing faculties in all European universities. The hallmarks of the Order were its rigorous medieval scholarship and uncompromising orthodoxy in belief. It focused its activities particularly on areas where the Church was weak. The "perfection" of the Cathari and the Waldenses' knowledge of the Bible were the first alarm signals to the Dominicans. The members of the Order knew they needed to lead perfect, irreproachable lives even though the sins they sought to eradicate were relatively minor; for example, Dominic is believed according to legend to have confessed shortly before his death that he gained greater pleasure from converting attractive young women than from others!

The interpretation and dissemination of church dogma was of key importance to the Dominicans who feared that false teachings would otherwise gain currency. They had realized that there had to be a solid basis for preaching, teaching and even debate with the masses. To this end they began to use the lives of orthodox saints as exemplary heroes; the famous *Legenda aurea* by the Genoese Jacobus de Voragine is but one example. This account presents in simple form the temptations faced by saints, with scope for reference to local figures. The clergy could use the legend in preaching sermons and its dramatic style meant it could be read aloud. It was excellent propaganda material, and the fact that by the end of the 15th century not hundreds but thousands of copies of it were in existence proves its effectiveness and its popularity. The Dominicans did not serve the Church only as preachers, scholars, saints and martyrs but also as inquisitors. Dominic was canonized in 1234, the first of a series of saints from the 13th century who were rewarded for their efforts in the struggle against heresy.

Here again we can draw a parallel with the 16th century; towards its end there was a flood of "new saints" who had gained renown and recognition for their execution of various religious and ecclesiastical duties.

The Minorites—the Friars Minor—composed another Order whose services were appropriated by the Curia. The founder of the Order, St. Francis of Assisi, was born Giovanni Bernardone, a man of quite different talents than Dominic. This patrician's son from Assisi represented a different class of man from the Spanish nobleman. St. Francis (the "divine fool") played a central role in European history in the 13th century, and through him one understands the emerging middle-class mentality. He was not as simple as contemporary dignitaries of the Church would have us believe; his opposition to feudal society, his return to nature and to the simple life of the people, his humility before God and his fellow human beings, his charity and his calls for simplicity all expressed a very specific reaction to social conditions in the early 13th century.

In the literature on this period there is no lack of speculation as to what extent the French background of his mother and the pragmatic influence of his merchant father had on the development of his religious ideas. His views certainly caused a stir, not only in the small town of Assisi but also in the surrounding area and in the Church, which, given its experiences with the Waldenses, eventually accepted the teachings of his Order and used them for its own ends. Initially, there was some resistance. Francis, who led the life of a hermit, appeared before Innocent III unwashed, unkempt and with a beard, to ask for approval for his Order; the pope was understandably repelled. Francis's highly visible opposition to 13th-century society clearly betokened his immense scorn for that society. The pope had the young man thrown out, telling him he should go and join the "pigs." But Francis was soon back and Innocent III was shrewd enough to change his mind. He had realized that having a fanatic like Francis under his wing was preferable to letting him loose without any kind of control. Under the supervision of the papacy, the newly authorized Order turned its attention to direct support of the Church. Once again it was Cardinal Ugolino who recognized the potential as well as the danger of the Minorite Order. He was astute enough to see that he could use the Order for his own ends; his efforts to merge the Dominicans and the Minorites into one Order remained unsuccessful, however, for the two Orders were simply too diverse. While the Dominicans based their teachings on reason and knowledge, the Minorites appealed to the emotions, especially love. But in the mid-13th century the two Orders collaborated on a special project, the task of running the newly created courts of Inquisition which had been entrusted to them jointly by Pope Gregory IX, thereby continuing the work of his predecessors. It is worth noting in passing that the hostility of the two Orders for each other was so great that they were constantly making mutual accusations of heresy. The Minorites are even suspected of having accused the greatest of the Dominican thinkers, Thomas Aquinas, of heresy. The rules of the Inquisition itself eventually put a stop to this internecine feuding.

The two Orders took an equally fanatical view of their services to the Church, but from the outset there was a crucial difference regarding the spread of heretical thinking in the convents of the two Orders. It could be argued that the Dominicans produced heretics only in isolated cases, whereas the Minorites had always tended to ignore certain church regulations, although they were not allowed in their preaching to touch on any fundamental church dogma. But soon things went even further. Entire groups of Minorite origin such as the Italian Fraticelli turned to heresy and had to be per-

secuted vigorously by the Church. While St. Francis at least recognized the hierarchy of the Church, the Fraticelli did not, and so were guilty of overt heresy. Francis died in 1226, and was canonized only three years after his death. The versatile but volatile Order, in a constant state of flux, spread rapidly across Europe.

Both the Minorites and the Dominicans soon had convents in virtually every major town of Europe, although later the Minorite convents were subsumed by Franciscan or other convents. Both Orders were urban-based but primarily mendicant, and their members were not permitted to own any property. This enforced poverty distinguished them from other older Orders and also left them free to earn a basic living in the service of the Church and of the faithful. This work earned them their bread and no more—although this was soon to change.

The Courts of Inquisition—Origins and Procedures

Innocent III imposed penalties on any practices of the clergy that represented a departure from the rules of the Church even in questions of minor importance, as illustrated by his dispatch of the prelates in southern France, although he knew from his legal training that this move would only be effective in punishing those guilty of disciplinary offenses, but not heresy.

Existing canon law was wholly inadequate for the persecution and punishment of heretics. At that time, a church trial was set in motion on the basis of a charge made under old Roman law. After that, legal processes could be initiated and the prosecutor had to prove the guilt of the accused. As a trained lawyer, Innocent knew how to apply the general principle that the accused could be punished on the grounds of a denunciation—*per denuntiationem*. Prior to the early 13th century, however, the bishops had tended only to impose penances on those who had been denounced, without actually initiating a trial. After Innocent III there came a split in the legal procedures: Denunciation could result either in a conventional trial with a charge or in a completely new procedure, an Inquisition. These new Inquisitions were totally different from any existing ecclesiastical legal procedures and were to be used first and foremost for trying and sentencing heretics. The Latin verb *inquiro* means "I investigate" or "I examine," and the term *inquisitio haereticae pravitatis* signified the examination of alleged heretical practices.

The judge presiding over such procedures found himself in a very different position to that of earlier judges. When a charge or a denunciation was made, the initiative came customarily from the court; in the case of Inquisitions, however, it came from the judge himself. He heard not only the denunciation but also the accused's statement, and he accused, tried and sentenced him. The powers of the inquisitor were unlimited and

unprecedented, a departure from both secular and canon law. The accused had to conduct his own defense and prove his innocence, which was frequently difficult since the verdict on his "guilt" lay in the hands of one person—the accuser and inquisitor. In addition, the main role of the inquisitor was to extract a confession from the accused, and he had all the necessary means to do this at his disposal. The Church soon resorted to torture to elicit confessions, even of trumped up charges, although it had already abolished the practice of "divine condemnation" and ordeals. Sentences passed at Inquisitions were completely illegal yet extraordinarily effective. Those unfortunate enough to fall into the clutches of the Inquisition never escaped. One such victim made a poignant assessment of his position thus: "quod beati Petrus et Paulus ab haeresi defendere non possent, si viverent, dum tamen inquiretur cum eis per modum ab inquisitoribus observatum" ("not even the Apostle Peter and the Apostle Paul, if they were alive today, would be able to defend themselves against a charge of heresy under the sort of examination carried out by the Inquisition"); quoted from P. Hinschius: *Das Kirchenrecht der Katholiken und Protestanten*, Berlin, 1893, p. 492).

This is hardly surprising, given that the inquisitors were soon granted very extensive rights and powers to which they persistently clung, claiming that these derived directly from God, who had been first inquisitor when he threw Adam and Eve out of the Garden of Eden. Obviously if the powers of the courts of Inquisition had been restricted to the clergy and had not been extended to the whole population, they would not have assumed the proportions and influence that they did. Toward the end of the 12th and beginning of the 13th centuries, secular potentates were realizing that they were themselves threatened when they uttered heretical

17

Page 17:

1 Pope Innocent III (1198–1216) is one of the most famous medieval Roman popes. He was responsible for the reorganization of church legislature and jurisdiction and extended the network of the courts of Inquisition. He devoted the main thrust of his efforts toward the struggle against the heretics in southern France.
Fresco by an unknown master, 1228. Sacro Speco, Capella S. Gregorio, Subiaco.

2 In the Middle Ages, Milan was one of the major centers of North Italian heresy. Public burnings of heretics took place here as early as 1034.
Basilica di S. Ambrogio (11th or 12th century).

3/4 The Church was always symbolized by a female figure wearing a sovereign's robes. "L'Eglise," stone sculpture in Notre Dame, Strasbourg (left) and "Ecclesia," Bamberg Cathedral (right).

5 According to legend, this orange tree was planted by St. Dominic himself. Chiesa di S. Sabina, Rome.

6 The fortress and the town of Carcassonne were a major center for the southern French Cathari in the early 13th century. During the Albigensian Crusade, the town was destroyed and its inhabitants were persecuted and killed by the crusaders, regardless of whether they were Catholics or Cathari.

7 Domingo de Guzmán, later St. Dominic (1170–1221), was a major figure in the struggle against the southern French heretics. As founder of the Order of the Friars Preachers (the Dominican Order) he also laid down the procedures to be followed in Inquisition hearings.
"The Life of St. Dominic." Painting by S. Lescadio. Museo Provincial de Bellas Artes de San Carlos de Valencia, Valencia.

8 St. Dominic was buried in Bologna. The
section of his sarcophagus depicted here
shows him during the trial by fire to find out
the orthodoxy of the content of books and
other writings (according to legend).
Relief by Niccolò Pisano in S. Domenico,
Bologna.

9 The Dominican Order produced a number
of leading Catholic theologians, the most
eminent of whom was Thomas Aquinas
(1225–1274). Detail from the allegorical representation of the Catholic faith by Andrea da
Firenze depicts him with three heretics,
Sabellius, Averroes and Arius, at his feet.
Capellone degli Spagnoli in S. Maria Novella,
Florence.

OPTAU
ET VAT
Ê M SEN
SUS.ET
IUOCADI
CUERIT

IME SÎS
SPIE ET
PPOSUI
ILLA RE
GNIS ET
SEDIRUS

S IOHES EUAGLISTA

S MATHEUS EUAGELI

10 "St. Dominic praying." Spanish high relief dating from the 16th century.
Středočeská galerie, Nelahozeves.

11 St. Francis, whose real name was Giovanni Bernardone, was a merchant's son from Assisi. His mother came from Provence, an area where many Cathari and Waldenses lived. This led to considerable speculation as to whether it was the French milieu that influenced the subsequent views and beliefs of St. Francis.
"St. Francis standing between Angels." Chiesa de S. Maria degli Angeli, Assisi.

S ANTONIVS · · S FRANCISCV

12 Following St. Francis of Assisi, other members of the Minorite Order were soon canonized, including Anthony of Padua. "St. Anthony of Padua and St. Francis." Fresco by Simone Martini. Chiesa di S. Francesco, Assisi.

13 The seal of Emperor Frederick I. Státní ústřední archiv, Prague.

14 Emperor Frederick I (1152–1190) in the year 1184 issued special laws aiming toward a joint operation of secular and ecclesiastical powers to combat heresy. Miniature from the Schäftlarn Monastery. Biblioteca Apostolica Vaticana.

15 Around the mid-14th century, the
Church had reached the zenith of its power.
The painting "La Chiesa Militante e Trio-
fante" (the militant and triumphant Church)
by Andrea di Buonaiuto (1369) symbolizes
the Church's secular and spiritual power and
its direct link with Christ.
Capellone degli Spagnoli in S. Maria Novella,
Florence.

16 Although the Staufers were engaged in a bitter struggle with the papacy, their interests coincided with those of the pope when it came to the persecution of heretics. The culmination of this union of interests came with the passing of the laws by Frederick I's grandson, Emperor Frederick II (1212–1250). Golden seal of Emperor Frederick II.
Státní ústřední archiv, Prague.

17 A lead bull of Pope Innocent III, dating from 1205. The seal was used to authenticate a document in which the pope gave over lands to a monastery—that is, intervened directly in local affairs.
Staatsarchiv, Dresden.

18 Clement V (1305–1314) received his appointment as pope through the influence of the French Crown. It was at his order that the Order of the Knights Templars was dissolved and its members persecuted.
Bull of Clement V. Státní ústřední archiv, Prague.

19 Bull of Pope Clement V, announcing to the kingdom of Bohemia the dissolution of the Order of the Knights Templars and the way in which the assets of the Order were to be disposed of.
Státní ústřední archiv, Prague.

20 Joan of Arc was burned on 30 May 1431 in Rouen. Only a few years after her execution, in 1436, she was rehabilitated and ultimately declared a saint as well as the national heroine of France.
Bibliothèque Nationale, Paris.

21 The trial of Joan of Arc was the most famous Inquisition trial in France during the Hundred Years' War. Joan of Arc had successfully led the French army against the English. The girl who had visions and claimed to hear the voices of saints speaking to her, fell easy prey to accusations of witchcraft. The Sorbonne was involved in her accusation and sentencing. A page from the account of the heresy of Joan of Arc.
Bibliothèque Nationale, Paris.

33

23 "Cardinal Don Fernando Niño de Guevara." Painting by Domenikos Theotokopulos,
known as El Greco, dating from around
1600.
Metropolitan Museum of Art, New York.

22 On 1 January 1492 Isabella of Castile
(1474–1504) and her husband Ferdinand of
Aragon (1479–1516) triumphantly entered
the Alhambra in conquered Granada, whose
town walls had been besieged by Christian
troops since the spring of 1491. In November
of the same year, the last Granadian emir,
Boabdil, súrrendered to the conquerors. The
conditions for the surrender of Granada were
moderate with regard to questions of faith and
belief. However, the "unbelievers" in the city
were warned by the fact that, when she entered the city, Isabella was accompanied by
the Grand Inquisitor. "The Conquest of
Granada." Painting by Pradillo Senado,
1643.
Prado, Madrid.

24 "Baptism of the Moriscoes."
Relief by F. de Borgoña. Main altar in the Capilla Real, Granada.

25 The Spanish king and queen
attached so much importance to
the annexation of the Emirate of
Granada to their sovereignty that
they had the family vault, which
they originally had intended for
Toledo, built in Granada. Their
children lie buried here alongside
their parents.
Capilla Real, Granada.

opinions and criticized the Church. They responded by backing church policies with the full weight of secular punishment. Hence the feudal powers, and in particular the emperor at its head, sought to couple the Church's severest penalty, excommunication, with its own, the death sentence (thus blasphemy could be interpreted as implied criticism of the secular powers). And it was only this statutory joining of the two forces, Church and State, in sentencing that gave the courts their extensive and generally unchecked powers. The role of the Church was to identify the heretics and condemn them as dangerous. On the basis of that condemnation—but without verification of it—the State would then take the charge before a court of Inquisition and, if the accused were found guilty and excommunicated, also execute him.

It is impossible to describe all the milestones in this evolution, but it should be pointed out that the Hohenstaufen emperors (who were, incidentally, great opponents of papal power), played a key role. In 1184, Frederick I passed a special law in Verona, under the influence of the papacy, to check the spread of heretical sects throughout Lombardy. Heretics were to be persecuted by secular jurisdiction, enabling the Church to impose secular punishments, including confiscation of property, a bar on trading, or even the dissolution of the episcopal palace in towns where heresy was widespread.

An important element in the combination of secular and ecclesiastical interests was a decree passed by Frederick II in 1220 on his coronation as emperor. It concerned the adoption of church procedures against heretics by the State, and its significance lay in the fact that no secular ruler could persecute a heretic without the involvement of the Church. It was several years before the Church was able to usurp the power of the courts for itself. Frederick's decree was implemented initially in Italy—hesitantly at first and only under pressure from the Dominicans in Rimini. But by 1224 the statutes of Brescia incorporated a statement of obligation to persecute and accuse heretics: "Secundum leges et iura imperiali et canonica et specialiter infra scriptum legem d. Friderici imperatoris et secundum eius tenorem. . ." ("in accordance with the laws of the State and of the Church, in particular the law passed by the Emperor Frederick. . ."; quoted from P. Hinschius: *Das Kirchenrecht der Katholiken und Protestanten*, Berlin, 1893, p. 348).

Pope Gregory IX had this wording incorporated into the Papal Registers in 1230 and 1231, and so it became a general regulation, to be carried out by the Church and adopted by all the secular powers. The regulations concerning papal Inquisitions gave them the general protection of the emperor and contributed to their expansion not only throughout Italy but also throughout Catholic Europe.

Even at this relatively early date the Church had begun to extend its use of excommunication to cases other than of heresy. Since Honorius III, excommunication had been used in cases of infringement of church liberty, including attacks on church property or its confiscation, arrest of the clergy, and so on.

By the mid-13th century the courts of Inquisition had become an established institution, and by the end of the Middle Ages its procedures were known and implemented everywhere, although the scope of the Inquisition had been modified in some areas by the local secular authorities. From the 1230s, the Dominicans bore the bulk of responsibility for the Inquisition, joined in the 1240s by the Minorites. Other Orders, however, were also involved in the work of the Inquisition. For a long time there was uncertainty as to whether the pope could nominate inquisitors alone or whether he required the approval of the head of the Order concerned. Certainly the secular clergy and the clergy belonging to religious Orders (unless specifically exempted), all Christian princes and all their subjects and officials were subject to the courts of Inquisition. The latter group was never granted exemption, and all possible verdicts could be passed on them even *post mortem*. The only groups exempted from the scope of the courts of Inquisition were the pope, the bishops, the papal legates, the officials and of course the inquisitors themselves, provided that they had been appointed by the pope himself or by the head of an Order.

As already indicated, the courts of Inquisition had unlimited powers. Only the pope, his legates or a general church council could reverse a decision. The accountability of the courts of Inquisition to the local authorities—the bishops—was somewhat more complex; in 1231 the courts of Inquisition functioned independently of the local bishop. But this proved to be unworkable as far as ecclesiastical practice and the relationship of the Church to the local secular authorities was concerned. So the Council of Vienne, meeting under Pope Clement V, decided to rule on the relationship between the bishops and the courts of Inquisition. It was deemed necessary that the episcopal court should agree with the courts of Inquisition on the arrest and torture and confirmation of the final sentence passed on the heretics. In fact, this ruling did not in any way limit the powers of the Inquisition.

As the main task of the papal Inquisition was to eliminate heretics, anyone who knew anything at all about the spread of heresy was required to come to the inquisitors. It was the duty of all to support the Inquisition, to keep it informed and to seek out witnesses. This applied to all the clergy, from the bishops' officials down to the pastors, to the secular rulers and their staff, and indeed to all Christians.

The task of the inquisitors was not only to seek out and punish the heretics, but also to convert them to orthodox thinking and belief. An inquisitor lost his legal powers only through death, appointment as a bishop or other promotion, or the stripping of the office. Inquisitors could impose any canon sentence, including excommunication, and the power to do this extended to all secular and religious persons unless specifically exempted. Over time, the inquisitors also gained the right to grant indulgences, to exonerate a suspect of heresy (except in cases where the pope himself intervened, such as misuse of benefices) and to free someone of interdict. They were also empowered to give absolution to crusaders, to read mass during times of interdict and so on.

The appointment of the first inquisitors for southern France led to the establishment of rules relating to their character and person. They had to have a fanatical devotion to the Church and to be convinced of the singularity and vital importance of their calling. They also had to have theological training (like the Dominicans) and to be diligent and above corruption. Among their number were some whose cruelty verged on sadism, a judgment supported by the requirement on the presence of the inquisitor during torture. Although the view medieval man had of corporal pain differed from our contemporary attitude, only designated individuals could witness the punishment inflicted on a fellow human being.

The attitude of the inquisitor to his own life was also important; his life was unusual in that it was spent "in God's service" and this meant a low view of material goods as well as of the lives of those condemned to a gruesome death for the sake of their afterlife. A number of inquisitors were themselves victims of murder. Petrus of Verona, a Dominican, was one victim who was later canonized and in whose dubious honor a religious brotherhood was founded to accompany condemned heretics to their place of execution. Other examples include Konrad von Marburg, a German whose harsh and cruel work soon found a vengeful echo in his own violent death, and others murdered in France and the Bohemian kingdom. Although the inquisitors aroused some opposition and resistance among the common people, their fanaticism enabled them to wield power by the fear of eternal damnation and a fear that the very presence of heretics meant misfortune. Their unlimited powers meant that the inquisitors were feared, if not universally respected. But they were also lonely and isolated.

There is an outstanding portrait by El Greco which conveys an enormous amount about the character and appearance of an inquisitor, and though it dates from the 16th century, there is no reason to assume that the appearance of earlier inquisitors was any less austere. Clearly, then, the inquisitors needed the special protection of the church administration. Anyone attacking an inquisitor or a court of Inquisition could expect to be brought before the court and dealt with harshly.

The inquisitor could have a deputy appointed by the pope and qualified to carry out his duties. He also had available the services of a notary and of consultants (mostly theologians) to advise him. But the inquisitor was under no obligation to consider their advice. Finally, he had a number of officials directly beneath him, who presented cases and did other work on his behalf. These included prison governors and the inspectors who took charge of confiscated property and money. The officials in charge of confiscated property kept a record of costs and would sell off part of it if necessary to cover the expenses incurred by the accused in meeting the cost of imprisonment and trial.

All Inquisition officials, from the most senior to the most junior, had to be respectable in the eyes of the Church, come from decent and irreproachable families, lead orderly and decent lives, be able to speak Latin, and not be related to any other officials. When they took up office they had to take an oath of allegiance and swear that they would keep confidential everything they saw and heard in the execution of their duties. They were not permitted to accept gifts from other officials or share in the goods and money confiscated from the accused. Their only payment was their official salary.

There was no official appeal against the courts of Inquisition, and the highest advisory authority was of course the pope himself. It soon became necessary to release the pope from the onerous task of administering the work of the courts and, in 1262, Urban V appointed Cardinal Orsini as the Grand Inquisitor—*inquisitor generalis*—to rule in difficult cases. The post was occupied until 1294, but was later revived again by Pope Clement VI.

The courts of Inquisition and their officials were mostly paid out of public finances, and often received a share in the assets confiscated from a heretic. Individual countries adopted different practices on this: in Italy, for example, the courts received up to two thirds of the property confiscated; elsewhere they received a flat-rate cash sum.

What were the crimes and offenses that were tried and punished at these investigations? The courts were, of course, working toward the elimination of heresy, and so their job was to assess whether papal dogma was being taught correctly and in line with Christian teachings and also to rule on what constituted heresy. Thus they became involved on the mere suspicion of heresy. Their primary function was to demonstrate and prove heresy and to distinguish between blasphemy, abuse of the sacraments, and false teaching on baptism, on the Eucharist or on consecration. The courts were also empowered to punish offenses such as the falsification of Inquisition documents; usurpation of the Inquisition; attacks on the Inquisition itself or the inquisitor; failure to comply with the rulings of the Inquisition; misuse of the oath to the Inquisition and alleged or deliberate false witness to a court. In addition, the courts could prosecute anyone who had been excommunicated for more than a year or anyone who possessed, read or propagated banned books. If it could be proved that a person had attended a burial or any other Christian ceremony held for a heretic, then that person could be summoned before the Inquisition, as could those who had neglected religious duties. Anyone who had served the papal Schism was also brought before the court of Inquisition, including all the individual counter-popes themselves. Backsliders or apostates formed a special group, including those who had deviated from the rules of their Orders. In any given district it was the judge's task to bring all suspects before the Inquisition, and it was the duty of all secular persons and clergymen to bring to his attention known heretics or suspected ones. It then fell to the clergy to publicize the Inquisition's rulings.

The trial began when a person was denounced and arrested for heresy or for the merest suspicion of heresy or for his sinful public reputation—*publica fama*. In contrast with other legal procedures, the denouncers or witnesses were kept secret. The inquisitor assumed also that the family and immediate neighbors of a suspect were themselves under suspicion. The denunciation, often anonymous, and the summons to the court were always followed by a ten-to fifteen-day period of grace during which the suspect was expected to recant. If he failed to do so, he was arrested and trial procedures were begun. Witnesses were heard first, and those who spoke in defense of the suspect came immediately under suspicion of heresy themselves. All witnesses were under oath to tell the truth. Trials were generally kept short, with some notable exceptions. It was not always easy to extract the required confession, and so in 1252 Pope Innocent IV issued the *Ad Extirpanda* Bull, which permitted torture. The bull was based on the *Codex Justinianus*, which laid down that torture was permissible in cases of *crimen laesae maiestatis* (lese-majesty) or treason, and hence sanctioned use of torture where royal majesty was under attack. The forms of torture used often in Inquisition trials were broadly the same as those used in medieval times. In general, torture was used only once, and in some cases a doctor helped the victim. Unlike the secular courts, which also resorted to torture, the main purpose of the Inquisition in torturing a suspect was to extract a confession of guilt from him, not to kill him. Having confessed, he could then be given an appropriate sentence, one which would serve as a deterrent and a warning. In practice, the inquisitor was present throughout the torture, primarily to ensure that it was kept a secret.

It would be mistaken to assume that the sentences meted out by the Inquisition were all equally severe or were all for the maximum penalty—death by burning.

Sentences varied, in fact, according to the gravity of the offense committed. In cases of calumny, the accused was forced to retract his calumny and was then rehabilitated. "Slight suspicion"—*levis suspicio*—also involved retraction and relatively mild penance. Punishment was harsher in cases of "serious suspicion"—*suspicio vehemens magna*—but even here, the suspect could get off with his life and a stringent penance provided that he recanted. The consequences were more severe at the third level of accusation, that of *suspicio violente*, "very grave suspicion." These suspects were either true heretics or recidivists. The accused could be condemned to wear a yellow cross on his robes in public, as a sign of his shame, for a fixed period, or he could be required to exhibit himself to public view at a specific spot by the church door on feast days, for humiliation. He could also be condemned to imprisonment for any period up to life. He received such penalties only if he expressed his willingness to recant. If he refused, he was turned over to the secular arm for execution.

The death penalty was given in cases of public and clandestine heresy. Those who could be proved to have engaged in heretical acts on more than one occasion could be sentenced to death, even if they recanted. The inquisitor assumed in such cases that the previous publicly expressed repentance had not, in fact, been sincere. Furthermore, anyone whom the inquisitor suspected of recanting merely to avoid death at the stake automatically incurred the penalty. If the accused repented of his heresy but was not sufficiently penitent, he could be sentenced to life imprisonment on bread and water, a sentence that was applied often to clergymen, even if they repented. Life imprisonment was a truly terrible punishment, and in many ways was no better than the death sentence. The prisoner was kept in complete isolation from the outside world, often in chains. If a death sentence were passed, the judge and his consultant pronounced the judgment in the prison, the Church disowned the heretic, and the prisoner was then surrendered to the secular authorities for execution. At the place of execution, the inquisitor would preach a short sermon while the fire was readied. If the person under sentence were a member of the clergy, he was deprived of his ordination and officially condemned, then publicly surrendered to the secular powers before the sentence was carried out.

It was not long before these medieval executions of heretics became monstrous public spectacles. The convicted prisoners, wearing the heretic's robes of shame, would be led through the streets or brought on a cart to the place of execution as a public warning, amid mocking and jeers.

Burning, which was the most common form of death penalty for heresy in the 13th century, was a dreadful death with a symbolic significance, and was used to show that the Church was avoiding actual bloodshed (although it was, of course, the secular authorities who were responsible for the actual execution). At certain periods, and in regions where the Church was under particularly severe attack, the maximum sentence was often imposed upon entire groups of people.

The less severe sentences covered a broad range of penalties over which the judge had discretion. As well as enforced wearing of special robes, heretics could often be required to participate in pilgrimages which were made more difficult by humiliating penances. Their property was always confiscated and secular and clerical privileges and honors were negated partially or wholly—in other words, the heretic was stripped of his rights as a medieval citizen. Initially, the houses of convicts were destroyed, but the courts later realized that greater advantage was to be had from the property.

One singular aspect of the Inquisition trials were those held of persons who were already dead and whose remains were in some cases exhumed and burned. For example, if it transpired during a trial that some dead person had actually been a heretic, then his bones would not only be exhumed and burned after being "sentenced," but his family was forced to pay the material penalties on his behalf and could in fact be stripped of all their possessions.

It also happened in some cases that those suspected of heresy did not actually appear before the court of Inquisition. These people were sentenced *in absentia* and their trial was carried out *in effigie*. The customary sentences were imposed on the accused, pending his eventual arrest, and in some cases he was also burned *in effigie*—that is, an effigy of the accused was burned instead.

Inquisitions throughout the Roman Catholic world were run along these lines, although there were certain procedural differences resulting from national customs. The degree of consistency in procedures is most vividly demonstrated by the number of Inquisition manuals still in existence, and which were used not only in the Middle Ages but also during later Inquisition trials.

When the Inquisition had been in force for almost one hundred years, the inquisitor of Toulouse and subsequent Bishop of Lodève, the Dominican Bernard Gui, wrote a handbook sometime after 1323 and based mainly on his experiences, *Practica inquisitionis haereticae pravitatis*. Gui was a tireless inquisitor whose wide experience had been gained in the south of France, an area marked by the activities of the Cathari and Waldenses. His work produced not only the handbook mentioned above, but also a catalog of Inquisition rulings issued under his jurisdiction in Toulouse between 1307 and 1323. It includes rulings of heretics to be executed, and those of six others whose bones were to be exhumed for burning.

Gui's handbook is not merely a summary of inquisitorial practice but can be regarded as a training manual for the task of an inquisitor and a guide to the heresies of the time. There existed a whole number of "infringements" of church regulations that an inquisitor could cite and which seem to us preposterous as criminal acts for which one could be burned. Gui names among the worst heretics of the time the Cathari, the Waldenses, false apostles, Beghards, Jews, witches and clairvoyants, providing documentation on each and setting out how their trial should proceed. Included is his portrait of an ideal inquisitor, and it is anything but an attractive one.

Another commonly used book, *Directorium inquisitorum*, was written by Nicholas Eymeric, a Spanish Dominican. He, too, was able to draw on a wealth of experience, as he had been the inquisitor in Tarragona in the latter half of the 14th century. Like Bernard Gui, Eymeric lists the various heresies and provides a guide to the methods of the inquisitor. A useful handbook, it found wide usage among church judges.

The Introduction of the Courts of Inquisition in the Catholic World

France was the first country in which the Inquisition tried out its powers. The Inquisition gained its first practical experience in the crusades which were decimating southern France. It was here, too, that the practices of the Inquisition incorporated the view that heresy could not be eliminated until the heretics themselves were destroyed and that the heretics would not be completely wiped out until all those who supported and sympathized with them were also eradicated.

The first Dominican inquisitor traveled systematically through the land and laid the foundations for the courts' work. He conducted the search for heretics, and established trial procedures and the scale of penalties. Although torture had not yet been officially sanctioned by the pope, it was widely used. The fanaticism and fury of the inquisitors was unprecedented. By the 1220s, there were still people in a position to drive the inquisitors out of Toulouse, but a few years later they were sending friends and neighbors to the stake with their accusations and denunciations. Discord and fear were rampant, and within a few years the inquisitors had sentenced thousands of people to be burned. People gradually became accustomed to what had originally seemed unthinkable and unacceptable, and they simply turned their faces metaphorically from the fires.

The church councils in southern France supplemented and clarified the measures to be taken against heresy; the Council of Toulouse held in 1229 in fact made them more or less generally applicable and clarified a number of rulings against heretics. Every parish was to have one priest plus at least two or three laymen who promised under oath to spare no effort in persecuting the heretics and their sympathizers. Their task was not only to investigate parishioners and their conduct but also to search houses, identify possible hiding places for the heretics and report them. The local authorities had to persecute and penalize the heretics; if they failed to do so, their own property was confiscated. Even common believers had to swear to persecute heretics and suspects and to denounce them, an oath which had to be renewed every two years.

Secular law was invoked to supplement church law, in particular the 1226 Royal Ordinance of Louis VIII and the 1229 Royal Ordinance of Louis IX. Under these Ordinances, all the officials and subjects of the French king were required to seek out heretics, hand them over to church courts, and assist in implementing sentences.

The 1315 Royal Ordinance of Louis X, which applied the rulings of Emperor Frederick I to the whole of France, was probably the most effective measure taken by the State of France against heretics. Thus the net of the Inquisition was drawn even tighter, and for the next hundred years all categories of heretics were tried and persecuted continually.

Two particular trials that took place at this time occupy a special place in the history of the Inquisition. In 1304 and 1305, Esquin de Floyran of Béziers denounced the Order of the Knights Templars, among other reasons because new entrants to the Order denied Christ, spat on the cross, worshiped an idol and committed moral offenses. The Knights Templars was an exclusive Order of knights which had acquired fame and glory in the Holy Land and in the crusades. The Order had been founded by French noblemen at the beginning of the 12th century. Their name—Templars or, in Latin, *templarii*, *milites templarii*, *fratres templi* or *equites templi*—had been derived from the seat of the Order near the Temple of Solomon in Jerusalem. The Order had between 3,000 and 4,000 members when this accusation was made, 2,000 of them living in France.

The burning of 180 Albigenses in the year 1210. Albi was one of the most important centers of the Cathari in southern France at the beginning of the 13th century. Engraving by Jan Luyken, 17th century. Moravská galerie, Brno.

Efforts to achieve a church reform often overlapped with the political sphere. This includes the case of the Italian, Girolamo Savonarola. He was sacrificed to the reason of the State and burned in Florence on 25 May 1498.

The best-known of the German inquisitors, Konrad von Marburg (C. 1180–1233) was linked with the town of Marburg. His ceaseless pursuit of heretics and witches unleashed fear and horror throughout the German lands. Engraving by Matthäus Merian the Elder from *Topographia Germaniae*. Lutherhalle, Wittenberg.

HIERONYMVS SAVANAROLA FERRARIENSIS.
Quæ tibi facunda vis & quæ gratia linguæ
Senfit mota tuis confilys patria
Sed quorfum rapidi eloquy ruat ingeny & fons,
Exitus admonuit, Sauanarola, tuus.

Charges against the Templars were motivated apparently by political considerations. Its members were bankers to the French king, and by 1305, King Philip IV owed them more than half a million guilders! The French king and his councilors—especially Nogaret and Dubois—agreed willingly to the denunciations. At the instigation of the Dominican inquisitor, William of Paris, the king had all Templars in his kingdom arrested on the night of 12 October 1307; all their money and possessions were confiscated by the French Crown.

The violent trials, which lasted for years, have never faded from the memories of historians or belletrists. Many Templars were burned, but many legends were born from their ashes. The Grand Master of the Order, Jakob Moley, died at the stake cursing his unjust judge to trial at the Last Judgment, and within a year of his death on 18 March 1314, Pope Clement V, Nogaret and King Philip IV were themselves all dead.

The second famous trial in the French kingdom took place more than one hundred years later and concerned a simple young French woman, Joan of Arc. Here again, political interests lie behind the events of the Inquisition; in this case, the problems were those of the Hundred Years' War between England and France.

Improbably, this "maid of Orléans" became commander of the French army, a feat that only someone

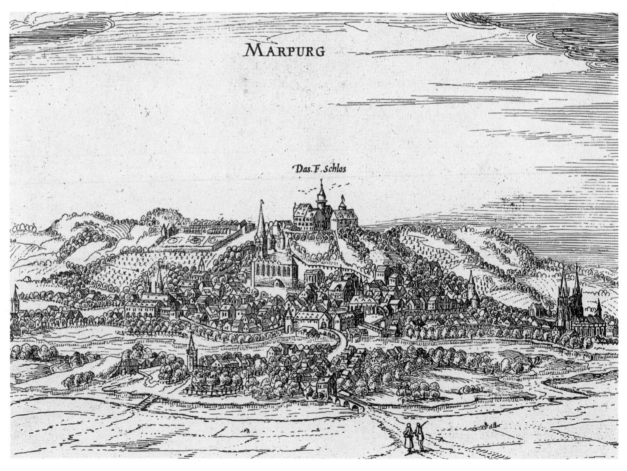

MARPURG

Das. F. Schlos

claiming divine guidance in the form of voices and visions could have achieved. It was, therefore, not difficult to accuse Joan of Arc of being a witch and of other crimes against the faith. She was burned at the stake on 30 May 1431 in Rouen but was rehabilitated four years later and eventually was made a saint and a French national heroine.

In Italy the progress of the Inquisition was swift and terrible. Since the 1230s the country had been swamped by both Dominicans and Minorites. In addition, the direct influence of the Curia and the existence of the Pontifical State made it possible for the papal anti-heretical rulings to be implemented vigorously. The existence of heretics and of people like the Waldenses, the Dolcinists, the Fraticelli and others gave the Church a unique opportunity to set up courts. As early as 1231, Brescia became the first Italian city to adopt a law —under the guidance of the Dominican Bishop Guala —on the burning of heretics. In 1233 in Verona the inquisitor had sixty people, men and women alike, burned, while in the same year heretics died at the stake in Milan.

Even in the heyday of the Renaissance, Italy was not free of burnings which had, as in France, become a political means of persecution. Cola di Rienzo was slain here as a dangerous rebel, although in 1354 he had been released from prison and had returned to Rome and subsequently served the popes in Avignon. The Italian prophet and reformer, Savonarola, also died at the stake in Florence in May 1498. The introduction of the Inquisition in the German regions be-

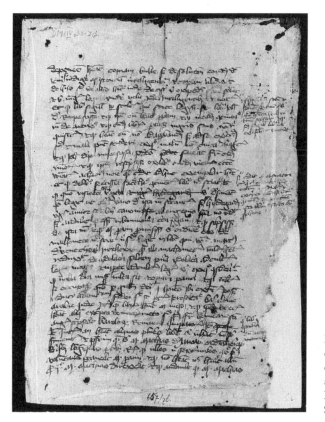

Page from an account of an Inquisition trial recorded during the early 1390s during the hearing of a lecturer at Prague University. Památník národního písemnictví, Strahov-Prague.

gan under Inquisitor Konrad von Marburg. He was hard and uncompromising, a model for his future colleagues in the Inquisition. He had no mercy on suspects nor did he hesitate in condemning an innocent man, saying that God knew whether in fact he was guilty or

Merchants' house in Constance; on the first floor, the so-called council chamber where Martin V was elected in 1417. The Council of Constance in the early 15th century was a council of reform to renew the Church. The election of a new pope in 1417 at least marked the end of the Great Schism.

CONSTANTIA
IOHANN. HVSSI ET HIERONYMI PRAGENSIS.
IN CONSTANTIENSI CONCILIO,
ET IN IPSO VTRIVSQVE INCENDIO
ANNO 1415. d. 6 Julii. et ANNO 1416. d 30 Maii.

The Council of Constance acted as Inquisition tribunal in the case of the Czech scholar and university lecturer John Hus and of Hieronymus of Prague. It condemned both to death by burning. The copperplate engraving by Hans Daucher shows the burning of Hus in 1415 in Constance.

Page 45:
Title page of a book about John Hus and the Hussite movement, published in Wittenberg in 1609. Státní ústřední archiv, Prague.

innocent and would Himself decide on how he would spend eternity. Thus it is hardly surprising that Von Marburg and his companions were murdered in 1233. His merciless actions were undoubtedly one reason why the Inquisition was unable to become properly established here; by the 14th century, other methods had been found and in the 15th century the empire began to lead Europe in witchcraft trials, which represented another disastrous development.

The situation in Bohemia, which acquired the title of "14th-century Languedoc," created many problems for its clergy. The Archbishop of Prague, Jan IV of Dražice (1301–1343), was forced to stay in the Curia in Avignon for eighteen years to free himself and his diocese of the suspicion of heresy. Those fragments of the account of the Inquisition that have so far been pub-

lished give some indication of the extent of heresy in Bohemia and of the presence of the Inquisition, the impact of which was unparalleled in central Europe.

The records of Inquisitor Havel of Jindřichův Hradec between 1335 and 1355 show that he alone tried in excess of 4,400 people during that period. About one in twenty was condemned to be burned. Virtually the whole of Bohemia was affected: Prague Neuhaus (Jindřichův Hradec), Budweis (České Budějovice), Saaz (Žatec), Königsgrätz (Hradec Králové) and Brünn (Brno).

Those involved were mostly property owners from the towns and the country; only very few came from the mighty patrician class. Most of those affected were Germans, the descendants of immigrants to Bohemia in the previous century. The burning of Master John Hus in Constance in 1415 may have marked the beginning of a new era, but Hussitism had its roots in the 14th-century Bohemian heresies. The Council of Constance served as a court of Inquisition in the case of Hus, and he was tried on several different charges. Even after his death, the Church tried on several occasions to destroy the Hussites by crusades. The efforts were in vain, however, for the Hussites actually deprived the Church of its power and wealth to such an extent that by the mid-15th century the Church no longer had the power to excommunicate the heretic Czech king George of Poděbrady and strip him of his title and of the international connections which went with it. The Hussites belonged to the early stages of the Reformation in Europe. Already one hundred years before Martin Luther the Hussites secularized church property and claimed liberty of Bible interpretation and preaching. This was an utterly new situation.

Conditions in the Balkans were politically and ecclesiastically more complex. The Inquisition was unable to assert itself there, or in the kingdom of Hungary, which claimed subjection to Rome. Heresy persisted in these regions, for they lay at the margins of papal influence. A similar situation obtained on the Pyreneean Peninsula during the Reconquest.

It proved easier to introduce the Inquisition in the kingdom of Aragon. Inquisitor Nicholas Eymeric emerged here in the latter half of the 14th century. In Castile and in the kingdom of Portugal, the Inquisition was not particularly successful in the Middle Ages, and it was not until after the completion of the Reconquest that the situation on the Iberian Peninsula finally changed.

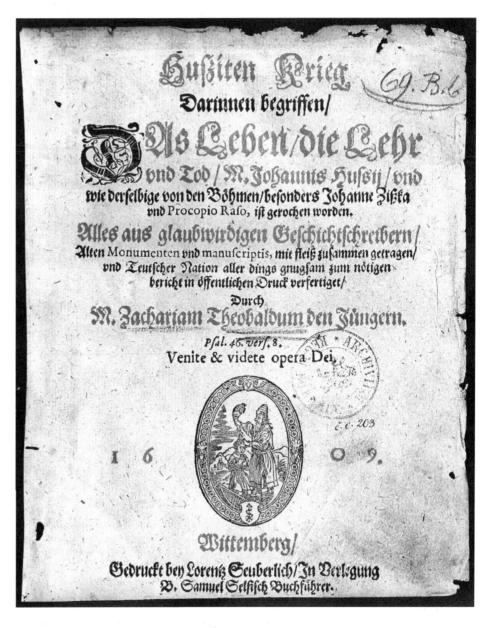

THE REIGN OF TERROR OF THE EARLY SPANISH INQUISITION

Isabella of Castile and Ferdinand of Aragon had given outstanding service in the victory of the Catholic Church on the Iberian Peninsula and to the consolidation of its power. The Curia recognized their achievements by bestowing on them, in 1496, the title "the Catholic Kings." Yet they remained, first and foremost, feudal lords who were careful in their services to the Church not to encroach on their own secular powers.

The State retained control over the Church in virtually all areas. From the outset, they used the weakened standing of the Curia after the 15th-century Reform Councils to force the Church into highly significant concessions. In 1482 they extracted an agreement from the pope that all church benefices on their territory would be occupied only with royal assent and by people subject to themselves. They also managed to gain a concession that papal bulls would in future only be issued with the approval of the kings and that any bulls in conflict with the interests of the State would not, in fact, be endorsed. Moreover, they succeeded in applying a ruling on the powers of the State against the misuse of clerical courts, and thus subjected the clergy to secular control and also brought the interests of the Spanish clergy into line with those of the State. This operation was to affect the dangerous and problematic courts of Inquisition as well as the major Spanish Inquisition.

Ethnic conditions on the Pyreneean Peninsula at this time were complicated, but the prevailing political and religious conditions were no less complex. The methods used by the Spanish Inquisition to achieve unity of belief were appallingly excessive. Suspicion of the non-

To eradicate all possibility of doubt, Pope Sixtus IV decreed a papal breve on 1 November 1478 in which he empowered Ferdinand and Isabella to commission two or three archbishops, bishops or other theologically trained clergy to watch over the newly baptized converts. They were told to set up a special court for this group, and as a result they appointed the first two inquisitors from the Dominican Order, Michal Morillo and Juan Martin, plus two more clergy on 17 September 1480. Their field of work was the city and diocese of Seville, and they condemned and sentenced all those who showed even the slightest unorthodoxy in their belief, sending them mercilessly to the fires. Suspects were brought from the entire region, including the farthest-flung parts of Castile. Even those who repented and turned aside from their former ways were punished severely, not only with prison sentences and corporal punishment but also with confiscation of all their property.

Rapidly, the conduct of the trials generated a number of complaints in Rome, including a submission by the Archbishop of Seville. Although he was not fundamentally opposed to the activities of the courts of Inquisition, Sixtus IV nevertheless realized that the conduct of the two Dominicans could have a negative effect on the Church. In a breve sent to Ferdinand and Isabella in January 1482, he expressed his dissatisfaction and stressed that they were failing to comply with the guidelines laid down in his first decree and had only appointed Dominicans as inquisitors for courts that lay outside the jurisdiction of the bishops. The pope had understood that the position of the Curia was under threat from the secular powers. However, nothing changed significantly, and a further step was taken toward the emergence of the Spanish Inquisition with the appointment of a Grand Inquisitor by the Crown. In the autumn of 1483, Pope Sixtus IV bestowed additionally on the prior of the Dominican convent in Santa Cruz, Tomás Torquemada, all the clerical honors associated with the office of Grand Inquisitor. His jurisdiction extended over the entire kingdom, and he was the direct agent of the pope. His task was to make sure that the activity of the Inquisition was as far-reaching as possible. He had a council to help him, consisting not only of clergy whose authority derived from the Grand Inquisitor but also of secular officials who were empowered by the king. Thus the Grand Inquisitor was appointed by the king, but his jurisdiction came from the pope.

From the outset the Spanish Inquisition was clearly established as a joint religious and secular court. This merciless and harsh tribunal—in Spanish, the *Supremo de la Santa Inquisición*—was in its extremism entirely characteristic of and consistent with the absolutism of the Spanish monarchy, which represented a combination of royal and religious power.

One of the earliest illustrations of the torture of Jews, showing victims attached to the wheel. Anonymous woodcut, 1475.

Christian population and of those who had converted to Christianity was always harsh. The Jews had to live in ghettos again and were forced to wear identification badges. Jews who had converted to Christianity and the Moriscoes were all subject to stringent control by both Church and State. Vestiges of the non-Christian population who had not left the country were, in fact, the reason for the introduction of courts of Inquisition. Another reason was that many who elected to stay had contacts with the leading families of the land and were wealthy. This aroused the interest of the Crown who saw advantages to be gained from confiscating their property. These and other reasons explain the request of the Spanish kings to the Curia to renew the courts of Inquisition. In Aragon, the courts had never really stopped their work, although in Castile the situation was more complex.

The *Suprema*, as the court became known, was not only feared from its very inception but also perceived as a threat in the sense that no one was entirely sure as to the full extent of its power. With its methods and virtually unfettered powers, the *Suprema* became a power unto itself; not only did the court dissociate itself increasingly from the influence and the intervention of the Curia, but also from the power of the Spanish kings.

Even before the *Suprema* began its activities, the work of the Inquisition had already been associated with some of the most ruthless men in history. Joining this infamous group was Tomás Torquemada who became Grand Inquisitor at the age of eighteen. About 100,000 people were sentenced under his jurisdiction.

It can be said without exaggeration that he was not only the "practitioner" of the Inquisition but also the "theoretician" behind it. His guidelines, which represented a summary of the philosophy and methods of the Inquisition in Spain and elsewhere, soon became an established handbook for the work of the courts. It details the secret workings of the Inquisition, its role as a court of first and last resort for accused heretics, the finality of its irreversible decisions, the immediate excommunication and burning of all who refused to confess their guilt and the penalties of those who did. Thus it sets forth the general procedures of all medieval Inquisitions which were shamelessly carried out by the secular authorities in conjunction with the Church.

Although some of these principles were extended following the spread of the Reformation in Spain, Torquemada's guidelines never lost their authority. The *actus fidei*—in Portuguese the *auto-de-fé* (Spanish: *auto-da-fé*)—soon passed into the language as a byword.

It is evident that under these circumstances, the Inquisition was not only feared but also, very rapidly, came to be hated. In Spain, as previously in other countries, inquisitors met unpleasant deaths. In 1485, for example, Inquisitor Peter Arbueze was murdered in Saragossa Cathedral. Nor did the Spanish clergy ever really fully accept the methods used by the inquisitors, although their reservations were of no avail in bringing about change. The Spanish alliance of "the throne and the altar" proved highly effective; the confiscation of property from heretics provided the king with an appreciable source of revenue. Not only that, but the Inquisition did achieve a kind of peace, albeit uneasy, in the country. The common people grudgingly accepted the activities of the Inquisition, and the auto-da-fé became a popular, if gruesome, form of public spectacle.

In many ways, the initial work of the Spanish Inquisition can be explained though not exonerated. Nevertheless, there were—and still are today—many ready excuses as to the necessity for such an institution. It is clear that the complex circumstances on the Pyreneean Peninsula toward the end of the 15th century and at the beginning of the 16th did not exactly make the task of unification under one government easy, but that fact did not automatically justify all the means that were brought to bear, including the *Suprema* itself. As for the inquisitors themselves, the conduct of Tomás Torquemada can be condemned without hesitation, but the case of another major inquisitor and politician, Francisco Jiménez (Ximenéz) de Cisneros, is not so clear-cut. Jiménez was a member of the Minorite Order and had progressed from being Queen Isabella's confessor to being one of her advisers. He was also a man of learning and had extraordinary political abilities which he sought to use in the reform of the Church in Spain. He founded the university in Alcalá which for a long time remained a center of humanistic theology. Jiménez himself, working with other scholars, compiled a polyglot Bible text and had it printed at his own expense. His role as a politician was such an important one that before the government of Charles V took over in Spain, he had been at the head of the government. He was Archbishop of Toledo and a cardinal, and later held office as Grand Inquisitor. He decided the life or death of many guilty or innocent people.

Francisco Gonzales Jiménez (Ximénez) de Cisneros (1437–1517). Copperplate engraving by François Edelinck based on a contemporary painting.
Staatliche Kunstsammlungen Dresden, Kupferstichkabinett.

François Ximenés de Cisneros, Cardinal, Archevêque de Tolede, Grand Jnquisiteur et Regent d'Espagne

One of the certificates of Pope Sixtus IV (1471–1484) that were sent to Spain; it refers to the competence of the newly established Spanish Inquisition. Archivo general, Simancas.

IN ROME, THEY FORGIVE ATHEISTS, SODOMITES, LIBERTINES AND ALL OTHER KINDS OF OFFENDERS, BUT THEY WILL NEVER FORGIVE ANY-ONE WHO SPEAKS BADLY OF THE POPE OR OF THE CURIA OR WHO EVEN CREATES AN IMPRESSION OF HAVING DOUBTS ABOUT PAPAL OMNIPOTENCE.

Gabriel Naude

THE PAPAL INQUISITION
ON THE THRESHOLD OF A NEW ERA

The merger of the State and the Catholic Church and hence the expansion of the Inquisition were made possible by the particular conditions in Spain. But the existence of courts of Inquisition also seemed to be called for in other countries, especially with the advent and spread of the European Reformation. The Church cannot be made solely responsible for the events sparked off by the Reformation of which some—such as the German Peasant War—took on revolutionary proportions; it was simply unprepared, theologically, practically and politically.

The power and ideological significance of the pope in Rome dwindled as medieval society declined. From the late 14th century and, later, after the major reform councils of the 15th century, secular rulers began increasingly to subject the Church to their own needs. They still took note of papal edicts but were increasingly reluctant to submit to all the demands of the Curia, especially financial ones. Links between Rome and the secular powers were not severed, but the papal court was increasingly subject to secular rulings and found its

IACTA·CVRAM·TVAM·IN·DOMINVM·ET· IPSE·TE·ENVTRIET·

ASSERVIT·CHRISTVM·DIVINA·VOSE·LVTHERVS· CVLTIBVS·OPPRESSAM·RESTITVITQVE·FIDEM· ILLIVS·ABSENTIS·VVLTV·HÆC·DEPINGIT·IMAGO· PRÆSENTE·MELIVS·CERNERE·NEMO·POTEST· MARTINVS LVTHERVS· M·D·XXXX·

Martin Luther (1483–1546). Copperplate engraving by Heinrich Aldegrever.

PETRVS·BEMBVS·CARDINALIS ANNVM·AGENS·LXXVII

activities on the Appenine Peninsula restricted and itself representing one of the Italian states. Since the mid-15th century, when the Holy See was reserved exclusively for members of the leading Italian families who passed the tiara down from generation to generation while another major section of the patrician class gained its living at the papal court, Italian politics and the struggle on the Appenine Peninsula had become the over-riding concerns of the Italian popes. In the waning years of the Italian Renaissance, papal Rome proved deaf and impervious to the warnings of the humanists and to the impetus being gathered by the Reformation.

Otherwise, the Medici Pope Leo X would not have greeted Erasmus's *Praise of Folly* with a smile and ignored its warnings and criticism of the Church and feudalism.

His kinsman, Pope Clement VII, who also became a Medici pope at the Holy See, remained unaware of the threat which was posed to the Church by the Reformation. He was captured during the *sacco di Roma* (sack of Rome) in the year 1527.

The supporter of reform, Cardinal Pietro Bembo (1470–1547), frequently came to the defense of critics of the Church. Engraving by Giulio Bonasone. Istituto Centrale per il Catalogo e la Documentazione, Rome.

Pope Leo X (1513–1521), who was descended from the famous Florentine Medici family, saw the beginnings of the German Reformation. Influenced as he was by Italian politics, he could neither understand nor combat the movement with ecclesiastical means.

His nephew and later Pope Clement VII (1523–1534) was forced into a more active policy of the Curia by the *sacco di Roma* by Emperor Charles V. German mercenaries mocking Pope Clement VII during the sack of Rome in 1527. Engraving from J. L. Gottfried's *Historische Chronik*, 1619.

After the emergence of Luther in the 1520s and the *sacco di Roma*, and under the influence of other changes, clergymen of the younger generation of church dignitaries began to think seriously about the unsatisfactory standing of the Church and the Curia. The militant wing of the Church—represented by Giovanni Caraffa, subsequently Grand Inquisitor and later Pope Paul IV—gained prominence. Pressure to change also came from those who had left the Church, such as Bernardino Ochino, an excellent preacher, and the papal nuncio, Paulus Vergerius, who ultimately became professor of theology at the Lutheran university of Tübingen. Between the two groups there was also a large number of people addressing the problem of church reform and making their own contributions to it. Among these was Matteo Giberti, Bishop of Verona and a close political adviser to Pope Clement VII, and who had lived through the dreadful and unexpected events of the *sacco di Roma*. Giberti devoted his efforts to ecclesiastical reform in his own diocese, and his achievements as bishop served as an example of the duties of Counter-Reformation bishops as described subsequently by Carlo Borromeo. His reforms proved very effective and were later repeated by the Council of Trent. In many ways, the Church was uncertain whether the Lutheran Reformation really signified a defini-

tive break with Rome or whether, in fact, a return to the methods of previous centuries would not actually help the Church bridge the yawning gap. New Orders—the Capuchins, the Theatines and, especially, the Jesuits—all offered help to the Church, and the older Orders were challenged to review their activities so as to give more support.

The call for a new council was voiced increasingly by both secular and ecclesiastical dignitaries, while in Rome the papal Inquisition began its work. It would be wrong to assume that until now the Inquisition had been restricted only to Spain and Portugal. The episcopal courts had not become as important as the courts of Inquisition—nor could they hope to—but they did turn their attention to witches and sorcerers. Witchcraft and clairvoyance were commonly dealt with in medieval manuals of the Inquisition and were often the subjects of trials.

In the *Coena Domini* Bulls, the Curia had already issued public warnings against heresy and had condemned entire groups of heretics as well as individuals. This grew more effective as the Reformation took increasing hold in Italy, especially in the north where a heretical tradition existed and there was geographical proximity to the countries of the Reformation; all this prepared a fertile ground for Reformational ideas. The spread of Protestantism in centers as Lucca and Modena was the final signal for the Church to resume the Inquisition as a way of asserting papal power.

Emperor Maximilian I (1493–1519), founder of the Habsburg dynasty.

The Reintroduction of the Papal Inquisition

The foundation of the Inquisition of Rome is linked with Pope Paul III, who was descended from the famous Farnese family. During his papacy, the Curia finally embarked on its Counter-Reformation, using the Inquisition, the newly authorized Jesuit Order and the Council of Trent. On 21 June 1542, the pope issued the *Licet ab initio* Bull, in which he announced the establishment of the Inquisition in Rome as a central authority for all countries committed to the struggle against heresy.

The pope himself could not assume the entire administration of it, so he formed a commission made up of six cardinals, chosen for their faith and scholarliness. Heading the commission were Cardinal Caraffa and Cardinal Juan de Toledo; the other cardinals were Paolo Parisio, Bartolomeo Guidiccioni, Dionisio Laurerio and Tommaso Badia. The work of the *Sanctum Officium*, as the commission was officially known (it was also referred to later as the *Sacra Congregatio Romanae et universalis inquisitionis* and as the *Congregatio S. Officii*), was to have jurisdiction over both clergy and laity. The commission rapidly acquired a range of privileges and powers; its main task was to flush out heretics, carry out their trials and punish all those who had committed offenses against the Catholic faith. The

The execution of Conradin of Staufen, a grandson of Emperor Frederick II, depicted on a satirical leaflet made in the Cranach workshop, dating from 1545. The death of the young Staufer was used as anti-Curia propaganda.

Sanctum Officium could also act in the absence of the local bishop if the bishop himself renounced his right to be present. The papal bull also laid down penalties for heresy, ranging from prison sentences to death. The newly established Inquisition of Rome also enjoyed special powers that gave it a full mandate and guaranteed it the support of the secular authorities.

This bull formed the foundation for the powerful new institution that enjoyed the widest legal powers in the Pontifical State. The influence of the *Sanctum Officium* spread slowly in the other Italian states, though with resistance and restrictions. Caraffa himself, as Grand Inquisitor and later as Pope Paul IV, experienced the resistance at first hand. The decision of Paul III to let the founder of the Jesuit Order, Ignatius of Loyola, know of his plans to found an Inquisition was a deliberate one: the Jesuits welcomed the activities of the Inquisition, as they had a wide knowledge of the work of the Inquisition in Spain. However, the Jesuits' field of interest spread beyond the Inquisition, which remained the preserve of the Dominicans.

The Jesuits—the Society of Jesus, known in Latin as *Societas Jesu*—were a militant Counter-Reformation Order, set up in 1530 by the Spaniard Ignatius of Loyola and shaped by him until its approval in 1540 by Pope Paul III. From the outset, the clergy of the Order put all their energies at the disposal of the Roman Catholic Church, and concentrated on preaching and the education of the young. It could be said that they were particularly active in those areas where the Church was under threat and where immediate intervention of the Inquisition did not seem advisable. Their service to the Church took the form not only of preaching but also of service as confessors, in particular to influential political personalities. The Order was organized along military lines with a general at its head; the strictly enforced military obedience not only shaped the internal discipline of the Order but aided the defense of church interests. Its central organization and military discipline became a symbol of the Counter-Reformation, particularly in those areas with a substantial non-Catholic opposition.

Inquisitor Caraffa Becomes Pope

The brief pontificate of the Neapolitan Giampietro Caraffa brought a whole host of problems, not only for the Curia but also for a society shaken by doubts and difficulties. As Pope Paul IV he was a strong defender of unrestricted papal power and an adamant believer in papal supremacy and divine origins. As such, it was hardly surprising that he took popes such as Gregory

IX and Innocent III as his examples. This medieval conception of papal power in the mid-16th century was at best an unpleasant and dangerous anachronism for the Church.

Paul IV's convictions had been made public even before he became pope; as a young prelate, he had been known as an ardent believer in church revival and a strong opponent of any concessions to the Reformation. He was a co-founder of the Theatine Order that was fighting for inner revival in the Church. Caraffa had been called by Paul III to the college of cardinals, a group of scholars and moderate clergy including such people as Giovanni Morone, Gasparo Contarini and his successor, Giovanni Angelo Medici, who tried to learn the language of the reform movements and communicate with them. In the 1540s they sought a compromise to bring about the reunification of the Church. Caraffa, however, had never shared the tolerant views of this group, and after the failure of the debates with Protestants in 1541 in Regensburg, in which the Curia had been represented by the totally unsuccessful Cardinal Contarini, Pope Paul III turned his attentions increasingly to Caraffa, even placing him at the head of the new Inquisition, the highest court body. Even the former conciliatory friends of the cardinal left Rome when his inquisitorial trials began. Moreover, his personal hatred led him to persecute even those working for the future strength of the Church, including the founder of the Jesuit Order, Ignatius of Loyola, whose origins and religious zeal aroused distaste in Caraffa. He combined medieval conceptions of the extent of papal power with that of the Renaissance attitude that the papacy should, first and foremost, be an Italian affair.

The coat-of-arms of Pope Paul IV.
Státní ústřední archiv, Prague.

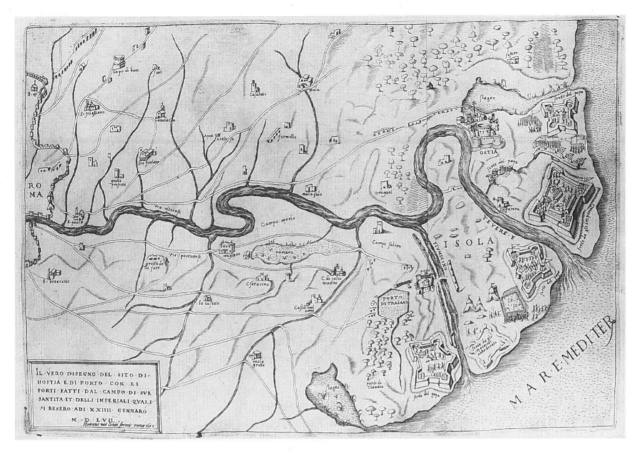

Illustration of the deployment of troops during the threat to Rome under Pope Paul IV by the troops of Philip II in 1557. Engraving by Henricus van Schoel. Gabinetto Nazionale delle Stampe, Rome.

In this Italian chauvinism lay the root of his enmity of all things Spanish, and so he had difficulty in finding allies at the Spanish court. Nor did Caraffa win allies at the court of the central European Habsburgs when he refused to give his approval to Ferdinand I, the choice of Protestant and Catholic princes for Holy Roman Emperor. The pope broke off diplomatic relations with Ferdinand's court, nearly declared him a heretic and refused to consecrate even a single bishop from the empire during his pontificate. His blind hatred prevented him from seeing that this not only made the king's task more difficult but that the Church lost all the positions that it had until then occupied in the countries most threatened by the Reformation. Nor would his uncompromising view of papal power permit him from calling together a new general church council.

His inflexible view of the Italian papacy prompted Paul IV to side with France in the struggle for Italy. He only escaped by a whisker defeat by the Spanish, as Clement VII had done. In the last year of his life, however, the pope became convinced of his errors in political judgment when France had to cede the decisive political influence in western Europe to the victorious Spanish. The pope became reconciled with Philip II, allowing him to set up not a Roman but a Spanish Inquisition in the Netherlands.

Paul IV then withdrew from public life, deciding to focus on reform of the Church. Although Spain and France agreed on the necessity to reconvene the church council, the pope remained unenthusiastic. His political withdrawal had in no way weakened or moderated his view of the primacy of papal power. Most of the cardinals of the Curia were also excluded from the preparations. They feared the pope, and at the sessions of the consistory they were scared to express opposition or even their own opinions. It was clear to them all from the outset that the slightest doubtful statement could result in the arrest of completely innocent cardinals and imprisonment in the Castel Sant' Angelo, interminable trials and sentencing as heretics—for only the pope could be right.

In the last months before his death, Paul IV withdrew to the darkest recesses of the Vatican Palace to make his plans for reform of the Church. He let it be known that the pope required nobody's services and that he alone was entitled to set out reform. His main assumption that the activities of the supporters of the Reformation were the product of insufficient discipline prompted him to focus his reforms primarily on the Church's own ranks. In several bulls he ordered restrictions of the religious lives of secular priests and of monks, stepped up fasting, made it illegal for church offices to be sold and also forbade the sale of "indecent" pictures. In his misguided zeal he even toyed with the idea of destroying Michelangelo's frescoes in the Sistine Chapel—he found the nakedness depicted there offensive. He also compiled in 1545 the first Index of Forbidden Books.

The Inquisition was to provide a valuable support in the execution of his plans, and he devoted a great deal of time and attention to it in the last few months of his life. He appointed Cardinal Michele Ghislieri, subsequently Pope Pius V and a Dominican friar, to be head of the Roman Inquisition for life. Ghislieri met Paul IV's requirements in a number of ways. The pope also extended the work of the Spanish Inquisition.

By 1559 Paul IV was completely alone. Most Europeans agreed that it had been a mistake to choose a cardinal of nearly eighty to be pope. By the end of his pontificate, the people shook in terror of Rome and of the soutane with which the pope seemed to want to cover the city. The whole of Catholic Europe waited impatiently for him to die.

On 18 August 1559, before the official announcement of his death, the citizens of Rome demonstrated in the streets against the tortures and suffering to which the pope had subjected them. It was an established and respected custom that when the Holy See was vacant, the people of Rome had a special right to ignore the previous order. However, the events that followed Paul IV's death were unprecedented. The citizenry came close to staging a revolt, with people set not on plundering and looting but on storming the prisons of Rome.

The first places to come under attack by the enraged populace were the new "House of the Holy Rochus" and the Via Ripetta, which housed the *Sanctum Officium*, the Roman Inquisition. Inquisitor Ghislieri barely

managed to escape with his life. The prisons of the Inquisition were opened and about seventy prisoners were released; those who promised to live as good Catholics were allowed to return to their homes and families. Among them were Jacob Palaiolog and Wilhelm Pestel, Loyola's former friend and the predecessor of Campanella.

Drunk on the wine from the cellars of the inquisitor's house, the people triumphantly set to the torch the building housing the *Sanctum Officium*, burning documents, Paul's Index of Forbidden Books, and books that had been confiscated on suspicion of containing heretical material. The Dominican Convent, Santa Maria sopra Minerva, which was thought to be another center of the Inquisition, only narrowly escaped the same fate. That evening, after the announcement of the pope's death, the people vented their hatred on his marble statue; an executioner was brought to the capitol and he cut off the marble nose and the hand outstretched in blessing.

The unrest in Rome lasted for several days. The statue was eventually destroyed; the marble head was cut off, spat upon and decorated with a yellow Jew's cap, then carried down from the capitol and burned for three days at a symbolic stake. Then it was thrown into the Tiber.

Within a few days, as the college of cardinals maintained silence, the people of Rome had managed to sweep away all of Paul's "reforms". The Roman Inquisition and its methods were shortly abolished. The Curia had lost all support for its unenlightened attempts at reform.

The Search for New Ways and Means—the Council of Trent

The reconvened Roman Inquisition on the Appenine Peninsula was unable to stem the spread of the European Reformation. The Curia feared the Reformation, and did what it could to encourage the machinery of the Inquisition. But the remaining Italian states had always restricted the operation of the courts of Inquisition, mainly because their leaders feared that otherwise the resulting unrest and dissatisfaction could damage the economic and political equilibrium. Similarly, the Spanish Inquisition, which enjoyed virtually unlimited powers, was equally incapable of preventing the defenders of the Reformation from spreading their ideas both publicly and privately in the regions under Spanish domination.

In the mid-16th century the Church was equally unsuccessful in its attempts to establish the methods of the Inquisition in the regions north of the Alps. Criticism of the Church there went back for a hundred years and, in addition, the rulers of the individual countries sympathized openly with the reformed Church. Thus all attempts by the Curia to regain its former position of power proved virtually futile.

The voices raised in favor of convening a general church council aroused mixed feelings in the pope and prelates of the Curia. The Church was hesitant, remembering the reform councils at Constance and Basle. But there was also increasing evidence that convening a general church council was the only way out of the serious crisis faced by the Catholic Church in Europe.

The Council of Trent began its deliberations in 1545 under Pope Paul III. They were temporarily broken off, but in 1551 Pope Julius III wanted to resume and complete them. His knowledge of the deliberations of councils was considerable as he himself, as Cardinal del Monte, had been president of a council. However, his efforts were in vain and in 1560, long after his death, efforts were still being made to reconvene the council.

There were many reasons why the completion of the work of the council was hindered. The conflict between the Protestant princes and Emperor Charles V ended in 1555 with the Peace of Augsburg. The hostilities not only brought about a shift in borders within the empire but also changed attitudes among other Euro-

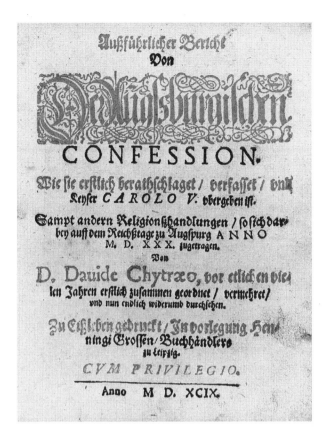

enable the Church to become unified. At the emperor's court in Vienna it had already become clear by the mid-16th century that the Church would be saved not by weapons but only by negotiations, compromise and reform.

The demands of the French court for church reform tended to match the ideas of those advanced by Ferdinand I. The French view of the bishops' power, however, corresponded more to the Spanish view.

Even the Curia's own conduct was by no means unanimous, although the prelates by now agreed as to the need for change, and expressed a number of possibilities for reform. The pope feared that the secular powers would themselves embark on a program of reform which they would force the Curia to accept, so he and his advisers eventually took action themselves. Former unsuccessful attempts at reform had convinced the Curia that reconvening the council or convening a new one was the only way of achieving a reform which would be acceptable to the secular rulers while maintaining the standing and influence of the Curia. However, the cardinals and the pope were unable to agree on the precise points of the reforms to be submitted to the council.

Toward the end of 1559, Cardinal Giovanni Angelo Medici was elected pope in one of the most dramatic conclaves the papacy had ever seen. He remained pope as Pius IV from 1559 until 1565. His very first bull outlined his policies, which were devoted to reform of the Church. The major difference between him and his predecessors was not in his mission but in the methods he chose to achieve his goal. These were rooted firmly and realistically in the political conditions prevailing in

pean potentates toward the council. Although the demands of the secular powers for church reform had become more insistent, they had not yet been clearly articulated. Not even the Catholic rulers had a clear and uniform vision of the reform, and the spread of the Lutheran and Calvinist Reformation, together with the resignation of Emperor Charles V widened the gulf not only between Catholics and Protestants but also among the Catholics themselves.

Philip II, successor to Charles V in Spain, called for stringent measures against the Protestants, without regard for the conditions prevailing within the empire. The reform of the Church demanded by the young Spanish king was based on a more precise definition of church dogma and greater obedience to it. His demand that the power of the pope should be limited and that of the bishops increased, with a greater emphasis on the divine origin of all religious power, was consistent with his own political interests. Clearly Philip II would want to increase his support of the individual bishops who were coming under the direct control of the State.

The stance of Emperor Ferdinand I, who had been crowned without the approval of the pope, was based more on social considerations. He demanded of the council not that it should debate dogma but that it should carry out an effective reform of the Church and in particular allow lay people to take communion and priests to marry. He sought to avoid debate over controversial theological issues because he and those around him still hoped that concessions would again

Title page of the report on the Augsburg Confession.

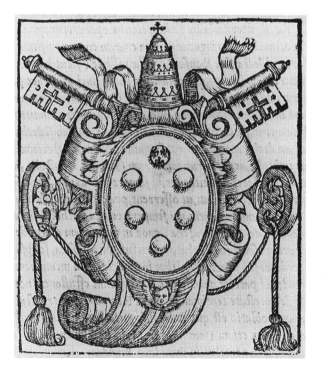

Pope Pius IV (1559–1565), Giovanni Angelo Medici, was not related to the famous Florentine Medicis but was born in a large and poor but respectable patrician family in Milan. The relationship between the two families was an invention of later times to the advantage of both. Giovanni Angelo was the only one of the sons to study law and, like countless other Italians, he gained a foothold at the papal court. He was ordained relatively late, in 1545. Until this date he had led a completely secular life and had always enjoyed a close if not demonstrative relationship with his three children. The illustration shows his coat-of-arms.
Státní ústřední archiv, Prague.

HÆC ROMANORVM EST FERDINANDI REGIS IMAGO
DA QVISQVIS DEBES HVICQ; DEOQ; SVVM.
M.D. (ISL) LVI

Emperor Ferdinand I had conveyed his own vision of reform to the council. His document, which he had presented by his orators to the cardinal legates in June 1563, caused great perplexity. His compromise proposal demanded major concessions from the Church and, in many respects, was similar to the position of the Reformation. Only the observance of imperial majesty prevented open opposition and hostility from the side of the Church. Engraving by Hans Sebald Lautensack, 1556.

Europe at the time and in a realistic assessment of the powers of the Curia, for which he seemed committed to preserving a privileged and independent status. He made it known that he would reconvene the Council of Trent, and so he resumed diplomatic relations with the court of Ferdinand I. The sincerity of his intentions could also be demonstrated by the fact that his new nuncio, Stanisław Hosius, Bishop of Ermland, was in Vienna by Easter 1560. The nuncios to other courts had also received instructions to raise the question of reopening negotiations on a new council, for neither was it possible in the mid-16th century to convene a general council without the consent of the rulers of Europe nor indeed to carry out any kind of reform in their countries.

Convening the council meant overcoming a formidable array of obstacles. The choice of the venue for the council was a major problem; the emperor, for example, proposed Cologne, Regensburg or Constance. Merely reconvening the former council and resuming where it had left off would from the outset have ruled out any participation by Protestants, who had not given their consent to dogmatic articles in the two previous sessions of the council. There were also a number of other more or less serious problems. It was not until 29 November 1560 that Pius IV issued the *Ad ecclesiae regimen* Bull which summoned representatives of the whole of Christendom to Trent again. The diplomatic negotiations that had preceded the issuing of the bull and indeed the achievement of its goals proved to be exceedingly complex. Following the bull, the reconvened council met only because it was the will of the pope and the Church. The pope felt that this formulation was extremely important. He also apparently laid equal stress on the fact that Christians of all denominations should be represented in Trent, including those who had already expressed open criticism of the pope and the Curia or had opposed them with weapons.

Perhaps the pope wanted to show that the Church had not itself caused the deep divisions and problems. In any case, it was ready to compromise. The pope issued official invitations to the council not only to all the Protestant princes in the empire but also to the kings of Denmark and Sweden, the queen of England and even the czar of Russia. The council was to open on Easter Monday 1561, but there were the inevitable delays. The fact that the council eventually met in Trent in January 1562 was evidence of the pope's extraordinary political agility and also of that of his nephew, Carlo Borromeo. It was also due in part to the work of the special legates and nuncios who had raised the question of participation in the individual royal courts and had worked untiringly to bring about the reconvening of the council.

On 18 January 1562, a solemn Mass was held in the cathedral to mark the opening of the third and final session of the Council of Trent. This monumental building, constructed in the 13th century in Romanic-Lombardian style, was the location for the sessions of the council, while all other deliberations were held in the newly completed Renaissance-style Church of St. Maria Maggiore. The pope did not head the work of the council himself, thereby hoping to prove that he had no wish to influence it. He had entrusted that task to five cardinals well before the council opened.

The council's third session lasted two years. From the outset, the pope granted it special protection and immunity. Its members were allowed freedom of speech and anyone could express his opinion without fear of being brought before the Inquisition. The pope wanted all the members to approve the council's final

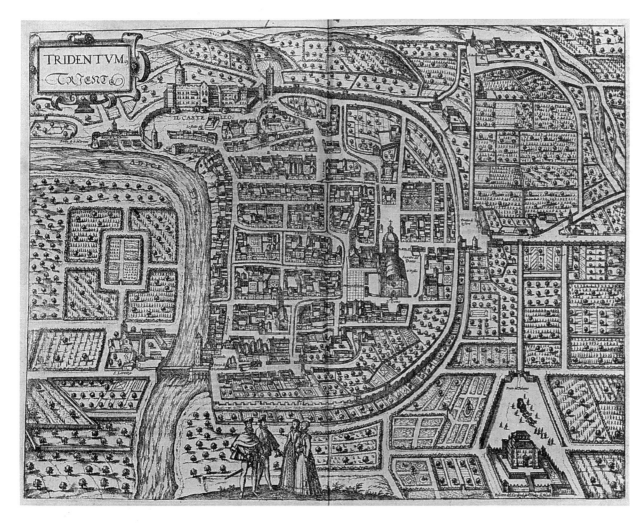

The small town of Trent with its picturesque townscape formed a decorative background to the council. The site of the town was also a compromise for the participants from Spain, France, for the princes of the empire and for the emperor in Vienna. Trent was far enough away from Rome to avoid accusations of the direct influence of the pope on the council. Mail between Rome and Trent took a week, although urgent news could be conveyed within four days.

Státní ústřední archiv, Prague.

decisions, but Philip II subverted this proposal. He saw the Inquisition as an indispensable aid and wielded his influence as the secular power for some of the Italian bishops and for all of the Spanish bishops. They were able to exert a disproportionate influence for the first half of the session since virtually all the German clergy, with one or two exceptions, boycotted the council, although they did acknowledge their loyalty to Catholicism. The German clergy feared that the religious peace achieved in the empire would be disturbed. The handful of votes from Hungary, Poland, Portugal and England were insufficient to make any real difference, and it was not until the French intervened that the real counter-weight emerged. Emperor Ferdinand I had three representatives or "orators" on the council: the Archbishop of Prague, Antonin Brus of Müglitz; Count Sigmund Thun; and the Bishop of Fünfkirchen, Georg Draskovics. Marquis Pescara represented the king of Spain. The French king sent three representatives, and Portugal, Poland, Venice, Florence, the Swiss Catholic cantons and others were represented, mostly by bishops sent from the individual organizations, particularly monastic Orders. It is interesting that the old universities were not officially represented.

By mid-1563, the council found itself in an impossible situation and the emperor was even thinking of suspending it, as he was not finding it easy to carry out the decrees of the council in his empire. That the deliberations of the council were not broken off and its work was not suspended is due in no small measure to its new president, Cardinal Morone. When Pius IV appointed him, he was acknowledging not only Morone's specific abilities but also his previous service to the Church, his wealth of experience, his diplomatic flair and his political abilities.

Pius IV entrusted him to extract the council from a cul-de-sac of impossible demands and to pacify the reigning princes and offer them a specific, realistic and acceptable plan for ecclesiastical reform which would not damage the Church and would prove acceptable to the secular potentates. Within a very short time after his appointment as president of the council, Morone went to visit Emperor Ferdinand I in Innsbruck. In a personal audience, Morone was able to smooth the emperor's ruffled feathers to such an extent that Ferdinand said later that "our excellent Cardinal Morone will take responsibility for an acceptable reform of the Church."

On 29 November 1560 Pope Pius IV issued a bull in which he called representatives of the whole of Christendom to Trent, although it was not until 18 January 1561 that the clergy and representatives of the secular princes began to gather in the town. The Council of Trent. Etching by C. Laudy, 1565.

List of participants in the Council of Trent.
Kapitulní knihovna, Prague.

Official report on the Council of Trent.
Státní ústřední archiv, Prague.

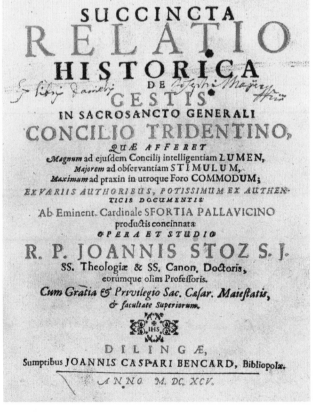

By June 1563, Morone had presented the council with the forty-two points of his new proposals for reform, and they were completely different to any others presented previously. He had managed to put aside the most controversial theological topics and the demands of the emperor; he had reached a personal agreement with Ferdinand that the pope would accede to some of his wishes once the council had completed its work. Ironically, Pius IV had already made so many concessions to the emperor during the session of the council that the fulfillment and confirmation of privileges for the emperor's territories came close at times to satisfying the demands that had been laid down in the "Reformation Book."

The proposals put forward by Morone were aimed particularly at the internal reform and renewal of the Church. He touched on the relationship between the pope and the bishops, the appointment of bishops, their jurisdiction, the monitoring of heretics, the authorization procedure for publication of books, and the legal powers of bishops. The proposals also concerned the role of the secular and monastic clergy, the strengthening and consolidation of the discipline of priests, the need for dioceses to be visited regularly and reported on, the establishment of seminaries for the priests, synods, the supervision of education in schools and reform of the Catechism, among other issues. The proposals defined the legal powers and rights of the bishops and the extent of their direct and personal control over the responsibilities of individual priests so

that the well-being of the papal and Curial dioceses could be ensured. The proposals also touched on issues such as singing at church services, the responsibility of the bishop for church building and decoration and for the future development of the Church; and its day-to-day routines and guidelines on the worship of saints and holy relics. Finally, the reform proposals also included a regulation on marriage.

After six months' debate, Morone's reforms were finalized and adopted. In December 1563, the deliberations of the Council of Trent were brought to a solemn conclusion in the cathedral and in January of the following year, Pope Pius IV issued a special bull in which he confirmed all the council's statements, canons and decrees. At the same time, the bull also suspended any privileges and special dispensations that were not in accordance with the decisions of the council.

The implications and the outcome of the council's deliberations did not completely meet with the satisfaction of contemporary observers, and Ferdinand I was confident that a new council would amend some of the rulings. However, a new council was not to meet for another three hundred years!

The immediate future and political practices were to show that the rulings issued by the council—applied to a Church that was only a shadow of its former self—were to remain strictly limited. Nevertheless, the council had created a contemporary Church which was to be both effective and practical for the Catholic states of the time.

The Council of Trent and the Inquisition

Pius IV had used his sacrosanctity to ensure that the council was free and that the Inquisition should not interfere with it. An examination of the commentaries published on the council's sessions contain little reference to the *Sanctum Officium*. However, the deliberations of the commission on the Index of Forbidden Books, which fell under the jurisdiction of the Inquisition, was another matter. The actual influence of the Inquisition on the deliberations remained limited, largely because of the Archbishop of Prague—Antonin Brus of Müglitz, who was one of the few prelates from that side of the Alps—was appointed president at the express wish of the emperor by the pope and the cardinals.

Nevertheless, even this powerful and protected institution could have restricted its activities at least for the duration of the council's deliberations, out of consideration for the papal promises and with regard to the aging emperor. However, there are two strong arguments against this which also demonstrate how powerful and independent the Inquisition had become. Pius IV was a friend of Venice, although this renowned republic enjoyed then, and for a long time afterwards, relative independence from the Curia. The church dig-

Cardinal Morone prevented the failure of the final negotiations of the Tridentine Council. Like Pius IV, the well-educated man, scarcely older than the pope himself, came from Milan. As a representative of church reform and well acquainted with the conditions north of the Alps, he had been suspected of heresy and was arrested by Paul IV and imprisoned in the Castel Sant' Angelo. This effectively barred him forever from becoming pope. He continued to devote his life to the renewal of the Roman Church. The illustration shows his coat-of-arms.
Státní ústřední archiv, Prague.

Pauli et Iulij III. Caroli V. et Ferd. I. assensu inchoantur A
Dñi 1546. sub Pio IV. tandem promulgatur SS Trid Con
taini, cui successive intervenere 13. Card. Leg. 4. non Legati
29. Phil. ablegati. Patriarche 3. archi Episc 3. Epi. 235.
Abbat. 15. Relig. Grales 12. SS Thlgiæ et I.I. Doct. 145.

nitaries in Venice enjoyed the protection of the Curia
and were mostly clerics from the highest Venetian patrician families. The patriarchy of Aquileia, dominated
by Venice, was chiefly influenced even in the 16th century by members of the patrician Grimani family. In
the mid-1500s, Giovanni Grimani of Aquileia became
patriarch. In the 1540s he was accused of having made
statements on man's free will, no small problem for the
patriarch from Venice and from a very important family, at a time when the republic was demanding cardinal's status for the Aquileia patriarch. His criticisms
were taken up and exploited by the enemies of the republic, who brought a charge of heresy before the
Sanctum Officium.

The trial lasted for several years and was remarkable
in many respects. The republic was able to prevent the
patriarch from being arrested by the Inquisition, but
could not secure his appointment as cardinal. The
statement made by Pope Julius III at the beginning of
the trial seemed to be true: "If all the waters of the Tiber were to gather together, they could not wash Grimani clean of the taint of heresy."

The republic continued to demand cardinal status for
Grimani. A suitable moment arose when the papal conclave elected Pius IV as pope. But even he was unable to
bring Grimani into the college of cardinals. Grimani
again pleaded his case before the Inquisition, but his efforts were in vain. His theological knowledge proved
insufficient to enable him to deflect the crafty questioning of the judges. The pope himself was forced to intervene, and asked the Council of Trent in a special letter
to release him. The pope even appointed a commission

of particularly trustworthy and reliable cardinals on
whose recommendation the council eventually acquitted Grimani of the suspicion of heresy. However, Pius
IV died before he could appoint Grimani to the college
of cardinals. Grimani, already en route for Rome, immediately returned to the safety of Venice where he
learned that the next pope had appointed Ghislieri as
the Grand Inquisitor.

The council members gathered in Trent were reminded by the incident of the need to be alert to the
work of the *Sanctum Officium*, and another incident
involving a senior prelate also accused of heresy
brought the same problem to their attention. Bartolomeo Carranza was Archbishop of Toledo, and the
Spanish Inquisition accused him of not conforming his
Catholic Catechism to church dogma. He was also suspected of being sympathetic to and conciliatory with
Lutheran influences in Valladolid. The unfortunate
prelate was imprisoned without trial for years and his
case never came before the Inquisition. In the highest
echelons of the Curia it was felt that the massive property of the Archbishopric of Toledo and its income
were the prime reason for the interest of King Philip II,
who was the sole beneficiary of the archbishop's long
imprisonment.

Pius IV wanted to release the unfortunate man from
the clutches of the Spanish Inquisition, but his interventions on his behalf through emissaries and in a personal letter to Philip were in vain. It was to no avail that
he demonstrated to the king that only the pope himself,
not the prince, could make a judgment as to the theological orthodoxy of his clergy. In his answer, Philip II
made it clear that the whole affair was the concern of
the King of Spain, not of the pope.

The negotiations continued during the Council of
Trent and Carlo Borromeo himself acquainted the le-
gates with Philip's arrogant comments. The Index
Commission tried in vain to prove the orthodoxy of
Carranza's Catechism and to have him brought before
the council to defend himself. Philip and the Spanish
Inquisition remained steadfast. It was only under Pope
Pius IV that some alterations were achieved. It is hardly
surprising, then, that Philip II's announced intention
to introduce the Spanish Inquisition into the areas of
Italy dominated by the Spanish throne caused serious
unrest among the Italian prelates who were affected.
Philip II was thinking primarily of the region around
Milan which bordered on the Calvinist cantons of
Switzerland. Not only the clergy but also the citizens
of Milan, some of whom made emigration plans, react-
ed with horror. Appeals to the pope, who was no
friend of either the Spanish Inquisition or the major Inquisition trials in Italy, resulted in the refusal of the
council, under the pope's influence, to extend the
scope of the Inquisition. The pope reserved for himself
the right to rule on orthodoxy and to judge whether his

bishops were heretics; he did this either personally or through special commissions appointed by him in accordance with the decrees of the Council of Trent. The fundamental decisions in these matters were the responsibility of the local church authorities. It was widely known that the Curia was terrified of the Escorial, which is why there is no mention of the activities of the *Sanctum Officium* in the final decrees of the council.

The fact remains, however, that within a short time, new methods were sought to implement its work wherever it could be established.

The "In Coena Domini" Bull

The emperor was not the only person to be dissatisfied with the rulings of the Council of Trent. Some of the members of the college of cardinals had also accepted the canon of reform with a heavy heart: As it turned out, the council in fact represented a victory for the papacy, although this was never officially acknowledged. Thus it was that Pope Pius IV issued his *Benedictus Deus* Bull on 26 January 1564 to confirm all the canons and decrees passed by the council, despite the opposition of some of the cardinals. Moreover, on 17 February 1565 the *In principis Apostolorum sede* Bull removed all the privileges, exemptions and dispensations still in force that did not conform to the rulings of Trent. Thus a whole host of old church rules lost their validity, although the bulk of the canon of church law remained in force, as the *In coena Domini* Bull confirmed. The bull contained rulings on the question of heresy and also concerned itself directly with the Inquisition. Not surprisingly, it created apprehension in the Curia and among the secular powers.

The *In coena Domini* Bull—shortened to *Coena Domini*—might also have been called the "Maundy Thursday Bull," since it was read every Maundy Thursday by the pope in Rome and concerned general excommunication. No other papal bull or secular regulation could compete with it in importance. After it had been read solemnly for centuries, it became established as a warning and a deterrent, for in the Middle Ages excommunication put individuals and entire groups of people outside the powers of the secular authorities.

The origins of this bull are unclear; the only thing that is known for certain is that it dated from the 13th century at a time when the Church was strong and was competing with the State and at a time when the Inquisition was just beginning to establish itself. In 1363 Pope Urban V linked his bull with those of his predecessors and stressed the regular annual reading "per nonullos pontifices, praedecessores nostros et postremo per nos . . . excommunicationis et anathematisationis sententiae in certis annis solennitatibus promulgatae fuerunt . . ." ("by several popes, our predecessors, and finally also by us . . . that should be solemnly declared as excommunicated and banned for years"). Pope Martin IV had used this bull against the Count of Monteferato in 1282. Boniface VIII solemnly reiterated all excommunications in Rome on Maundy Thursday each year. So it was that from the late 13th and early 14th centuries up to the end of the 18th, the popes al-

ways read *Coena Domini* publicly and solemnly. They not only made public the known sins and offenses against the Church in this general excommunication but also extended, added to and clarified the bull. It was finalized in 1627 by Urban VIII. It was, however, also used by the councils, decreed in 1415 by the Council of Constance and in 1431 by the Council of Basle. Post-Trent popes, like their medieval and early 16th-century predecessors, used the bull as a powerful weapon not only against heresy but also against any attack on the rights and freedoms of the Church in favor of the State. Under certain circumstances it could also be used against Catholic secular rulers. In the 15th century popes were asking to have it read at least once a year in the dioceses, and in 1568 Pius IV managed to incorporate it into a general penal code for the Church. Pope Julius II ordered all the bishops to read it at least once a year on church holidays. More than fifty years later, Pope Gregory XIII demanded that all vicars, clergy and confessors should have a copy of the bull and should study it closely. It was at this time that the publication of the bull and its public reading in churches began to arouse the opposition of the major Catholic princely courts.

What did the bull actually say and how did it manage to have an undesirable effect on the interests of the absolutist Counter-Reformation leaders?

The *Coena Domini* Bull and its powers of excommunication did not apply only to heretics: It also excommunicated all those who could be shown to be acting against the Church and who represented a threat to the dominance of the Church and the Curia in Rome. Church lawyers were constantly extending and elucidating the procedures it laid down. During the time of Urban V, the bull contained seven classes of offense; this was extended to nine under Gregory XI, ten under Martin V, twelve under Julius II, seventeen under Paul III and in 1583, under Gregory XIII, to twenty-one offenses that could be punished by the Church with excommunication.

Of course, the first of these was heresy and the causing of schism in the Church (an interesting clause that could be used both for and against the pope), followed by offenses against church dignitaries. Theft from prelates, restriction of their jurisdiction, the imposition of taxes on the clergy without the approval of the pope, acts of violence against clergy and pilgrims, offenses against trials of clergy, confiscation of papal lands and estates and similar offenses were also listed. The bull required that all Catholic authorities should protect the Church. It provided for public identification of guilty parties, both groups and individuals, excluded them from society by excommunicating them, freed their servants from submission and forced the State to prosecute the guilty parties. If the secular powers failed to do this, then they themselves were subject to the penalties in the bull.

The passages relating to heresy are the most interesting. All medieval heresies and sects were included, from the Cathari to the Waldenses. At the beginning of the 16th century, Julius II added the followers of Wycliffe and the Bohemian Hussites to the list, including those who protected and helped heretics. Hadrian VI was already able to include Martin Luther and his adherents, and at this time, the printing and reading of heretical books and their dissemination was also banned. With the Hussites, the European Reformation was mentioned in the *Coena Domini* Bull. This is significant in that the Catholic Church defined its enemies so precisely, it was able to pinpoint the beginnings of the European Reformation. The listing of all the Reformation movements in the bull issued by Gregory XIII was very detailed. To avoid any omission, Pope Paul V's Easter Bull in the year 1610 included a general reference to all European Reformation movements and condemned all those such as French Huguenots or Bohemian Hussites who had strayed from the Church. With respect to the reading of heretical books the bull was both comprehensive and specific; the reading of all such books, as well as of any religious books that had not been approved by the pope, was forbidden.

The publication of the *Coena Domini* Bull was inevitable. The ecclesiastical principle that "ignorance is bliss" and free from sin could not in fact be taken seriously where practical questions of orthodoxy were concerned.

The resistance of the authorities was to the articles that dealt not with heresy but with the position of the State with regard to church property and land and with obedience of the clergy to the pope. As early as 1551, Charles V had refused to have the bull printed in Spain for this very reason. A powerful opposition formed against Pius V who, as we have already indicated, made the bull the basis for a canon of church law that would not even protect orthodox Catholic monarchs such as King Philip II. Philip himself also forbade the 1568 bull to be printed in Spain and went so far as to say that the pope should either retract it or amend it. Publication of the bull was also prevented in Naples and in Portugal, where the bishops who were in favor of it were threatened with having their incomes blocked. Prison sentences were even imposed on those found selling copies of the bull. The Republic of Venice took a similar line. In 1575, after some hesitation, the Venetian council consisting of ten members reached an unusual decision: the *In coena Domini* Bull could be read in the churches, but only at times when no one could hear it and when no one would pay it any attention. The situation was more complicated in those regions where religious peace was so tenuous that disparagement of other faiths could not be allowed. The papal nuncio in Prague had the bull published and fixed it to the door of St. Vitus' Cathedral. He even recommended the Archbishop of Prague to have it printed. The anger of Emperor Rudolph II erupted almost immediately; he forbade the publication of the bull in all the lands belonging to the Bohemian Crown. In his view, the interests of the State took precedence over the defense of the interests of the Church as represented by the publication and content of the *Coena Domini* Bull.

Major Trials under Pope Pius V

The configurations of power in the world had changed considerably since the 13th century. Christians of the Latin tradition had religious controversies not only with the orthodox schismatics in the East and with Muslims in Spain but also with the inhabitants of the newly discovered continents and with the Ottoman Turks, who had advanced as far as central Europe. Moreover, at the time of the Reformation half of Europe had turned away from the "one holy Catholic Church." So one of the priorities of the Council of Trent was to reconsider its definition of heresy and to devise new ways of combatting it.

The council reiterated the distinction to be drawn between the Church's attitude toward heretics on the one hand and pagans on the other. The Church did not want to persecute and punish those who had never belonged to it but those who had been baptized and had thus become members of the faith. This distinction was consolidated and clarified by the official *Catechismus Romanus* which resulted from the rulings of the Council of Trent. According to this Catechism, heretics weren't unbelievers, but were sinning against the faith; this misbelief came under the jurisdiction of the Church which was thus entitled to punish them. A heretic was not someone who held views different from the teachings of the Church but rather someone who rejected church teachings and insisted on his own mistaken views.

This distinction was not in fact a new one; what was indeed different was the emphasis placed on it by the Church. The Church's interpretation of the Decalogue (the Ten Commandments) also traded on this theme of the struggle against heretics, who were regarded as servants of the devil. However, this new concept of heresy was of only limited significance for the Inquisition.

26 Clement VII (1523–1534) was an opponent of the Italian policy of Charles V. After his defeat in the *sacco di Roma*, he had to agree to a joint policy with the emperor. "Encounter of Clement VII and Emperor Charles V." Painting by Giorgio Vasari. Palazzo Vecchio, Florence.

27 Pope Paul III (1534–1549), born Alessandro Farnese, strengthened and empowered the papal Inquisition during his pontificate. Painting by Titian.
Museo Capodimonte, Naples.

28 During the riots that followed the death of Paul IV, the head of his statue was severed from the body—an insult and a degradation to the pope as the highest inquisitor.
Castel Sant' Angelo, Rome.

29 Pope Paul IV (1555–1559), born Giampietro Caraffa, was the son of a respected and eminent Neapolitan family. Engraving.
Österreichische Nationalbibliothek, Vienna.

ZELATVS SVM PRO DOMINO DEO
ZELO EXERCITVVM

SANCTISSIMVS PAVLVS IV. PONT. MAXIMVS.
Ex Ordine Clericorum Regularium Assumptus, Neapolitanus. B. P. N. Caietani Thienei eiusdem Ordinis Institutoris primi, Theatino abdicato Episcopatu, Socius. Apostolici pectoris Vir, Catholicæ Religionis Vindex, Priscæ Pietatis Assertor, Disciplinæ Restaurator, Quo Vno sua stetit Ecclesiæ Sanctimonia, Sapientia Maiestas, Ævi sui Τρισμεγιστος. Sedit Annos quatuor Menses Tres. Obijt Anno Domini M. D. L. IX. Passus ab Hæreticis in lapide Martyrium, tot Trophœa enumera quot segmenta.

30 Ignatius of Loyola (1491–1556). Painting by Francisco Pacheco.
Seville Cathedral.

31 "The Last Judgment." Fresco by Michel-angelo.
Sistine Chapel, Vatican.

32 Emperor Charles V after the victory
over the Schmalkaldic League in the Battle
of Mühlberg, 1547. Painting by Titian.
Prado, Madrid.

33 Through the mediation of Pope Paul III,
Charles V and Francis I met in Nice to agree
to an armistice. The papal initiative in fact
foreshadowed the Council of Trent. Zuccari
later painted the meeting in Nice for the so-
called Council of Trent chamber in the Villa
Farnese Caprarola near Viterbo.

D · O · M

PIVS · IIII · PONT · MAX ·
MEDICES · MEDIOLANENSIS ·
SEDIT · ANN · V · MENS · XI · DIES · XV ·
VIXIT · ANN · LXVI · MENS · IX ·
OB · V · ID · DECEMB · MDLXV ·
IOANNES ANTONIVS SORBELLONVS ·
EPISCOPVS PRAENESTINVS ·
CONSOBRINO
CAROLVS BORROMEVS · S · PRAEXEDIS
MEDIOLANENSES ·
M · SITICVS · DE · ALTAEMPS · GERMANVS ·
CONSTANTIEN · S · MARIAE TRANSTIB
TITT · PRESBB ·
AVVNCVLO ·
S · R · E · CARDDD · POSVERE ·

34 Pope Pius IV was elected by one of the most dramatic conclaves ever. The cardinals, banished to their cells for more than three months, experienced momentous events in the confines of the Sistine Chapel. Two cardinals died during the conclave. Even Calvinist Geneva had sent its spies to Rome in monastic garbs.
Monument to Pope Pius IV by Michelangelo.
Chiesa di S. Maria degli Angeli, Rome.

35 Bull of Pope Pius IV.
Státní ústřední archiv, Prague.

36 Pius IV commissioned five cardinals to head the Council of Trent: the Cardinal of Mantua, Ercole Gonzaga; the head of the Augustine Eremites, Gerolamo Seripando; the theologian, Stanislaw Hosius; Lodovico Simonetta and Mark Sittich Hohenems, a nephew of the pope. "The Council of Trent." Painting by Titian.
Louvre, Paris.

37 The interior of the church Santa Maria sopra Minerva in Rome was the most common venue for the *actus fidei*.

38 An *actus fidei* in Santa Maria sopra Minerva. Michele Molinot is recanting of his false teachings. The engraving by Arnold van Westerhout, dating from 1657, is one of the oldest representations of such a scene. Gabinetto Nazionale delle Stampe, Rome.

39 Pope Sixtus V
(1585–1590). Section of
his sepulchre, erected to
him by Domenico Fon-
tana.
Sistine Chapel in Santa
Maria Maggiore, Rome.

40 Pope Gregory XIII
(1572–1585), born as
Ugo Buoncompagni,
cardinal of San Sisto.
Thanks to his efforts the
reform of the calendar
could be completed in
1582. Monument by
Giuseppe Rusconi.
Basilica Vaticana,
Rome.

NOVI
OPERA
EIUS
ET
FIDEM
APOC.CAP
V.19.

GREGORIO XIII. PONT. MAX.
IUSTITIÆ CUSTODI PIETATIS CULTORI RELIGIONIS VINDICI
ET PROPAGATORI IN UTROQUE ORBE MUNIFICENTISSIMO
IACOBUS III. S. MARIÆ IN VIA PRESB. S.R.E. CARD. BONCOMPAGNUS
ARCHIEPISCOPUS BONONIÆ ABNEPOS POSUIT

41 View into the courtyard of the Archivio Segreto in the Vatican, where part of the Inquisition archives is stored.

42 On the Roman Piazza Campo de'Fiori, where many of the condemned heretics met their deaths, a monument was erected to the most famous of all—Giordano Bruno.

43 Prison cell in the Castel Sant' Angelo.

44 Pope Paul V (1605–1621). Bust by Giovanni Lorenzo Bernini. Galleria Borghese, Rome.

45 Galileo Galilei (1564–1642), who strictly adhered to experimental methods, laid the foundation of the natural sciences and was a passionate defender of the heliocentric system. This brought him into conflict with the Inquisition which forced him to recant. Painting by Justus Susterman. Galeria degli Uffizi, Florence.

47 Commemorative plaque erected by Jacob Palaiolog for his friend Collin of Chotejřina in the Prague Carolinum.

48 The prison rooms in the lower stories of the Castel Sant' Angelo were probably also used by the Roman Inquisition.

49 The French king Francis I (1515–1547) made successful attempts to limit the impact of the Reformation without too much bloodshed. Engraving by Etienne Fessard after Antoine Boizot. Lutherhalle, Wittenberg.

50 During the reign of King Charles IX (1560–1574) of France, militant Catholics tried in vain to stamp the Huguenots out by force. The bloody religious wars they un-leashed were to go on for another fourteen years after Charles's death but failed to bring about a solution. Drawing by François Clouet. Staatliche Kunstsammlungen Dresden, Kupferstichkabinett.

FRANÇOIS I.
LVII.ᵉ Roy de France,
Mort à Rambouillet, le 30 Mars 1547, après 32 ans de rég.

51 In December 1559 one of the leading Huguenots, Anne de Bourg, was executed in public. Despite periodic persecution of the Huguenots, the Inquisition was unable to gain a foothold in France. Contemporary copperplate engraving. Bibliothèque Nationale, Paris.

Anne du Bourg Conseiller du Parlement de Paris bruslé a S. Iean en Greue le 21. Decembre. 1559.

Anne du Bourg ayant esté mené sur vne charrette en la place
Sainct Iean en Greue à Paris, & s'estant luy mesme despouillé
iusqu'a la chemise : est guindé en vne potence, la ou il est estran-
glé, & puis son corps getté au feu.

Horribles cruautez des Huguenotz en France.

49

Ces tyrans insensez, n'estants iamais contens,
Inuentent tous les iours autres nouueaux torments,
A leur ardant courroux ne suffit nulle paine:
Ilz s'esgaient à voir souffrir cruelle mort.
Aux pauures innocents, qu'ilz font mourir à tort,
Montrant par tel tourments leur tant mortelle haine.

G.   Dv.

Horribles cruautez des Huguenots en France.

45

Cacher ne peut le mal qu'il porte en la poictrine
Le Tyran Huguenot; qui d'enuie mâtine
Se montrant comme Iuif ennemy du Seigneur,
Le prestre ayant forcé à celebrer la Messe,
Mysteres prophanant, & le batant sans cesse,
L'a mis finalement à la croix du Sauueur.

F 3   A cle-

52/53 Many Catholic priests paid with their lives during the Huguenot wars, a fact which was exploited for propaganda purposes by the anti-Huguenot factions in leaflets. Bibliothèque Nationale, Paris.

54 The Huguenot propaganda represented and illustrated the fate of those persecuted by the Catholics as martyrdom for the true faith.

EPITAPHE AVX FIdeles Martyrs de Iesus Christ.

Le zele ardent que ie voy en ce lieu
Emmi les feux, tout estonné i'admire:
Car il esclaire aux bons pour les conduire:
Et les enflamme au seruice de Dieu.
   Et le voyant des tourments au milieu
Victorieux par dessus son martyre,
Ie voy au feu vn autre feu reluire.
Ie voy vn feu brusler vn autre feu.
Car si l'ardeur, si la celeste flamme
Des saincts Martyrs & esclaire & enflâme,
N'est-elle pas vn feu clair & bruslant?
Et si, s'armant d'vne vertu supreme.
Elle a vaincu la flamme l'assaillant,
N'est-ce pas feu, plus feu que le feu mesme?

55 A particularly significant event in the persecution of the Huguenots was the so-called blood court of Amboise in 1560 as a result of which several Huguenots, some of them members of the aristocracy, were executed. Contemporary woodcut by Jacques Tortorel and Jean Périssin. Staatliche Kunstsammlungen Dresden, Kupferstichkabinett.

56 St. Bartholomew's Day, depicted here in a contemporary engraving, was the culmination of the bloody confrontation between Catholics and Huguenots. On the left, the murder of Admiral Coligny; on the right, the massacre of Huguenots in the streets of Paris. Státní ústřední archiv, Prague.

The reconvening of the papal Inquisition was not so much a direct result of the Council of Trent as an expression of a general feeling that the Church was under serious threat. This feeling had been growing since the first disputes with the Huguenots had broken out in France and in countries such as the Netherlands where political opposition had won concessions in religious matters. Moreover, Ferdinand I who had been an advocate of reform had now been succeeded as emperor by Maximilian II, whose Catholic zeal was the subject of some doubt in Rome. Increasing numbers of cardinals (and, incidentally, also the secular princes who had remained true to Catholicism) found it necessary to take drastic action against the heretics, at least in Italy. These trends, then, influenced the choice of the new pope after the death of Pius IV, who had made great efforts to restrict the arbitrariness of the Inquisition and the power of the *Sanctum Officium*. He was replaced in January 1566 by Michele Ghislieri, the Grand Inquisitor, former friend of Paul IV and a known opponent of Pius IV. The last excess of the papal Inquisition will forever remain closely linked with his name and his personal actions.

Ghislieri, who took the name Pope Pius V, made no secret of his intention to make the Inquisition an important instrument if not the major instrument of combatting the effects of the Reformation in Italy. Just one month after his election the Austrian legate was giving the emperor a report on the plans for a new papal reform of the *Sanctum Officium*. The inquisitor of Brescia said in March of the same year after an audience with the new pope that the latter would have to tighten the reins when it came to matters of the Inquisition, rather than give it free rein; and indeed, the pope soon translated his intentions into concrete measures that were all designed to achieve one goal—giving the Inquisition a leading position in the arsenal of weapons to be used by the Church to maintain its control over the faithful and their spiritual life. In this, he based his actions on his long and extensive experience as an enthusiastic inquisitor convinced of the infallibility of his views and the importance of his mission.

Above all, the Inquisition was to be enabled to work more quickly and effectively. To this end, Pius V reduced the number of cardinals in the *Sanctum Officium* from nine to four, hoping in this way to create more flexibility and efficiency in rulings and to speed up the decision-making processes of the courts. In many respects, Pius V simply reverted to the practices he had already instigated in the 1550s with Paul IV but which had been watered down by Pius IV. The inquisitors were once more entitled to hand over for torture anyone whom they could reasonably suspect of heresy. Thus all those against whom a trial had already been opened elsewhere for heresy or other reasons were to be handed over to the *Sanctum Officium* in Rome. The

.TEMP·DIVÆ·MARIÆ·AD·MINERVA

The main portal to the Church Santa Maria sopra Minerva through which virtually all the victims of the Inquisition of Rome had to pass. Museo di Roma.

secrecy of its deliberations was increased, and anyone found breaching this confidentiality, including copying documents relating to trials, was tried for lese-majesty against the pope.

The wealth of experience that Pius had gained as an inquisitor was put to good use in amending the rules relating to trials. The conditions of prisoners in custody were changed so that they had no contact with one another—virtual solitary confinement for those awaiting trial. They were not to be allowed either to read or write, and the prison guards were instructed not to go into the cells of these prisoners alone. Evidently the pope feared that they might be bribed into allowing prisoners contact with one another or even with the outside world. The pope also made no secret of his mistrust of the church authorities. It happened on more than one occasion that a suspect was saved by being vouched for by his vicar or bishop or by the leaders of his Order. These "testimonies" of orthodoxy were in future to be disregarded, as were any interventions in favor of suspects made by church dignitaries. Pius V could not bear the idea that even one suspect had been acquitted on such testimonies in the past, and so he imposed on the Inquisition the power—even the duty—to resurrect old, closed or suspended cases. He made it clear that he was in no way to be associated with the liberal policies of his predecessor.

It is difficult to trace how all these new rules and regulations were implemented in practice; historians will probably never have access to all the rulings of the Inquisition in Rome, for only fragments have ever been published, and it seems that the written records were not very extensive, quite unlike the records of the Spanish Inquisition, which are very comprehensive and well preserved and freely accessible for study. Our picture of the Inquisition of Rome is based essentially on indirect accounts—the reports of people living at the time and references in memoirs, diaries and contemporary correspondence.

Disparate and fragmentary documentation indicates that Pius V was not satisfied with mere proclamations but also wanted to influence the practices of the *Sanctum Officium*. The investigations of the inquisitors were carried out with remorseless efficiency and the trials were speeded up considerably. The prisons within the Curia were constantly taking in new inmates. The old premises of the *Sanctum Officium* were no longer adequate for the influx of suspects nor was there enough room for all prisoners and all the necessary documentation. So Pius V built new premises with a larger courtroom and more archives, but which could also be fortified to rule out any possibility of a repeat of the mass escape that took place in 1559 and which Ghislieri had good cause to remember. The premises were built next to the Vatican at the Porta degli Cavalleghieri in a street leading down to the harbor Ripeta del Borgo. The pope footed the bill, and in his eagerness to have the building ready as soon as possible, he instructed even craftsmen who worked on St. Peter's Cathedral to be brought in. Thanks to their work, the *Sanctum Officium* was able to move into its new premises in 1569. A guide to the principal sights of Rome dating from the 1560s says that his inscription was to be found over the door: "Pius V, P.M. Congregationis Sanctae Inquisitionis domum hanc qua haereticae pravitatis sectatores cautius coercerentur a fundamentis in augmentum catholicae religionis erexit anno 1569." ("Pius V, Pontifex Maximus, had this house erected for the prestige of the Catholic religion, to purify heretics from their sins.")

The new, improved Inquisition quickly made its mark on the public life of Rome, and in the first few years of Pius V's pontificate, processions of prisoners streamed into the Dominican church of Santa Maria sopra Minerva at least three times a year, where they were sentenced to be executed in a huge public auto-da-fé. The pope made these ceremonies even more spectacular and awesome by publicizing them in advance in the streets and churches of Rome and by inviting not only members and officials of the *Sanctum Officium* but also as many cardinals and secular and religious dignitaries as possible.

The gloomy room in the cathedral, barely penetrated by daylight, was too small to hold the curious crowds, so many were left outside, and on more than one occasion the final stages of an auto-da-fé were concluded outside the cathedral. In one case, the church was so overcrowded that the cardinals could find no seats. Were these really the same citizens who, ten years previously, had destroyed the Inquisition archives, set its premises alight and released its prisoners? Had they come out of sympathy for the accused, out of curiosity of perhaps malicious delight to witness the humiliation of once famous and powerful men? It is thus difficult if not impossible to assess the extent to which public opinion had changed since the death of Pope Paul IV.

The first official auto-da-fé organized by Pius V and held on 23 June 1566 in the Church of Santa Maria sopra Minerva was described at first hand by Cardinal Santori in his autobiography. He found the great interest of the people self-evident, but what did surprise him was that seats were reserved not only for the cardinals and members of the *Sanctum Officium* but also for the leading prelates and city officials. Half the accused, he writes, had repented and recanted but the rest had to be ordered to do so and were sentenced to prison or to service as galley slaves. The accused included two Spaniards, at least two notaries and several clergy. The climax of this inglorious and solemn spectacle was the passing of sentence on Pompeo de Monti, son of the Marquis of Corigliano and a close relative of the famous Cardinal Colonna. Cardinal Santori records that Pompeo had gray hair and a gray beard, looked very pale, and shook. While the sentences were being read, he stared at Cardinal Colonna as though he hoped to read his fate in the cardinal's face. As a recidivist heretic, he was surrendered to the secular powers. As he had already claimed once to have repented, he was beheaded and his body was burned.

The coat-of-arms of Cardinal and Grand Inquisitor Michele Ghislieri, later Pope Pius V. Státní ústřední archiv, Prague.

Subsequent autos-da-fé were run along similar lines. Virtually all of them had some relative or member of a noble family among the accused, one or more well-known preachers and in some cases famous scholars or officials. The number of those accused varied—sometimes barely ten and at other times more than twenty—but one of the accused was always hanged and usually one or more burned on the fires lit in the square in front of the Castel Sant' Angelo or on the Campo de' fiori. Sometimes the bodies of those who had already been hanged or beheaded were burned, but sometimes there was also the gruesome spectacle of the burning of live prisoners.

One year after De Monti, the Neapolitan noble and writer Mario Galeota was condemned; in the autumn of 1567 the aged humanist and former first secretary to Pope Clement VII, Pietro Carnesecchi, became the central figure at another auto-da-fé. In fact, his trial was one of a number of re-trials of those acquitted in the past to the outrage of Pius V. Carnesecchi was one of the last of the generation to advocate church reform and compromise with the Lutherans, to the disgust of the new pope and his militant advisers. Neither the favor nor the testimony of the Medicis, who had protected him for years, could save the old man from the zeal of the Inquisition, which set about compiling a list of his offenses. The reading aloud of the sentence in Santa Maria sopra Minerva purportedly took two hours, at the end of which he was turned over to the secular arm for punishment. Ten days later Carnesecchi was beheaded and his body was burned. He was not the only close associate of former popes who fell into disgrace under Pius V. In May 1568 the former treasurer of Pius IV, Minale, was condemned to life imprisonment following a trial during which he had been severely tortured and whipped after his repentance. Only two months into his sentence, he died as a result of the torture.

At the end of the pontificate of Pius V, the rhythm of the Inquisition hearings began to slow down, and by 1569 autos-da-fé were being held only once a year. As if to compensate, the stature and importance of the accused was all the greater. In May 1568, Bartolomeo Bartoccio was condemned to be burned; as one of the leading proponents of Calvinism in Liguria, he had been arrested in Genoa and transported to Rome only after long delays by the authorities there. In the following year Aonio Paleario and Niccolò Franco also became victims—both had been tried earlier in the 1550s. The poet Niccolò Franco came before the Inquisition as the author of a booklet critical of the pontificate of Paul IV and his protégés. He had intended that the booklet —which had never been printed but had circulated in manuscript form—would settle his old scores with the pope who had had him imprisoned for thirteen months. After the prison had been stormed and he had been freed, Franco spent eight years in the palace of

Cardinal Morone, who had been imprisoned with him during the pontificate of Paul IV. But not even the protection of the cardinal was able to keep him from falling into the clutches of the Inquisition; although the unfortunate writer eagerly denounced all the readers and copiers of his booklet, he was subjected to long, drawn-out trials and torture on several occasions, in particular aimed at getting him to reveal who had prompted him to write the attack against Paul IV. Clearly there lay behind this an attempt to get Franco to testify against Cardinal Morone. Franco, to his credit, remained steadfast, and he may well have spoken the truth when he denied any collaboration with Morone. Franco was condemned to death for his disparagement

Pope Pius V (1566–1572) saw himself as the true successor of Paul IV and sought to follow his inquisitorial methods. Contemporary engraving by Giovanni Batista Rossi.

FACCIATA MAE^BA DEL PALAZZO DI ... SA SPIRITO IN SASSIA IN BORGO.

Contemporary representation of the building of the Roman Inquisition in Borgo. Musei Civici, Milan.

of the pope to whom Pius V owed his spiritual inspiration and church career.

Only in one case did Pius V try to release the accused, and it is significant that this trial was not completed during his pontificate. The trial in question was that of the Archbishop of Toledo, Carranza, who was accused by the Spanish king of heretical views. Pius V represented the interests of the Curia and the ecclesiastical hierarchy in this case against the unilateral intervention of the sovereign. He scored an undisputed victory when he forced Philip II to accede to Carranza's wish to be tried by the court of the papal Inquisition. The unfortunate archbishop traveled from Valladolid to Cartagena in the winter of 1566 and was then brought to Italy in the spring of 1567. However, the opponents of the Spanish Inquisition—present in large numbers in Rome—who had expected that the pope would immediately release Carranza and give him a lavish reception were disappointed; the sedan-chair carrying the prominent prisoner was brought into the Castel Sant'Angelo through a back entrance and Carranza remained a prisoner of the Inquisition. He was even allowed a Spanish guard. The *Sanctum Officium* began to examine all the Spanish material and within a few months decided that it was insufficient for the trial

to continue, for many of the views regarded in Spain as being heretical were viewed differently in Rome. Thus the decision was taken to proceed *ad fontes* and to take another look at Carranza's files. It was three years before all the files and documents had been studied and even then the cardinals could not agree on the degree of gravity of the heresy. Nevertheless, there was a feeling that while the archbishop expressed controversial opinions in many instances, he contradicted them elsewhere. The main reason for this further delay was consideration for the Spanish accuser. The Spanish legate Zuñiga made sure his sovereign realized the moderate nature of the proceedings against Carranza, accused the Inquisition of infringing its own rules and ultimately even accused the pope of being influenced by Carranza's friends. Philip II wrote directly to the pope, expressing his criticisms openly on several occasions. The dispute reached a head in 1570 when the *Sanctum Officium*, which had finished examining the archbishop's files, looked as though it would free him. The Spanish legate was instructed to put pressure on the pope and to remind him of the danger to the authority and prestige of the Catholic Church in Spain if Carranza were to be released and reinstated. During the whole of the proceedings against him, the archbishop had been treated according to his status and standing. There was, however, a chance of a compromise, with Carranza making a confession in secret so that he could be released, also in secret, and given his freedom. But Carranza had no intention of making his captors' lives any easier; he continued to insist on his own orthodoxy and complained bitterly about the abuse from his enemies. In the last two years of his pontificate, Pius V hesitated and wavered until ultimately he yielded to the pressure from Spain. Contemporary observers such as the emperor's agent in Rome, Cusanus, were of the opinion that the problem with Carranza affected the pope's health and eventually precipitated his death.

It was not until several years later that Pius's successor, Gregory XIII, summoned up the courage to speed up the trial and on 14 April 1576 he personally announced that the Archbishop of Toledo had been declared innocent of most of the charges after fifteen years' imprisonment. Carranza was to be required to repent of some "un-Catholic" (but not heretical) views and to do a penance by visiting seven Roman pilgrimages; then he was to spend the next five years living in a monastery. But Carranza was not to be allowed to enjoy his newly gained freedom for very long; on his visit to the first of the churches, just three weeks after he had been released from prison, he became ill and died.

The Inquisition of Rome Strengthened

At the very beginning of the pontificate of Gregory XIII, an event took place which filled the Curia with the same sense of optimism as the victory over the Turks in the Battle of Lepanto had done in 1571. That event was the massacre of Huguenots by militant Catholics in 1572 on St. Bartholomew's Day in Paris. The defeat of the hated Huguenots was not complete but it had been enough to stop their advance into Italy, which was feared so greatly by Pius V. It was clear that Gregory XIII was by nature and legal training a political realist and was closer to Pius IV than his immediate predecessor. His attitude toward the Inquisition was

in no way fervent, but the atmosphere in the Curia was already so full of religious zeal—above all from the Jesuits—that the new pope simply had to adapt to his surroundings. However, his authority in the Italian states and also within his own pontifical state declined considerably compared with that of his immediate predecessor.

The Inquisition trials continued along the lines established by Pius V during his period of office. Only a very few reports of autos-da-fé remain, but it is clear that they took place virtually every year. The only visible difference between this pontificate and the former

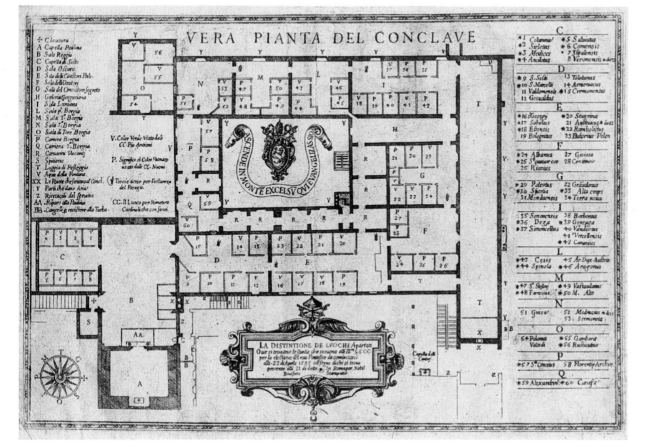

For the conclaves, the cardinals were put into improvised cells in the Vatican palace. This contemporary drawing of the conclave of 1585 shows the deployment of the cardinals.
Museo di Roma.

CASTELLO SANTO ANGELO DI ROMA

The Castel Sant' Angelo in Rome was also the prison of the Inquisition for several hundred years. A number of heretics were executed on the small square in front of the main gate. Unsigned drawing from the 16th century. Istituto Centrale per il Catalogo e la Documentazione, Rome.

one is that the autos-da-fé took place more frequently in St. Peter's. The groups of suspects were clearly smaller than in previous years, too, except in 1579 when more than twenty were sentenced at one time. Gradually, differences began to emerge in the attitude taken by Gregory to the Inquisition. He felt that the public trials were not the only way of eliminating heretical views and teachings. Therefore he—like Pius IV before him—recommended giving the accused the chance of repenting in secret in cases where they ran the risk of becoming stubborn heretics out of fear of public humiliation. He also feared that the public sentencing accompanied by details of the offenses of the condemned could arouse confusion among those watching and set them a bad example. When in early 1582 a Castilian rushed at the priest celebrating Communion in St. Peter's, knocking the chalice out of his hand, a decision was taken not to execute him in public. This was actually the third case within six months of heretics seizing a chalice or a monstrance, and it led to fears that public trials could simply stir up further anti-clerical feelings. The English Anabaptist Aretinson had made the first attack in St. Peter's in July 1581, and his burning had turned into a public holiday, with even children taking part.

One more major public auto-da-fé did, however, take place in 1583, toward the end of Gregory's pontificate. Among those on trial was the well-known Jacob Palaiolog. Another five prisoners were sentenced along with him because of heresy, while the rest were up before the Inquisition because of various other of-

fenses. A partial shift within the scope of duties of the Inquisition can be discerned here as well. It should also be borne in mind that the activities of the Inquisition of Rome were not merely limited to investigation of heresy but also concerned a range of offenses which were considered mortal sins. Correspondents from Rome described the horror of the higher echelons of Roman society when Pius V announced that the Inquisition would be taking action against the so-called "Greek sin"—sodomy. Those convicted of homosexuality were summarily executed. The Inquisition also punished mercilessly those who abused the giving of the sacraments, passing themselves off as priests when in fact they had not been ordained. The clergy who abused the confessional to have sexual intercourse with the young women coming to confess were also punished with very severe penalties, although very few were, understandably, ever brought to trial for this. Virtually every auto-da-fé had among its victims Judaists—that is baptized Jews who were convicted of reverting to Judaism in secret. While the orthodox Jews and others of different faiths were not normally persecuted by the Inquisition, their proselytized brothers were deemed to be part of the Catholic Church and so fell under its jurisdiction. The return to the Jewish religion was in this case viewed as heresy and was punished on more than one occasion by burning. As might be expected, there were fewer Judaists in Italy than in Spain. Another offense punished by the Inquisition was the link with impure powers, which could take various forms; cases of witchcraft occurred initially only sporadically in Italy, and although the number of cases had risen by the end of the 16th century, persecution here did not even approach the level it had reached in the German lands. (It is interesting that witchcraft was persecuted relatively frequently near Italy's northern border, for example in Venice.) Another manifestation of dealings with Hell was deemed to be the stealing of corpses for the purposes of black magic; cases of this kind became more numerous, especially under Gregory's successor, Sixtus V.

Sixtus V, like Pius V, was considered to be a pope of the people. His father was a poor tenant farmer, and his grandfather had been a poor Slav refugee from the Balkans. Like Ghislieri, Felice Peretti gained his education when he joined a Franciscan monastery. He, too, worked diligently and became known for his hard work, his talent and his religious zeal. The two men met and grew close under remarkable circumstances; after one of his very popular sermons, Peretti found on the chancel an envelope with the thesis of his sermon which bore the threatening words: "You lie!" As a true son of the Church, he turned to the Inquisition, and Grand Inquisitor Ghislieri himself sought out Peretti and subjected him to a grueling examination. Peretti passed with such flying colors that Ghislieri grew to like him and recommended him to his patron, Paul IV. Thus began a promising career for the young Franciscan that was to continue under the pontificate of Pius. Peretti became the consultant (adviser) to the Inquisition—among others, in the trial of Carranza—and also became the Vicar General of his Order and was finally appointed a cardinal. He extended and consolidated his position during the 1570s, mostly in his diocese of Forno, and after Gregory XIII's death the conclave faced a very simple task and elected him without even considering other candidates. When he assumed office, he carried out a consistent and at times bloody action against banditry, which had assumed serious proportions in the pontifical state, and also tried to gain the favor of the Italian states and their towns and cities by means of compromise and the granting of privileges.

As a former inquisitor, Sixtus V did not disappoint the members of the *Sanctum Officium*. Soon after his election, he had new courts set up in a number of provincial towns and commemorated Peter Martyr, an inquisitor who had been murdered by heretics. Finally he had the Inquisition's premises extended by the addition of new prison cells. However, the people of Rome had to wait another two years before the next great spectacle took place. It was not until 1587 that a major auto-da-fé was conducted in front of Santa Maria sopra Minerva. Of the twelve accused, four were surrendered to the secular administration, but none of them was a heretic in the classical sense. Two were burned for offenses against the Church, the other two for their libertine views, which in the case of one—the priest Pomponio Rustico—had clear materialist tendencies.

Although Sixtus V continued to monitor and support the activities of the Inquisition tribunals, he was no supporter of the show trials and was very reluctant to impose the death penalty. It seemed a contradictory attitude in a pope who previously had not only bandits but also small-time thieves hanged. It is difficult today to ascertain if the reason was the political prudence or whether the major heresies had already been largely eliminated under his predecessor. It may also be true that in this respect the role of the *Sanctum Officium* had undergone a certain change, which was to be completed under the pontificate of Clement VIII. The regular sessions of the tribunal concerned themselves not only with the investigation of individual offenders but also with more general questions of a dogmatic or political nature, whether a political alliance of the Catholic sovereigns with heretical sovereigns could be possible; under what conditions a mixed marriage between a Catholic and a non-Catholic could be approved; the attitude of the authorities of the Church to unapproved litany, etc.

By the end of the 16th century, the influence of the Reformation had been completely wiped out in most of the regions of Italy. The only exceptions were Venice, which remained open to the influx of foreigners from Protestant countries, and the mountain valleys of Piedmont, where the Waldenses were based. Although Clement VIII had to make a number of compromises with regard to his foreign policy—the most significant was the return of Henry IV to the bosom of the Catholic Church—Catholic orthodoxy triumphed in Italy proper. Nevertheless, the Inquisition continued its work and the sentences it meted out were often very harsh. There was an official auto-da-fé virtually every year and a large number of those on trial were sentenced to be surrendered to the secular courts. In 1595, six people were executed; in the following year, seven; in 1599, three; and in 1600, another six. A catalogue from the year 1599 reveals that eight prisoners were being held in the Inquisition prison, one of whom had been there since 1582, as well as nine prisoners who were waiting for their interrogations to be completed. Another nineteen prison inmates were being held in custody, most of them for up to one or even two years. In 1593 the former Dominican friar, later emigré and teacher of philosophy, Giordano Bruno, was arrested. Although his case was not entirely without precedent (it was similar to Pomponio Rustico), he was nevertheless the first major representative of a new category of Inquisition victim. He did not belong to any Reformation movement but had merely pursued his own line and activities as a philosopher and free thinker.

The Trial of Giordano Bruno

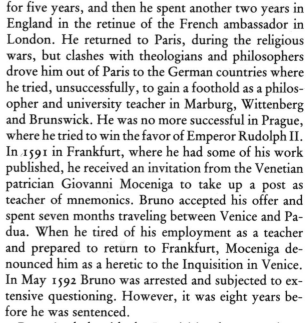

This trial was one of the most important, not only because the main protagonist was so well known but also because records exist of its decisive phases thanks to a written and published account. Giordano Bruno himself was certainly no typical Inquisition victim, neither for his views nor as regards his ultimate fate. He was one of the few Italian heretics who had decided to flee from his home following the first clashes with the ecclesiastical administration and the first brushes with the *Sanctum Officium*.

First he left his monastery in the kingdom of Naples, and then the Dominican convent at Santa Maria sopra Minerva. In 1576 he abandoned the habit of his Order altogether and traveled to northern Italy. When again he seemed to be in danger, he fled via Geneva to southern France, where he lived in Toulouse for a while. He won favor with Henry III who gave him asylum in Paris

for five years, and then he spent another two years in England in the retinue of the French ambassador in London. He returned to Paris, during the religious wars, but clashes with theologians and philosophers drove him out of Paris to the German countries where he tried, unsuccessfully, to gain a foothold as a philosopher and university teacher in Marburg, Wittenberg and Brunswick. He was no more successful in Prague, where he tried to win the favor of Emperor Rudolph II. In 1591 in Frankfurt, where he had some of his work published, he received an invitation from the Venetian patrician Giovanni Moceniga to take up a post as teacher of mnemonics. Bruno accepted his offer and spent seven months traveling between Venice and Padua. When he tired of his employment as a teacher and prepared to return to Frankfurt, Moceniga denounced him as a heretic to the Inquisition in Venice. In May 1592 Bruno was arrested and subjected to extensive questioning. However, it was eight years before he was sentenced.

Bruno's clash with the Inquisition has never been fully explained. Moceniga's denunciation was almost certainly not made from the motive he claimed during the investigation, that he suspected Bruno of failing to teach him all the secrets of mnemonics. The statement of the bookseller, Ciotta, shows that Moceniga was asking for information from Frankfurt as to Bruno's views and religious convictions soon after the latter's arrival in Venice. When he discovered that the teacher he had employed had the reputation in Frankfurt of being godless, he wanted to hand him over to the Inquisition, but not before he had wrested all the secrets of mnemonics from him. It may also be that he had actually invited Bruno to Venice in the first place with the collusion of the Inquisition; Bruno might have been able to serve as a decoy to help flush out heretics. However, there is one important detail that proves that Moceniga was not merely concerned with denouncing Bruno to exonerate himself of the offenses that he had committed in appointing Bruno. Moceniga had prevented Bruno from leaving his house and had instructed his servants to lock him in the attic two days before the Inquisition actually intervened. Bruno appealed before the Venetian inquisitors— who did not seem fully to grasp the extent of their prisoner's non-conformism—as a repentant sinner who regretted mentioning as a joke some arrogant and immoral thoughts and allowing his passion for the work of philosophy to lead him to make some dubious statements. He refuted any suggestion that he was a heretic and offered to clarify any points in his statements that remained unclear or doubtful. His own explanation for Moceniga's denunciation was personal hatred and envy. It is difficult to assess what hope of success such a defense could have had, for Bruno's trial in Venice was never completed.

Giordano Bruno (1548–1600), the Italian philosopher, was forced by his anti-clerical conduct to roam Europe to avoid capture. Following a denunciation he fell into the clutches of the Inquisition in 1592. After eight years of trials and imprisonment he was finally burned.

·SIENA·

Siena was one of the first Italian towns in which the Inquisition renewed its activities, although no one there was ever sentenced to death.
Gabinetto Nazionale delle Stampe, Rome.

The Roman *Sanctum Officium* was well aware of the danger of Bruno's thinking, and probably was well acquainted with it. In September, only three months after he was arrested, Rome demanded that Bruno be returned. The Venetians refused at first, for they always resisted such interference in their legal freedom, but then after six months' negotiations they agreed. In early 1593 the prisoner was transported to Rome, where he faced opponents much more dangerous than those he had faced in Venice. They had all Bruno's writings examined systematically and thoroughly and had some of them summarized and reproduced. Then the trial proper began. Although they were aware from the outset of Bruno's profound rupture with the Church, their investigations followed a set pattern. They accused Bruno of basic heresy, such as denying transubstantiation, negating the divinity of Christ and denying the existence of Hell. He had to face charges, too, of opposing the worship of saints, icons and relics, of the dogma of the Immaculate Conception, and of the effectiveness of fasting. He was also accused of not considering physical love to be a sin. The Inquisition was particularly bothered about his teachings on the infinity and eternity of the world. They also paid special attention to his activities in heretical countries abroad. Only some of the written accounts have survived and are available for study today, but it is evident that Bruno adopted quite different tactics in Rome to those he had adopted in Venice. He could not merely refute the well-documented charges while hoping that the graybeards among the inquisitors would not understand the finer points of his philosophy. So he tried to play for

time. As indicated in the summary of his trial, he first admitted the charges and claimed he was willing to repent of his offenses, but he later added written documents in which he repudiated his confessions. As a result of this strategy, the trial lasted much longer than others had done.

It is not clear why Bruno failed to see through the tactics of the Inquisition, particularly because it was a commonly used trick at that time to appoint a fellow-prisoner as informer. Bruno confided in at least two of his fellow-prisoners and they were able to provide the officials of the *Sanctum Officium* with increasingly detailed information as to his anti-clerical and blasphemous views. One Matthäus de Silvestris, for example, who spent some time in the same cell as Bruno, talked to him every day about the Church and claimed that Bruno maintained the Church was ruled by monks, ignorant priests and asses, and that church teachings were the teachings of asses. The same witness told the Inquisition that Bruno denied believing in God.

The inquisitors themselves delayed the outcome of the trial for other reasons; not because they were unconvinced of his guilt, but because they were keen for reasons of propaganda to see him repent. When in February 1600 they finally realized that he would not, they reached their decision, the only one possible under the circumstances, to turn Bruno over to the secular arm. It is typical that the sentence was read in private in the palace of one of the cardinals. Bruno immediately dropped all pretense and rejected all the attempts made to get him to repent and gain a more merciful death than that of burning as a "reward." The efforts made by the Congregation of St. John Decollatus were in vain, as had been previous attempts made by some leading theologians. Bruno is reported by one of his contemporaries, the humanist Kaspar Schoppe, to have spat the words at his judges before his death: "You're terrified by the sentence you've imposed on me, more terrified than I was waiting for it." Doubtless there was some truth in this observation.

Setting Up an Inquisition Bureaucracy

The trial of Giordano Bruno marked a new phase in the development of the Roman Inquisition. Of course, some trials continued to be run along the old lines, with the cardinals of the *Sanctum Officium* meeting three times a week for discussion and consultation. Sentences were still imposed in public, but the number of curious onlookers waiting in the Campo de' fiori for the gruesome spectacle was getting smaller and smaller, and the number of heretics being executed was also dwindling. In 1609 a recidivist renegade was burned, but by 1611 the crowd had to be content with the burning of a Jew from Pavia; and in the next few years the unfortunates were merely those who had desecrated the Host and individuals who celebrated Mass and heard confession without ever having been ordained as priests. Among the four executed in 1635—an unusually high number of executions for any one year by that time—was a *regens chori* convicted of obscenity and necromancy and three plotters who had planned an attack on the life of the pope.

Title page of the *Dialogue on the Two World Systems . . .*, Florence, 1632. In August of that year the work was banned by the pope. In February 1633 its author, Galileo Galilei, was brought before the court of Inquisition.

The legal authority of the *Sanctum Officium* was extended by Pope Urban VIII to include supervising the life of monasteries. The inquisitors were also instructed to seek out all forms of superstition, from astrology to the use and wearing of talismans. The range of inquisitorial activity at that time can be reconstructed in general terms from correspondence exchanged from 1626 to 1628 between Rome and the provincial Inquisitions. Apart from the question of the orthodoxy and purity of Catholic teachings, the correspondence concerns itself with the worship of saints, dispensations for marriage, sacrilege, witchcraft and magic, trances, false prophecy and moral sins. A papal bull on astrology was issued by Urban VIII in 1631 and instructions on the conduct of witchcraft trials in 1625.

Of course, this does not mean that the Inquisition had stopped pursuing the elimination of heresy and the restoration of religious orthodoxy as its main aim. One of the most important victims of the Inquisition in this period was the Archbishop of Split, Marcantonio de Dominis, who had already been investigated during the time of Paul V for unorthodox views on transubstantiation and penances. He had repented, but was accused again in the 1620s. He died shortly before the trial was concluded and was surrendered posthumously to the secular powers for his corpse to be burned on 21 December 1624.

But while the inquisitors had less work to do on heretical views in theology, they had increasingly to concern themselves with non-conformist thinkers in science and philosophy. The trial against Giordano Bruno marked the beginning of a series of trials in which the Inquisition was to show the same harshness and bitterness against all new emergent forms of thought as had done their predecessors in the 16th century. Perhaps the best-known example is that of Galileo Galilei. On one level his trial symbolized the fight against the scientific truth that the earth goes round the sun. On another level it dealt with the struggle against the Counter-Reformation principle of the supremacy of the Church and its control over human thought.

A celebrated and well-known scholar—even in religious circles—Galileo Galilei had been warned in 1616 by Cardinal Bellarmine not to allow himself to be drawn via his passion for astronomy into the debate over whether the earth orbited the sun. The work of Copernicus had been included on the Index of Forbidden Books by Pope Paul V, but many of the cardinals felt that astronomy had nothing to do with theology in this particular question. They raised no objections to a further study of the whole matter provided that the results of such a study were not published. (They could not be seen calling into question the action of the pope in banning the work of Copernicus.) These cardinals included Cardinal Barberini, who later became Pope Urban VIII. When he became pope, he asked Galileo, whom he greatly admired, to write a paper on the subject of Copernicus's work giving the arguments for and against the heliocentric system—with a conclusion that would negate Copernicus's viewpoint. This was in 1624, and Galileo set enthusiastically to work, linking the whole question of the earth orbiting the sun to the apparently innocent question of tides. The manuscript was approved and printed, and as soon as this was done, the Curia began its intrigues. The Curia told the pope that in his book Galileo had deliberately used far more telling arguments for Copernicus than against him. The aging astronomer was also denounced to the Inquisition and the Inquisition summoned him to Rome, although expressing its deep respect for and acknowledgment of his status and his work. Galileo was investigated in Rome between March and June 1633, and during the course of the questioning it was ascertained that he was in fact a recidivist; the diligent schemers had used false information to demonstrate that Bellarmine's warning in 1616 had actually been an inquisitorial sentence. So Galileo was in danger of receiving the maximum sentence. Can we seriously blame him for repenting under these circumstances? The book he had just written had, at least in appearance, refuted the work and teachings of Copernicus.

In a break with the normal practices of the Inquisition, Galileo was sentenced "only" to life imprisonment and penances, a sentence that the pope had reduced as much as possible first by allowing Galileo to move to Tuscany and second by allowing him to spend his sentence on his own property—under house arrest, as it were. However, the trial and its outcome were detrimental to the Curia and to the Inquisition itself, not merely because Galileo was an outstanding scholar and thinker, but also because the intrigues of the Curia had prevailed over the power of the pope. Urban VIII felt compelled to give into the orthodox wing of the Curia, a situation which would have been completely unthinkable under Pius V or Gregory XIII. The deciding factor in the sentencing of Galileo was not fear of scientific

The interrogation and torture of women accused of witchcraft was gruesome and quite ruthless. Burning of witches in Baden (Switzerland). Woodcut dating from 1574. Stadtbibliothek, Zurich.

progress—that would have been beyond the intellectual powers of the Curia—but the conflicts and intrigues between the cliques of cardinals and bureaucrats.

A mistaken assumption often made by casual observers is to limit the impact of the Inquisition in Italy to that of the papal Inquisition in Rome. Inquisitors and tribunals were, in fact, at work throughout virtually the whole of Italy, and their activities should not automatically be equated with that of the Inquisition in Rome. There were, of course, many similarities, but also many differences and contrasts, even contradictions. To illustrate this, we can divide the tribunals scattered throughout Italy into three groups. The work of the inquisitors in the cities of the pontifical state came closest to that of the Inquisition in Rome. There was less similarity with the Inquisition in the autonomous Italian states, such as those of Florence, Venice or Savoy. The greatest contrast with the work of the Inquisition in Rome came from the Inquisition in the Spanish territories within Italy, some of them by no means small or insignificant areas such as Milan, Naples and Sicily. However, it is impossible to attempt to describe the work of all the tribunals. We can only highlight some typical areas and situations.

The Neapolitan Inquisition between Rome and Spain—Campanella

The supremacy of Spain or, to be more precise, of Aragon, in Naples was a tradition going back centuries. The Spaniards felt "at home" there and so they had no hesitation in setting up their Inquisition as soon as they felt it was necessary. In the 1550s the Inquisition in Naples was run according to the Spanish pattern with anonymous denunciations, torture and confiscation of the property of the accused, which was made

available to the Spanish treasury. However, the proximity of Rome was too great for Naples to remain unaffected by the power of the pope. In a breve in 1554, Julius III had already forbidden the Inquisition to engage in certain activities, "di confiscare i beni degli inquisiti per causa di fede" ("to confiscate the property of those persons being on trial by the Inquisition on behalf of their faith"), although it is doubtful how much attention was paid to this breve in Naples. His successor, Paul IV, considered the Neapolitan Inquisition to be an institution of the diocese and the local bishop, and thus wanted to subject it to the papal supremacy and the *Sanctum Officium* in Rome. To enforce this, a permanent Inquisition commissioner from Rome was to be sent to Naples—a course of action that was not so easily achieved. Initially, cooperation between the representatives of Spain and the Inquisition of Rome was successful only in cases where both sides shared a significant common goal and interest, for example, in the case of the bloody massacre of the Waldense communities in Calabria when the Spanish officers were only too willing to listen to the denunciations of the Inquisition commissioners.

Things changed as soon as influential residents of Naples began to fall victim to the Inquisition; when in 1563 the Inquisition in Naples began a big campaign to arrest suspects in the city and sent a number of prisoners to Rome for further questioning, the opposition became more vociferous. This opposition was fueled by reports of the setting up of the Spanish Inquisition in Milan and by fears that the kingdom of Naples could meet a similar fate. It is significant that the prosperous and the poor alike shared these fears and, as is common in these tense situations, the rich began to take their families and their fortunes away from the towns, leaving the poor to demonstrate in the streets. The first public disturbances occurred when two "stubborn" Lutherans sentenced by the bishops' Inquisition—that is, the Roman Inquisition—were executed publicly. The outrage was directed against the Spanish supremacy as well as against interference by the pope in the affairs of Naples. On the one hand, representatives of the city were sent to the Spanish king to protest against the deliberate establishment of the Spanish Inquisition while on the other, the patricians of Naples and other cities protested against intervention by the pope in having prisoners transported to Rome for trial. Philip II's recent experiences in Milan had prepared him for negotiations with Naples and he assured them that there was and never had been any question of establishing his Inquisition in the kingdom of Naples.

The tide of unrest gradually receded throughout 1564 and by the beginning of the following year the Inquisition had become established as an office of the bishops, officially independent of Rome and, in practice, also independent of the Spanish Inquisition. The Roman *Sanctum Officium* was no longer able to appoint an inquisitor to Naples, although it continued to send commissioners there. It was not permitted to give the Inquisition instructions as to their procedures, but did inform them of new heresies. More complex and delicate cases were now sent to Rome, without any problems. The church authorities in Naples feared new outbreaks of unrest brought about by public executions and so they ceased the large-scale autos-da-fé and sent all their important heretics to Rome. For example, when at the beginning of the 1570s a group of Judaists was discovered in Naples, the Grand Inquisitor, the Cardinal of Pisa, recommended that the trial should not take place in Naples for fear of the unrest which could result. The accused were sent to Rome and were sentenced and punished there in 1572. In 1575, the Venetian legate Giovanni Lippomani wrote that the people of Naples were pious and diligent in their religion, but always ready to rise up in protest against the Inquisition. The number of those arrested and then sent to Rome had become so great that it proved expedient to establish a regular ship service between Rome and Naples simply for use by the Inquisition. It was safer, and also cheaper, to transport the prisoners by sea, since armed guards were not necessary.

The state organs continued to insist on their sovereignty. The transport of prisoners of the Inquisition to Rome was generally allowed only with the approval of the Viceroy of Naples. The emissaries of the Inquisition in Rome, too, always had to seek his permission for their activities. This was the case even for Pius V. On more than one occasion there was a dispute between the state authorities and the Inquisition as to who was responsible for punishing certain offenses. But the more delicate question of who benefited from the goods confiscated always lay behind such disputes.

Over time the influence of the *Sanctum Officium* in Rome over Naples had grown to such an extent that by the 1580s no one was in any doubt as to its authority. The Neapolitan bishops took to seeking advice on how they should proceed in even the simplest cases, and the papal nuncio instructed the police in Naples as to who was to be arrested on suspicion of heresy. Not even the high nobility was spared; in 1583, for example, the *Sanctum Officium* had Prince Spinello arrested on suspicion of unorthodox religious views. The viceroy asked the prince to raise bail and to travel to Rome by himself. When, in 1600, Tommaso Campanella was summoned before the court of Inquisition, it was the pope himself who decided the composition of the court. The tribunal was instructed to send the decisions of its investigations to Rome for consultation before it passed sentence. In 1628 the nuncio, in negotiations with the viceroy, declared it as common practice that the authorities of the Church should arrest suspects in Naples and send them to Rome without first obtaining the consent of the secular authorities. This was too arrogant a step for the Spanish king, and he felt constrained to intervene at least so as to maintain certain standards. However, little changed in practice.

The work of the Inquisition in Naples under the control of Rome was very similar to that of the Spanish Inquisition. The Neapolitan Inquisition confiscated the property of suspects, too, and like the Spanish Inquisition, it was willing to instigate an examination on the grounds of an anonymous denunciation. The hopeless situation of the accused who had no hope of any effective defense was, incidentally, the same in all the trials. The conflict between Rome and Spain was really all about prestige. The differences between them were the result of temporary situations or the personal initiatives of individual inquisitors. When, in 1659, one Monsignore Piazza was appointed commissioner in Naples, the appointment seemed to mark a return to the times of Pius V. He set up a tribunal in Naples complete with tax officials and notaries, disposed of the armed Familiari and began with great zeal to fill the prisons of Naples and interrogate those who had been denounced or were suspected of heresy. He organized autos-da-fé with humiliating confessions and processions through the streets, and even demanded that the state treasury should pay for them. However, he made a serious mistake when he failed to take due account of the standing of the prisoners he took. The opposition to his new Inquisition rapidly gathered force and there were demands that the viceroy should intervene. Fear of growing protest from the people was at that time a sufficient argument, especially with the Masaniello Revolt of 1647 still fresh in people's minds. The viceroy ordered Piazza to leave the kingdom, accompanied by a cavalry division. However, when in May 1661 the estates wanted to exploit the situation and demanded that Naples should respect the bull of Julius III (which forbade the assets of those accused of unorthodoxy to be confiscated), the viceroy turned down their demands.

The young Dominican friar Tommaso Campanella brushed with the Inquisition several times during the early 1590s; first of all, because of his insistence on reading forbidden books, then for his Pythagorean views and finally, in 1594, because he had failed to denounce a secret Jew. The third of these trials was the most serious because one of the charges against him was that of being the author of a number of anti-religious pamphlets. However, it was a nonsensical charge, and Campanella got away with penance and a more or less enforced period spent in the Monastery of St. Sabina. By 1597 he was in Naples, from whence he returned to his native Calabria and there, as the turn of the century approached, he became deluded by a Chiliastic psychosis. He combined his sermons with militant calls to rise up against the domination of the Spanish. Moreover, he took an active part in a plot to use Chiliastic arguments to stir up resistance to the Spanish domination of southern Italy. The revolt was due to take place on 10 September but was discovered and Campanella was arrested during his attempted escape to Sicily.

In prison in Naples he was tried and tortured as a political rebel. Ironically, he was saved from certain death by the fact that there were also charges of heresy against him. Since the investigation of heresy lay outside the field of competence of the Spanish secular authorities, he fell into the clutches of the Inquisition and was sentenced to life imprisonment. During his sentence he enjoyed a special status—he was allowed to read and write, to study and to keep up correspondence with the outside world, for he had a number of patrons among the members of the Curia and particularly among those who opposed Spanish domination. Finally, Pope Urban VIII, who greatly admired Campanella, managed to get him transferred to Rome where he was kept under more relaxed conditions. He was even permitted to publish some of his writings—censored, of course. His interest in astrology and the defense of Galileo involved him in new hostile intrigues, however, and eventually the pope quietly ordered him to be returned to France.

However exceptional the fate of Campanella may have been, he became acquainted during his life with both the Roman and the Neapolitan Inquisitions, both inspired by aiming at political power and by religious narrow-mindedness but also by a boundless and shameless desire for possessions and, paradoxically, also by a certain cautious tolerance for the scholarly and intelligent people before them. The society that had virtually driven Campanella to destruction was now smiling on him in tolerance and humanity and offering him the chance of working in prison on a book which was to become one of the greatest creative works of the

The burning of a **witch** in Amsterdam in 1571.

period. If there had been uncooperative prison guards or if Urban VIII had died earlier, then his book *Civitas Solis (The Sun State)* and other works by this important thinker might never have been written. The trial of Campanella—in some ways, similar to that of Galileo—marked a further change in the atmosphere of the *ecclesia militans*. In place of the domineering and destructive religious fanaticism of previous years, which was rigid and unbending and made no attempt to investigate the human motivations of its victims, there was now a new means of repression; its main driving force was its bureaucratic apparatus, dominated by dignitaries of the Church and including fewer and fewer scholars and more and more parvenus. They were completely lacking the passion and enthusiasm of true sons of the Church who sought a solution to its crisis and would have been willing, had it served the interests of the Church, to sacrifice their own brothers. The bureaucrats had apparently decided to forego the bold dreams of re-establishing Rome's domination of Europe and contented themselves with watching over what they had managed to salvage from the scrap-heap of medieval universalism. They ignored the quest for new ways and means, sticking firmly to well-trodden paths. Although more than one of them was plagued by doubt, they were nonetheless clearly aware of the scope and the limitations of their efforts to bring about

a change in the fortunes of the Church. The most important thing was to maintain the status quo and to fend off any deviation from the official line. The trial against Galileo had shown clearly that not even the pope was in any position to act against the consensus of bureaucratic opportunism; at best he could only limit its effects. The trial against Campanella showed that, if there was any hint of tolerance in the inquisitorial system, it was a result not of generosity but of flaws in the bureaucratic apparatus of rules and regulations.

Although the Peace of Westphalia had once and for all destroyed the dreams of the Habsburgs of world supremacy and had consolidated the stability of a European split along religious lines, the Inquisition's impact continued. The inquisitors pursued all suspected and denounced non-conformists with a determination uncharacteristic of the times, brought them to trial and sentenced them at public autos-da-fé, although the number of death sentences imposed did seem to dwindle somewhat at this period, especially in Italy, possibly under the pressure from public opinion in Europe. However, the fact remained that the Inquisition had become a detestable anachronism, not only because the forces of the Counter-Reformation in these countries had become stabilized, but also because of the rise of modern rationalism and the development of the natural sciences and philosophy.

Fra Giacomo di Chio

Jacob Palaiolog occupies a remarkable position in the ranks of the victims of the papal Inquisition. His views place him among those heretics whose break with the Church had been most radical. On several occasions, he had managed to escape from the Inquisition's prisons, and although he had been sentenced and burned in effigy by the Inquisition, he won the emperor's protection for a number of years. He was one of the exceptional few who were allowed to appeal to the Council of Trent against the sentence of the *Sanctum Officium*. If we are to believe his own account of his origins, he was a descendant of the Byzantine emperor and thus one of the highest-ranking victims of the Inquisition. However, there is not a great deal of evidence as to the truth of this claim, and more recent research would seem to indicate that he had merely appropriated the name of the famous, dynastic family.

Jacob Palaiolog was born in 1520 on the island of Chios as the son of a Greek Orthodox craftsman and an Italian maid-servant working in the palace of a Genoese merchant's family. At that time, Chios still belonged to the Genoese, and so it was decided that the young Jacob should be brought up in his mother's religion. This opened up to the poor young boy his only chance of social advancement, and he joined a Dominican monastery as Fra Giacomo. The Dominicans recognized his extraordinary abilities and made it possible for him to

embark on higher education which led him to Genoa, Ferrara and Bologna between his entry to the monastery and the early 1550s.

The only detailed information we have concerning his views and the activities which alerted the suspicion of the Inquisition dates from the time of his return to the monastery in Chios and his subsequent departure for the Monastery of St. John in Constantinople. His views were the result of specific situations facing Chios and Eastern Christianity at that time.

Palaiolog had grown up in the midst of three or four creeds and cultural movements which were all in conflict: eastern Orthodoxy, which was the cultural bedrock of the region; western Catholicism, which was the faith of the dominant minority on Chios; and Islam, which had arrived there following the victorious expansion of the Ottomans. The fourth factor was the omnipresent Judaism. The conditions on the island meant that these faiths had to tolerate one another, but it was precisely this tolerance that met with the disapproval of the papal Curia. The *Sanctum Officium* sent inquisitors to Chios in the mid-1550s and instructed them to eliminate the "unfavorable conditions" that were regarded as being a direct result of a plot between evil Catholics and the Orthodox, Muslim and Jewish faiths. The inquisitors proceeded exactly as though they had been in Italy, which aroused the anger of the Ottomans who really held the key to the future independence of the island. So the Republic of Genoa sent commissioners who threw the inquisitors off the island. In this dispute Palaiolog, a Dominican, sided firmly with the republic against the aspirations of the *Sanctum Officium*. It was not until later, in 1577, that he was to go so far as to accuse the Grand Inquisitor of the time, Ghislieri, of having weakened the influence of the Genoese government on Chios by his actions in sending inquisitors and thereby of bringing about the conquest of the island by the Ottomans.

Palaiolog also aroused the hostility of the Inquisition for his theological views. As early as his time in Italy and in Constantinople, he had clearly been concerned with the idea of seeking a means of reconciliation between the major religious movements of the time—Christianity, Islam and Judaism. He searched diligently for a way to unite aspects of these monotheistic religions, and pursued his idea with unwavering obsession throughout the whole of his life. Although he in no way opposed the Catholic Church in this, stressing on the contrary that he was seeking to defend its interests, these considerations were bound sooner or later to lead him into direct confrontation with the defenders of the "true faith."

His first clash with the Inquisition seems to have come during his studies in Ferrara. Later, in Constantinople, when he discovered that the Ferrara Inquisition had made charges against him, he immediately returned to Ferrara to defend himself. He was successful in his attempt; in 1557 he was first arrested by the inquisitors in Ferrara and then freed. From there he traveled to Genoa, but in the meantime Grand Inquisitor Ghislieri got to hear of his stay in Italy and decided to make him the scapegoat for the expulsion of the inquisitors from Chios. He therefore instructed the Genoese Inquisition to arrest Fra Giacomo—who by now was becoming known as Palaiolog—and to investigate him for participation in heretical plots in Chios.

It seemed as though the time for revenge had come. The Genoese inquisitor, Franchi, was one of Ghislieri's most devoted servants and admirers, and his agile servant Sixtus of Siena was the same Sixtus whom Ghislieri had saved from burning in 1551 for recidivism in Judaism. The two planned the investigation in such a way that they won the favor and approval of their Roman patron. There were five witnesses to accuse Palaiolog of heretical views, although he himself was never told on what writings or sermons these accusations were based. From these "testimonies," Sixtus of Siena wrote an official charge, though entirely without evidence. For months, the accused refused to sign the statement, and hoped that there would be an intervention on his behalf from Rome. However, when his friends approached the Grand Inquisitor, Ghislieri accused them in turn of siding with a heretic against the

Church. Eventually Palaiolog gave way to the pressure, and signed the written statement in the autumn of 1558. His friends rallied around and arranged for him to escape from the prison in Genoa in early October. He fled to Venice via Pavia, but found he was already too well known to escape the attention of denouncers. The Venetian police arrested him again on 2 November on an anonymous tip that he was hiding in the house of a merchant from Pera. This proved to be a false charge, but he was arrested again in Venice in December of the same year and immediately transported to Rome to face the Inquisition there.

Thus began his third prison sentence, this time with no hope of help from his friends. However, he was certainly among good company in the Ripeta prison during the final year of Paul IV's pontificate—besides Cardinal Morone he also found himself rubbing shoulders with the Bishop of Messina, Verdura, the poet Niccolò Franco and others. It seems likely that the Grand Inquisitor had recognized the validity of the protests against the Genoa statement, for he ordered a new interrogation of Palaiolog to be undertaken, which took only scant account of the Inquisition proceedings in Genoa. On 11 August 1559 Palaiolog came before the *Sanctum Officium* for the first time, and his situation was very serious. However, Paul IV died a short while later and during the riots that followed his death the prison gates were broken open. The Chios heretic used this opportunity to escape and hide, first in Rome and then, under a false name, in the countryside. He was evidently arrested again and imprisoned in Venice, but managed once again to escape—in his own words "summa cum miraculo" ("as if by a miracle"). In 1561 he turned up in France.

By that time the trial against him in Rome had already been completed and closed. The Inquisition ruled that Fra Giacomo di Chio had been guilty of heresy on twenty-three points, and as a recidivist should be surrendered to the secular powers for punishment. On 3 March 1561 he was burned in effigy. He himself described the condemnation as the evil work of Michele Ghislieri, who had acted in conflict with the decision of the *Sanctum Officium* of 11 August 1559 to lift the sentence imposed in Genoa. This was his main argument in an appeal against the trial which he made while in France. In January 1562 he took part in a debate with Calvinists in Poissy and made such a powerful impression that he won the favor of the papal legate, Cardinal d'Este, who appealed on his behalf to Pius IV. Palaiolog also appealed, through the intermediary of the head of his Order, to the Council of Trent to give a ruling on his dispute with the Inquisition. Carlo Borromeo could only partly endorse this appeal, since he himself had doubts as to Palaiolog's standing. The pope agreed on the condition that the formal procedure should be to make a humble submission to the council and to reconcile the Dominican friar with the Church. He guaranteed Palaiolog safe-conduct to Trent, but said that only when he got to Trent would the guarantee be extended for the period he spent with the council.

Palaiolog arrived in Trent about the end of May, but refused to conduct himself like a faithful son of the Church asking for forgiveness, behaving instead like a self-confident theologian and respected gentleman and demanding a revision of his sentence. A number of legates were in fact willing to have a public debate with him, which was undoubtedly a reaction to the unfavorable attitude most of the council had to the Inquisition of Rome. Palaiolog, however, was asking for more than was in their power to grant him. He tried to convince them that his ideas were right and that he was correct in trying to get the different faiths to share a common language—even if the Church had to make some compromises. The legates offered him the chance of repenting in secret to the legate Simonetta, so that he could be forgiven, but he was obsessed by what he thought was the unique opportunity of gaining support for his views and he refused. He even acted unwisely in trying to negotiate not only his own freedom but also that of an organized group of like-minded sympathizers. Finally, on 28 September, the legates told Carlo Borromeo that they felt further negotiations were pointless.

A short while before this, Palaiolog himself had sensed that he had failed and began to be fearful of his own safety. His safe-conduct did not cover his return from the council, and so he devised a clever escape route, joining up with messengers of Emperor Ferdinand who were traveling to Vienna to report back to the emperor on the rather unsuccessful efforts of the council. In Linz, they discovered that the emperor had fled from Vienna to Prague to escape an epidemic of plague, and so they altered their route. In early October 1562 Palaiolog appeared in the capital of the kingdom of Bohemia, which for him marked the start of several years' stay in the lands of the Bohemian Crown under the domination of the Habsburgs. The papal nuncio, Delfino, got to hear of his arrival and ordered him to enter a monastery while his case remained unresolved. He also informed the Grand Inquisitor that the dangerous heretic had arrived in Prague. The inquisitor responded with an instruction to have the man arrested and immediately brought back to Rome. While the letter made its way, hampered by the winterly weather conditions, Palaiolog had managed by his intelligence and eloquence to win a number of patrons at the court (including Maximilian II, the son and heir of Ferdinand) and also among the Utraquists in Bohemia. As a result, he was warned in good time of the intention of the nuncio and escaped arrest in the spring of 1563 by a well-timed flight to Saxony. His attempts in Saxony to gain employment at either the court or the university were unsuccessful; the liberal-minded Palaiolog was no less alien to the orthodox Lutheran milieu than to orthodox Catholicism. However, his two-months' stay in Saxony gave Palaiolog and his friends time for further negotiations. His first success came when the Bohemian governor granted him temporary asylum in Prague and Palaiolog then continued his campaign from there. He approached Emperor Ferdinand with a request for protection against the power of Ghislieri so that he would not be forced to go to Lutheran countries. But Ferdinand challenged Palaiolog either to leave the country or to ask the pope for forgiveness for his offenses. Palaiolog refused, on the grounds that he could not ask forgiveness for what he had not done. Finally, the old emperor gave way to the appeals being made on Palaiolog's behalf by those around him, and in 1564 he allowed him to stay in his lands on condition that he appealed to the pope for mercy. Although the emperor died before this could be done, when Maximilian II took office, Palaiolog's situation in Prague improved considerably. The new sovereign was sympathetic toward him, extended his temporary right to asylum and even made him a small annual allowance. He was considered to be an expert on oriental affairs, particularly the Turkish question. Meanwhile, the scholar had become acquainted with the Bohemian Utraquists and had won some friends in this circle, particularly scholars and burghers who followed the humanist Matthäus Collinus of Chotejřina who was especially impressed by Palaiolog's knowledge of Aristotle, of Roman law and of the Greek language. It was Collinus who also arranged a marriage for him with the daughter of the respected burgher Kuthen of Prague, a marriage which brought him not only material security but also a brief period of family happiness. Clearly, his time as a friar was over. Toward the end of the 1560s it seemed as though the refugee was going to turn into not only a respectable burgher but also a diplomatic adviser, for the emperor gave him the task of gathering information on conditions in the Ottoman Empire.

However, Palaiolog was not to be allowed to enjoy a quiet life. After Ghislieri had acceded to the Holy See, he immediately demanded Palaiolog's extradition again, and sent out nuncial spies after him. Palaiolog averted the danger with the help of the emperor, but then suddenly came into conflict with the authorities of Bohemia because he had helped the former Dominican, Bonifacio Benincasa, to escape criminal charges by granting him asylum. The agents of the papal nuncio and the legate of the Spanish king exploited the dispute and on 30 March 1571 Palaiolog was arrested once again and imprisoned until July of the same year. This time, his appeals for intervention by the emperor went unanswered, and he was expelled from Bohemia. He had to sell his house in Prague, received his last payment from the emperor on 15 September 1571 and then took his family to Cracow.

His stay in Prague marked the beginning of the second phase of Palaiolog's life, the phase in which he was to break finally and definitively with the Church. Apart from his reports on the Ottoman Empire and other occasional work, he had written only one polemic against Paul IV, which also gave details of his imprisonment in Ripeta, and one polemic against the primacy of the pope. Immediately after his arrival in Cracow, however, he published over several months three major theological and philosophical works, suggesting that at least part of the work had been completed while he was still in Prague. During his stay there, he had grown so close to the Utraquists in Bohemia that some of them even considered electing him as their archbishop. In fact he had not only had contacts with just this group, who were successors to the Hussites; he had also acquainted himself with the thinking of more radical groups that focused on anti-trinitarianism.

It is, therefore, entirely consistent that after his arrival in Cracow the former Bishop of Fünfkirchen in Hungary, Andreas Dudycz, should have become Palaiolog's main supporter, a man who had once been a legate in Trent and had gradually moved to a very radical position. It was he who arranged meetings between Palaiolog and the Polish anti-trinitarians as well as with groups in Transylvania. In the autumn of 1572, the scholar began the journey back to his home, but first he spent some time among the anti-trinitarians in Klausenburg, where he wrote several tracts and pamphlets mirroring their ideas. He then went to Turkey, stayed a short while on his native Chios and in Constantinople, and then remained in Transylvania until 1575. He returned to Cracow when Stephen Báthory began to persecute non-Catholics. But even in Cracow he found no peace, for Stephen was soon elected king of Poland, and so for this reason, and because of some disagreements with the Polish anti-trinitarians, Palaiolog decided to return once more to the lands of the Habsburgs, this time to Moravia under the protection of Jetřich of Kunovice, a friend of Wilhelm von Rosenberg.

Although his association with the anti-trinitarians had not been without problems, it had acquainted Palaiolog with the workings of this religious group. The isolated and persecuted seeker after truth had become a member and even a worker of an organized religious movement where he found friends, helpers and admirers. Ironically, it was precisely this new feeling of fellowship which in the end proved his downfall. During religious persecution in the previously tolerant Transylvania, one of the leading anti-trinitarians, Davidis, was arrested and was burned at the stake in November 1579; Palaiolog immediately wrote a passionate defense of his friend and an accusation of the judges concerned, which he published in Basle in 1581. This marked his public commitment to a movement suspected by the Habsburgs of being an ally of and a secret agency for the Ottoman Turks. Now they could bring new charges against the man and arrest him for spying for the Turks. It was primarily for this reason that Emperor Rudolph II instructed the Bishop of Olmütz (Olomouc) on 20 October 1581 to arrest Palaiolog discreetly and to confiscate all his writings. The bishop summoned Jetřich of Kunovice, presented him with the emperor's letter and managed to have Palaiolog surrendered to the bishop's forces in Louka, Jetřich's residence, on 13 December. There was no resistance. Not a word of protest or outrage came from the Moravian nobleman; he did not warn his protégé, making escape impossible. But how is this to be reconciled with the famed religious tolerance prevalent in Moravia? One answer may lie in the fact that the Greek was arrested not as a heretic but as someone suspected of spying for the arch-enemy of all Christians.

Shortly after he was taken to Vienna and had his writings examined, it became clear that Palaiolog was not a spy. Unfortunately, he was now in the hands of the Habsburg authorities, who immediately made themselves useful to the papal nuncio. Palaiolog was detained as a prisoner of the pope and of the *Sanctum Officium*. Unlike his predecessor, Rudolph II was a true and devoted son of the Church, and after long negotiations he agreed in April 1582 to have the prisoner extradited to Rome. Thus began the third and final stage in the life of Jacob of Chios. Nuncio Bonhomini made careful preparations for his extradition to Rome. Palaiolog, now sixty years old but with a legendary ability to escape from prisons, was chained up and locked in an iron cage for the journey. He was conducted by

Jacob Palaiolog, as an adviser to the Catholic side, took part in the religious debate in Poissy in 1561 between the Catholics and the Huguenots. Engraving by Jacques Tortorel and Jean Périssin.

waterways to Innsbruck and from there slowly to Rome via Trent. He set out on 27 May, and it was not until August that the streets of Rome filled with curious crowds to see the cage with the "heretical monster" who was so renowned. His jailers had bound his hands behind his head so that he could not even cover his face in shame.

Palaiolog's last trial was conducted as against a leading anti-trinitarian. Famous theologians, including a number of cardinals, visited him in prison and tried to persuade him to recant. He debated with them for hours on end, but remained firm on his views, making the decision of the *Sanctum Officium* relatively easy. At an auto-da-fé on 13 February 1582 in Santa Maria sopra Minerva he was found to be a stubborn and recidivist heretic, and was surrendered to the secular powers for burning. On the night before his execution—scheduled for 19 February—some of the pope's prelates made a last visit to Palaiolog in prison but he still stuck to his views "con eloquenza incredibile" ("with unbelievable eloquence").

In the early hours of 19 February, Palaiolog was prepared for his last journey. He was stripped to the waist and dressed in a linen robe painted with a depiction of hellfire. Then, holding a candle and accompanied by members of the Brotherhood of St. John Decollatus, he and other condemned prisoners left the prison for the Campo de' fiori where he was to be burned alive at the stake as an unrepentant heretic before a large crowd. Then he suddenly asked for his execution to be postponed, saying that he wanted to search his conscience and repent. General surprise greeted the statement, and no one seemed able to make a decision on the spot. He was taken to a nearby workshop to await Pope Gregory XIII's decision while the other executions went ahead. Gregory decided to go along with Palaiolog's wishes provided that he recant publicly. The text of a recantation was immediately drawn up in the presence of a notary from the *Sanctum Officium*, and Jacob read it aloud to the crowd assembled in the square. He also promised to write to his followers, telling them of his change of heart. He was then taken back to the prison.

An eyewitness account speaks of him leaving the Campo de' fiori looking happy and even chatting and joking with those accompanying him.

If Palaiolog as a free man had posed the *Sanctum Officium* with an extraordinary problem, as a prisoner he was no less of a liability. His recantation had created an unprecedented situation. The cardinals could not agree on whether he should still be executed, so the decision was left to the pope himself at a meeting of the *Sanctum Officium* on 23 March. Palaiolog's execution was postponed, and in the interim he was to write to all his followers north of the Alps to explain his change of heart to them and to refute his heretical views. Filippo Neri was given spiritual charge of his soul.

There is no clear picture of what caused his sudden volte-face. Was it simply human frailty in the face of death? If he had wanted a less painful death, he could simply have humbled himself in the hours before his execution. Or had he found a new spark of hope in his conversations with theologians on the eve of his execution? Did he simply want time to plot another escape, as Nuncio Bonhomini and others believed? Palaiolog was to spend two years in prison, yet little information survives which could shed light on his motives. There is no evidence of his refuting the heretical views. If in fact he wrote the letters relating his repentance, they would not have gone unanswered. Palaiolog was clearly still playing hide and seek with his captors.

At last, however, the inevitable happened. On 25 May 1585 Jacob Palaiolog was put to death, in private, in the courtyard of the Torra di Nona prison. He had been granted the privilege of an honorable death by the sword, possibly because his captors were still not convinced that they were really dealing with a heretic of imperial Byzantine descent. The Brotherhood of St. John Decollatus wrote an account of the trial and recorded that Jacob made confession, humbled himself, received Communion and then died with the words "Miserere mei Deus" ("may God have mercy on my soul"). In fact, other accounts contradict this. Nevertheless, his remains were removed the same day for burning on the Campo de' fiori.

IT IS TRUE THAT THE INQUISITION INTERVENES IN ALL AFFAIRS, RE-GARDLESS OF RANK OR STATUS; IT IS THE TRUE LORD RULING AND REIGNING OVER SPAIN.

Report by the Venetian Legate Giovanni Soranzo, dated 1565

THE INQUISITION AS AN INSTRUMENT
OF THE SPANISH STATE

The Spanish Inquisition was more extensive than all the other European Inquisitions of the 16th century, and for this reason it is impossible to give a systematic account of its development since the 1550s. At the same time, the focus of its work was very standardized as a result of its monolithic organization. For these two reasons, then, we have to content ourselves here with a brief account of the principles and general trends of the Spanish Inquisition and with some critical and typical examples of its activity. In Spain, unlike in Italy, neither the Council of Trent nor the accession of Pope Pius V had had any significant influence on the development of the Inquisition and its organization. By coincidence, the last session of the council coincided with several events in Spain that represented a milestone in the development of the Spanish Inquisition. These included the major trials of Lutherans in Valladolid and Seville, the arrest of Carranza, Archbishop of Toledo, and the publication in 1561 of the so-called new instructions for the activities of the courts of Inquisition.

The Trials of Lutherans in Seville

The arrival of the teachings of Luther in Spain in the 1540s was linked with the activities of two important preachers and theologians in Seville Cathedral—Dr. Constantino Ponce de la Fuentes and Dr. Juan Gils, known as Egidio. The former enjoyed such a good reputation that he was summoned to the court of Emperor Charles V in 1548 as father confessor. The new ideas gained popularity in some monasteries, especially the Monastery of the Hieronymites, among some leading families but also among the common people. A Lutheran community was formed which operated clandestinely for about ten years and had some 130 members. The Inquisition became suspicious in the early 1550s, but only of a small number of individuals.

In 1552 Dr. Egidio was denounced and arrested because the consultants of the Inquisition read heretical and fallacious views into his theses. Neither the intervention of the Chapter of Seville nor that of the emperor himself was of any use, and on 11 August 1552 the popular preacher had to recant *de vehementis*, was sentenced to a year's imprisonment and was further banned from preaching or having any of his work published for ten years. The trial against him had disturbed the clandestine Lutherans to such an extent that some of them fled across the border. Things soon calmed down again, but the incident had attracted the attention of the Jesuits who in 1554 set up a college in Seville to counter the Lutheran heresy. They began diligently to spy on all the preachers, though with hardly any success. In 1556 Dr. Constantino Ponce returned from the imperial court to Seville and the chapter immediately appointed him Dr. Egidio's successor. A year later he was denounced and interrogated by the Inquisition. Although he was allowed to continue to preach, he remained under suspicion. He tried to escape the Inquisition by applying for membership in the Jesuit Order, but after a long delay the Jesuits refused, on the secret instructions of the Inquisition.

In early 1557, the atmosphere in Seville began to become unbearable for the Lutherans. There were rumors about imminent arrests that caused all the monks in the town's Monastery of the Hieronymites to flee in one night. Then, toward the summer, the Inquisition spies had a tactical windfall. They intercepted a consignment of banned books from Frankfurt and monitored their circulation. This, then, was their first chance to find out the names of certain secret heretics. After careful preparations, they moved on 9 October 1557, and large numbers of Familiari were sent out on a manhunt. Many Lutherans were arrested, although some managed to escape. Numerous secret hiding places for banned books and heretical manuscripts came to light, and the inquisitors were able to discover even more names, resulting in rumors of mass arrest. There is no evidence that these rumors were true but, nevertheless, the government was shocked and horrified. Charles V, emperor emeritus, wrote a personal letter in which he demanded that those arrested be condemned not only as heretics but also as traitors to the country and enemies of the Crown. The Grand Inquisitor had no trouble in persuading Pope Paul IV to write a breve in which he permitted action taken against the heretics to be severe. Even heretics who showed signs of repentance and who had recanted could be burned, and any denunciation was grounds for an arrest.

The arrests and trials continued in the following year. The large number of pending investigations completely exceeded the scope of the courts, which urgently asked for more help. The trials were still incomplete by the spring of 1559. Many of those arrested recanted and repented during the trials, including Seville's foremost Lutheran, Don Juan Ponce de León, while others contested the labeling of their views as heretical. Some defended the new teachings, including the twenty-six-year-old Marie de Bohorques, who was able to make a good impression on her enemies; she defended her

The banner of the Spanish Inquisition. Copperplate engraving by Bernhard Picart. Staatliche Kunstsammlungen, Dresden, Kupferstichkabinett.

demned were stripped of their holy orders. When one of them tried to speak to the others, he was gagged. However, Don Juan Ponce de León was allowed to try to persuade Marie de Bohorques to recant as he had. The account of the auto-da-fé records that she called him "an idiot and a windbag," maintaining that "this was not the time to talk so much." After the sentences were announced, the victims were conveyed by donkeys and taken to the bonfires, which had been lit in front of the walls of the city.

The second major auto-da-fé was not until 22 December 1560, when twenty-nine victims were sentenced, including a large number of women. Only seven Lutherans were sentenced to death, however, and another three were burned in effigy, including the two leading clergy, Dr. Egidio and Dr. Constantino Ponce, who had both died before sentence could be passed on them. On 24 April 1562 a third group of thirteen Lutherans was present on the platform together with eighteen foreign heretics; sixteen Hieronymite monks who had escaped in 1557 were burned in effigy. Among those condemned was the former priest Sebastián Martínez; he had been writing pamphlets against the Inquisition and its trials of Lutherans since 1559 and had them printed on his own press and circulated. In late 1561 he circulated so many pamphlets in Seville that queues of orthodox believers formed before the gates of the *Sanctum Officium*, wishing to hand in examples of heretical publications that they had found or that had been handed over to them anonymously. In early 1562 Martínez was arrested and sentenced to death. After the third auto-da-fé, only a handful of people remained in prison, including the scholar, Dr. García Arias, who may not have been one of the most active members of the secret community but who nevertheless posed a great problem for the Inquisition because he proved that their theological knowledge was very limited. Finally he, too, was sentenced to death at the fourth auto-da-fé in 1562. Over the next few years, a few isolated Lutherans were exposed by chance.

Lutheran views with an admirable knowledge of the Holy Scriptures and remained true to her beliefs until she was executed.

The first public auto-da-fé took place on Sunday, 24 September 1559. Huge platforms were erected on the Plaza de San Francisco, for the event had been publicized weeks in advance. Early that morning, a procession led by fifty clergymen followed by officials of the court and twenty-three Lutherans—sixteen of whom were to be surrendered to the secular powers—left the prison. First the creed was read, followed by a sermon, and then two clergy who were among those con-

The Lutherans of Valladolid

Lutheran thinking arrived in Valladolid, the royal seat of Castile, sometime after it appeared in Seville. The first propagator of these ideas seems to have been the Italian nobleman Carlos de Seso from Verona, whose wife was directly related to the Spanish royal family. He himself became an employee of Prince Philip in 1551. He was a friend of the Cazalla family, one of the leading families in Valladolid, of which three members were clerics. Seso tried in 1554 to convince one of them, also called Carlos, that purgatory did not really exist. Carlos became alarmed and approached his former teacher, Professor Bartolomeo Carranza, to ask whether he should report his friend. Carranza, who later became the Archbishop of Toledo, counseled

caution and wisely summoned Don Seso to himself and advised the two to keep absolutely quiet about what had happened. This was the first but not the last occasion that Carranza's name cropped up in connection with the Lutherans in Valladolid.

Gradually, Carlos and the Cazalla family adopted more and more of the Lutheran teachings and ideas. The Cazallas took the new teachings to other patrician families and Seso won new followers in the surrounding towns and cities, particularly in Toro and Pedroso. One particularly zealous agitator was Juan Sánchez, originally a sexton for Pedro Cazalla and later a servant in the house of the clandestine Lutheran, Doña Catalina de Hortega. He also won the support of a whole group of Bernadine nuns from the Convent of Our Lady of Bethlehem in Valladolid. The Castilian Lutherans, unlike those in Seville, had no organized communities, but did meet regularly.

In early 1558 the disturbing news broke that the Lutherans in Seville had been flushed out. Those in Valladolid decided to be more vigilant but did not suspect that the Inquisition was already on their trail. Two respected ladies from Valladolid found out from comments passed by Francesco de Vivero, the youngest of the Cazalla brothers, that Lutheran sympathizers were in the city, and they told their confessor, who advised them to infiltrate the heretics and help expose them. They took on their roles as spies with relish and made their first denunciation on 14 April. Quite by chance Dr. Augustín Cazalla, court preacher to the governor and preacher in the Bethlehem Convent, got wind of this and tried to warn his friends and have the forbidden books and manuscripts burned. The Inquisition acted too quickly, however, and the few followers who attempted an escape were unsuccessful. Don Seso was among them. Only Juan Sánchez escaped, to Geneva, but he was eventually tracked down and brought back.

The arrests began toward the end of April, and the trials of the suspects commenced in May. Most of those arrested showed great weakness and inconsistency, denounced each other and confessed to all the alleged offenses. Unfortunately for those arrested, the Inquisition decided to crack down harder than it had done in

Seville. The first auto-da-fé was held on 21 May 1559 on the Plaza Mayor. Doña Juana, as representative of King Philip II, and the twelve-year-old Prince Don Carlos took their places on the podium at five o'clock in the morning. Fourteen of the thirty accused were turned over to the secular arm for punishment, but only one was burned at the stake. The others had to wait until October 1559 to learn their fate, when Philip II himself came to Valladolid to take part in the auto-da-fé to show the support of the Spanish sovereign for the Inquisition. The twelve condemned to death included the main author of the Lutheran infiltration, Carlos Seso, and several nuns from the Bethlehem Convent.

One notable feature of the Valladolid trials was that the newly appointed Bishop of Toledo, Bartolomeo Carranza, was compromised during the investigations. A number of those arrested, including the Dominican Dominic de Roxas, said that they had heard Carranza was secretly on the side of the new ideas. Yet when Roxas discovered on 7 October 1559 that he was to be surrendered to the secular authorities, he demanded to be tried again, and claimed that all his statements regarding Carranza were lies. The inquisitors chose not to believe the fact that had emerged during the investigations that, as early as 1554, Carranza had talked to Don Seso about the latter's heretical views but had not denounced him. Nevertheless, the first denunciation of Carranza took place in December 1558 and the following year he was thrown into the Inquisition prison.

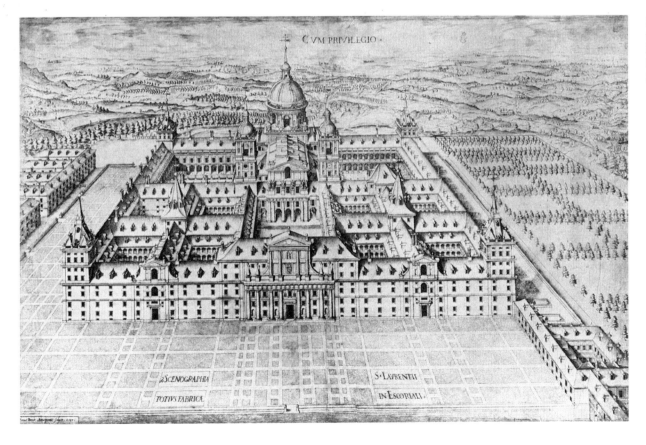

Philip II moved from Valladolid to the new capital where he had his new palace built.
Escorial. Engraving by Pieter Perret, 1587.

Doña Marina de Guevara became famous neither as a religious visionary, like Saint Theresa of Avila, nor as an organizer of religious life along the lines of Maria Ward. She did not write anything well-known and contributed nothing to either the development of heretical thinking or general education. Her name is included here to represent an entire category of victims of the Inquisition—victims who were in no way significant or outstanding and whose fates have long since faded from anyone's memory.

Doña Marina was descended from Castilian nobility, and her brothers occupied respected posts in the Spanish state in the mid-16th century. She herself was the sub-prioress of the Convent of Our Lady of Bethlehem in Valladolid, the former capital of Castile. She was a caring sister to the obedient and humble nuns, but a stringent superior to those who were in error. All the nuns admired her irreproachable life and the exemplary way in which she ran the Order, but this was not enough for her. At the age of about forty, she decided that she must try to get closer to God and so she started to punish her body by fasting and sometimes spent entire nights in prayer and repentance. This life-style gradually caused such harm to her health that the abbess forbade her to make her life any more stringent. She could have gone down in the history of the Order as an exemplary abbess or become a follower of St. Theresa.

It was only the discovery of a group of Lutherans in Valladolid that prevented her from living out this kind of life until the end of her days. The Bethlehem Convent had a twofold link with the Cazalla de Vivero family through two of the nuns. In 1557 Dr. Augustín Cazalla, former court preacher to Charles V and still a preacher at the court of the regent Doña Juana in Valladolid, began to work in the convent. He was a man of the world and seemed to be an excellent speaker and conversationalist and fascinating company. He soon gathered a circle of about six young admirers around him from among the nuns; they would ask him theological questions and were fascinated by the idea of achieving salvation through faith. The group also discussed the fallaciousness of the doctrine of purgatory and other articles of faith put forward by Martin Luther. Some of these young nuns saw Doña Marina de Guevara as a maternal protector, and she herself became a friend of Dr. Cazalla and gradually joined this inner circle. They also occasionally discussed religious questions with some of the female dignitaries of Valladolid who came to visit the convent. Dr. Cazalla clearly had great faith in Doña Marina, for she was the one to whom he sent a warning note when he discovered that the Inquisition had begun proceedings against him and some of the other followers of the new teachings. He assumed that the message would be intercepted, and

phrased it very carefully, saying that he had been denounced to the Inquisition and that he ordered the sisters of the Order to tell the truth about his preaching. It was implied that they were to keep quiet about the private meetings in the small group. Doña Marina passed the message on to the others.

At the end of 1558 the inquisitors began to make arrests and try the suspects. It is not clear who was the first to mention the name of the sub-prioress among those who had taken part in discussions now being labeled as heretical. Certainly she was one of the first group of nuns to be questioned as witnesses in the convent in mid-May. Thus it was that Doña Marina found her way into the clutches of the Inquisition. Clerks carefully and systematically got hold of manuscripts and began to gather together accounts of interrogations with her or with others about her. These documents have survived, enabling us to trace not only the sad history of this noble nun but also the practices of the Inquisition.

Doña Marina was first called as a witness on 15 May, at a time when the entire Cazalla family and their friends—including Catalina de Hortega who quite publicly admitted her support for Lutheran teachings—were in the custody of the Inquisition. Doña Marina spoke mostly about herself, her desires and efforts to get closer to God, her good works and penances, and the damage she had done to her health through excessive fasting. When she was asked directly who had Lutheran views, she named four people, including Catalina and Sánchez, who by that time had already left Spain. She made no mention of Dr. Augustín Cazalla although she had already spoken much of his words and thoughts. A month later she submitted a written statement in which she said that she had been told by many people that good works in themselves were not enough to guarantee her salvation.

This, it should be remembered, was at a time when the Inquisition had already demanded that she be imprisoned within the convent. Confusion and fear reigned in the convent, and all the nuns were called in for questioning. Those who were among Dr. Cazalla's "inner circle" tried to agree on their statements among themselves, and immediately after the questioning they told each other of the questions they had been asked and the answers they had given. However, these naive young girls could not hope to outwit the experienced inquisitors, who easily confused and intimidated them. Finally the nuns admitted that they had been warned and had tried to cover up certain facts. They now became the guilty parties. Sometime in July, Doña Marina became ill, seriously ill with some fever it seems, because the Inquisition records include a letter from the abbess of the Bernadines asking the inquisitors to let Doña Marina have a priest to give her the last rites.

We know only that the Inquisition sent a doctor, to confirm that she really was ill; the records do not tell us whether she was allowed a visit from a priest, although there is a short statement, dated 16 August, followed ten days later by another letter from Doña Marina to the Inquisition, obviously written in great distress. She admitted that she had sometimes discussed the possibility of going to Hell even if she had done good works, but that she had only meant by it that man was his own worst enemy. She had heard on many occasions that the only way to know God was to know oneself and to deny and forego oneself, "and so it seemed to me then —and still does seem to me now—that I am Hell." She also admits in this letter that she had voiced her views that, as she had lived according to God's commandments, purgatory was superfluous for her. But, she reiterated, she believed everything the Church taught and prayed earnestly for the souls in purgatory.

Following this, the inquisitor paid another visit to the convent on 31 August and demanded to talk to Doña Marina. He told her that her statement would be used as evidence against Catalina de Hortega, Sánchez, Dr. Cazalla and three other people whose names she had given. It is clear from the records that she was taken aback by this. She hesitated and then explained at some length that she could no longer stick by her former statements because she was not sure that everything she had said was absolutely true. It was as though she had suddenly become aware—too late—that her statements could harm others. This was, it is true, an attitude that aroused the anger of the inquisitor, who pointed out to her that she was in effect refusing to do her duty as a good daughter of the Church by not denouncing heretics. This was a serious matter, he said, but even this threat did not induce her to back up her former statements although she must have known this would cast her completely at the mercy of the court of Inquisition.

There seems to have been a long waiting period until February 1559, and Doña Marina was kept under house arrest during this period. Long delays between periods of interrogation were a common tactic used by the Inquisition to exert psychological pressure on its victims, although it may also be that the inquisitors simply were occupied with the other members of the "inner circle." Whichever it was, this period was the last quiet period of her life. On 11 February 1559 she was arrested and taken to the Inquisition prison, appearing at later investigations as a defendant. She was forty-three years old at that time.

The first interrogations may erroneously be taken as mere formalities. The accused had to give personal details and say whether she knew why she had been arrested. When she answered that she did not, and showed that she was not easily going to admit guilt, she was rapidly moved on to the second stage at which she

A Spanish auto-da-fé depicted in two scenes. The upper part shows the conduct of the trial itself, while in the lower part the condemned prisoners are taken to their place of execution on donkeys.

still rejected all the charges against her and refused to add anything to the statements she had already made. At the third stage of the trial, on 2 March, she asked to be reminded of her statements. But even then she refused to add anything to them. Immediately after that, the prosecutor Ramírez intervened and made the official charge against her. The twenty-four points of the charge can be summed up as follows: Doña Marina was accused of refuting belief in purgatory and prayers for the souls of the dead; of receiving Communion without having previously made confession; of possessing certain Lutheran books, reading them and passing them on; of telling the other nuns in the convent to remain silent during questioning; and of refusing to denounce the remaining heretics herself. After this charge was made, the prosecutor proposed the death sentence for her, on the grounds that she had proved stubborn and unrepentant and unwilling to admit and do penance for her offenses.

Doña Marina was really not conscious of having committed such grave sins against the Church, and she had no thought of pretending guilt she did not feel. When she was given the chance to answer the charge, she responded in a very self-contained manner; she answered most of the points of the charge by saying merely that she refuted the accusations. However, the dry, factual, documentary account does convey something of a challenging note in her voice. For example, she answered the charge of considering good works to be superfluous to salvation by saying: "Lord, I don't understand what sort of works those must be, and if I did say something about them, it was about my own useless good works of spending the whole night in the choir and fasting for three whole days." As for the charge of inciting the other nuns to silence during questioning, she said simply: "I really don't know what I can say." She admitted only what she had previously admitted—that some of the people with whom she had talked had questioned the existence of purgatory and the sense of good works, and that she had handled and seen Lutheran writings.

The very next day, it seems, she became fully aware of the danger she was now facing. She asked for another hearing, and assured the inquisitors that she really did not remember any further offenses. She also told them how deeply affected she had been by the charges against her: "While I thought I was getting closer to God, I am now told I am acting as a heretic." The account adds that she wept bitterly. Finally, at the end of the hearing, she requested paper so that she could write her answer to the charge. This was dated 7 March and had a codicil dated 10 March. In this written statement she insisted that she was a good Catholic and that the charges against her were all based on a misunderstanding. In addition, a new element appeared in her defense—that the witnesses against her were possibly biased, and that much of what they had said could be merely malicious rumors or misunderstanding of what she had said.

The inquisitors filed her statement and declared the trial closed. Other statements were to be taken, but at first nothing happened. Again, the accused was left alone in her cell for two months, and this time not in any sense to apply pressure to her; the Inquisition officials had their hands full trying to make arrangements for the auto-da-fé of the first group of convicted Lutherans.

Being left alone brought about a change within Doña Marina. On 8 May she asked for yet another hearing, saying that she wanted to get something off her conscience. She admitted to the inquisitors that she had indeed had doubts as to the existence of purgatory and that she had spoken with other nuns about these doubts. She also clarified some of the heretical statements that she had heard from Catalina, Dr. Cazalla and his brother Francesco de Vivero. Again she stressed that, despite all her doubts, she still believed in the teachings of the Church.

Another month went by. It was not until 12 June that she was again called for questioning, immediately after the first auto-da-fé, whose drastic sentences must have been conveyed to her. Both Dr. Cazalla and Francesco de Vivero had died. Asked once again to tell the truth, she answered humbly that she could no longer remember anything, that her memory had started to fade and that her soul was in anguish. She asked the Inquisition's advice as to how she could redeem her soul. Yet the inquisitors kept coming back to the question of

purgatory. Doña Marina answered once again that she could no longer remember whether she had really stopped believing in purgatory. She was sure of her doubts, but knew that she had always obeyed the law of the Church. The inquisitor wanted to know why she had had such doubts, and she answered that she had heard others talking of such things and named names for the first time. This was undoubtedly the reason why she was again, only three days later, asked why she had refused to confirm her statements the year before. She accounted for this behavior by her poor memory and confusion.

On 27 June the accused was presented with extracts from statements made by twelve witnesses, read with no indication of who had made them. The statements contained a good deal of concrete information on the subject matter of conversations in which Doña Marina took part. Most of the prisoners had tried to lighten their consciences by giving detailed information about the offenses that they had committed and also those of their friends. Dr. Cazalla, however, had to be tortured before he would say anything. Doña Marina's answer to the individual statements and denunciations was still one of rejection. Where what was said was actually true, she simply stressed that she had never felt that the nuns had spoken against the teachings of the Church or against their Order. She refused point-blank to comment on the complex and scholarly statements on the heretical content of the conversations she had had: "I could never have said such things, because I have never had the clarity of understanding fully to grasp these issues." She answered a witness's statement, which she had had a chance to study in her cell, in much the same way: "It seems to me that I have been given a copy of this statement so that I can recognize offenses I would not have recognized before, and I dare not read it for fear the devil will confuse something in my memory."

The trial was drawing to a close. The accused had an opportunity to construct her defense and then to give her final statement and suggest witnesses for the defense. In her written submission of 13 July, Doña Marina asked to be acquitted of the charge. She explained this request by saying that the witnesses had testified against her for revenge; they were nuns from the same Order who felt that she had been harsh toward them and who hated her for it. They were naive young girls, easily confused and misled. She said that she could see no evidence from the testimonies that her faith was anything but orthodox; on the contrary, she said, the testimonies were evidence of her spirituality and her firm faith. If she had heard heretical ideas being voiced, she had certainly never understood them and adopted them, as the statements alleged. This was Doña Marina's last, albeit faint, glimmer of hope, to prove that the witnesses from the convent were biased against her and that she herself was merely a simple-minded woman who had no feeling for fine theological nuances. The six witnesses had simply painted the blackest possible picture of her. Unfortunately, this last attempt was based on an entirely false assumption, for she had no idea that the anonymous witnesses included not just the nuns from the convent but other people, too.

The attempted defense was a failure. Only two of the six female witnesses understood—or wanted to understand—the "rules of the game" and said that Doña Marina had been a harsh superior and had been very unpopular. They also said that the younger nuns were frightened of her and were scared to go to her with their heretical views; and that she was a simple woman with no facility for expressing herself well, so that her words could easily have been misunderstood. Two further witnesses added to her problems by painting her in the best possible colors as a loving and beloved superior, a wise woman of sound judgment. One of the two was the abbess of the convent. We know from other statements that she actually hated Doña Marina and had already accused her previously of being a follower of Lutheranism.

Once the witnesses for the defense had been heard, the tribunal could pass judgment. Of the eight judges, seven decided on 29 July to surrender her to the secular authorities and to condemn her to death. Only one

spoke in favor of trying to get at the truth through torture. No final decision was taken, however, for the papers relating to the case had to be sent to the *Suprema* which had some objections to the trial. In September 1559, the Grand Inquisitor Valdés, Archbishop of Seville, summoned an inquisitor from Valladolid and told him to arrange a secret interview between Doña Marina and Don Alonso Tellez, who was clearly a trusted representative of the *Suprema*. When Inquisitor Riego told his colleagues in Valladolid about the interview in Seville, they were very angry, refused to let the interview take place and sent their official secretary, Julien de Alpuche, to Seville to represent their arguments there. He argued that this course of action was against the practices of the *Sanctum Officium*. Even if the interview persuaded Doña Marina to confess her offenses, he argued, this would be of little help to her, given that the trial had already been concluded and sentence passed. The inquisitors also doubted whether Don Tellez would maintain the confidentiality of the Inquisition. When the secretary had presented these arguments, the Grand Inquisitor washed his hands of the affair. He said he would leave it to the inquisitors of Valladolid to decide according to their own consciences and to the best of their abilities. The inquisitors had, of course, already done this but they still did not want to create an impression of disobedience to higher

The frequently reproduced illustrations of a male and a female heretic condemned to death are part of a series of copperplate engravings by Bernard Picart, dating from 1723. The isolated figures are an artistic rendering of the topic. No condemned heretic was ever portrayed in this way and in such surroundings. Staatliche Kunstsammlungen Dresden, Kupferstichkabinett.

authority. So on 7 October, one day before the second auto-da-fé was to be held, they went to a great deal of trouble to set up a meeting between Don Tellez and Doña Marina, advising her that the Grand Inquisitor instructed her to tell him the truth. Doña Marina swore that she had told the truth all along and was returned to her cell. Her fate was now sealed.

The next day Doña Marina left her cell for the very last time, the leading actress in a gruesome drama, to go to the second Valladolid auto-da-fé. It cannot have been much source of comfort to her to mount the platform with a number of friends and in the company of the leading and most-respected Lutheran in Valladolid, Don Carlos de Seso, and the most passionate preacher of the new teachings, Juan Sánchez, who had been unable to escape the Spanish Inquisition by fleeing to Geneva. Doña Marina went over to the platform where the young King Philip II was sitting and overheard the exchange between the king and Don Seso. The Italian —who was related to the king—was accusing him of personally authorizing such a massacre. The king's answer could be heard all over the square: "If my own son were to commit the sort of crime you have committed, I myself would have carried the wood to the stake"—a statement that was to go down in history.

There followed long, solemn formalities, opening with the solemn oath of King Philip and a sermon on the subject of the "false prophets." The reading of the sentences took a long time. Doña Marina was one of seventeen to be surrendered to the secular powers, and when the spectacle had come to a close they were all put on asses and taken to the walls of the city where the pyres were ready. Doña Marina was one of fifteen who had been granted a more compassionate death by strangulation; her corpse was subsequently thrown into the fire. Other dramatic events arose when the two most stubborn heretics, Don Seso and Juan Sánchez, were tied to the stake. Seso faced his martyrdom with dignity, but

Sánchez, a common man, fought to the very end. When the fire was lit, he managed to loose his bonds and jump down from the fire. He hoped this would make his death easier—being killed by a soldier—but when he saw how his teacher was taking the agony with dignity, he repented and is said to have thrown himself into the flames.

A study of the comprehensive records of the trial of Doña Marina makes one question to what extent she deviated from the truth of church teachings. Had she really given credence to some of Luther's articles, as charged and as sentenced? Careful study of the statements from witnesses shows that Doña Marina certainly told the truth in her defense. Those who were fully acquainted with the whole affair all made a clear distinction between the inner circle of admirers of the views of Luther, as explained by Dr. Cazalla, and Doña Marina herself. There is more than one statement to the effect that she often expressed disagreement with the views of the others. The sentence passed on her also gives no clear view of what she herself believed. So why did she receive the death sentence? It seems as though she rendered herself guilty in the eyes of the inquisitors by something else entirely—those under her were guilty of holding false and heretical views, yet she had failed to denounce them, and would not even confirm her earlier statements for fear of harming anyone. Her efforts to analyze the exact extent of her own doubts cannot have made a favorable impression on the uncompromising inquisitors. Her self-confidence must have sorely irritated them. The inquisitors also found it necessary to condemn the nuns of the Order and their spiritual leader, Cazalla, to death along with someone who took responsibility for him, at least institutionally. In her case, it was a pernicious judgment, motivated partly by personality and partly by politics. The doubts of the Grand Inquisitor—himself no great paragon of compassion—were certainly justified.

The 1561 Instructions on the Activities of the Inquisitors

The experiences gained by the *Suprema* from the work of the Inquisition over its first fifty years were reflected in new instructions on the activities of the Inquisition that were issued by the Grand Inquisitor in 1561. They deal not only with the theory of the Inquisition but also with its practical operation and are therefore a valuable source of information. The eighty-one points dealt with in the instructions cover all the various stages in an Inquisition hearing, though there are some peculiarities in the order in which things are listed.

If someone were accused of an offense that required a theological assessment, the inquisitors summoned scholarly and conscientious theologians. If the inquisitors were assured that the offense was in fact a religious matter, they could then apply to have the person arrested. If someone were accused of heresy but the state-

ment or evidence was insufficient, the suspect was not to be called for questioning, for this would put him on his guard. The inquisitors gave the order for arrest to the *alguacil* (the arresting officer) of the *Sanctum Officium*, and he confiscated all the assets of the accused when the arrest was made. A clerk made a full inventory of the goods confiscated. The *alguacil* took as much money from the confiscated assets as was necessary to transport the accused, provide him with clothing and food and with his plank bed in prison. After the arrest, no one was allowed any contact with the accused, and he was allowed to have nothing with him—no money, no paper or writing instruments, no gold or silver —and he had to spend the intervening period in a cell by himself. The jailer was under strict instructions not to allow any contact between prisoners.

58 The Granada Inquisition certificate dated 1569 bears the characteristic symbols of the Inquisition: cross, sword and branch. They are borne by small angels.

59 The coat-of-arms of the Palacio Real Mayor in Barcelona with the symbols of the Inquisition.

60 "If my son were to commit that sort of crime, I myself would carry the wood to the stake," Philip II is said to have declared at the famous auto-da-fé in Valladolid. His son Don Carlos—here depicted in a painting by Sán-chez Coello, in the Středočeská Gallery, Nelahozeves—was not a heretic as Friedrich Schiller portrayed him, but his fate was similar to that of a sacrificed son.

61 "Auto-de-fé." Painting by Feo Rizi, 1680.
Prado, Madrid.

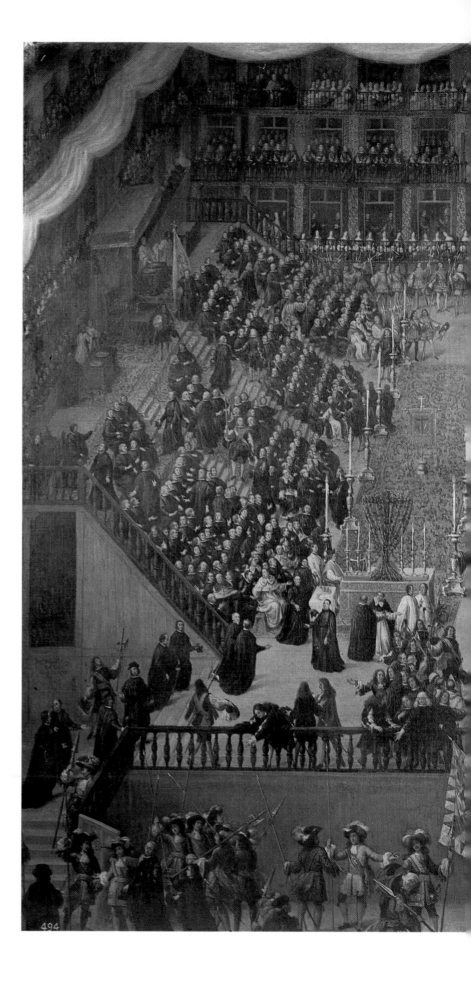

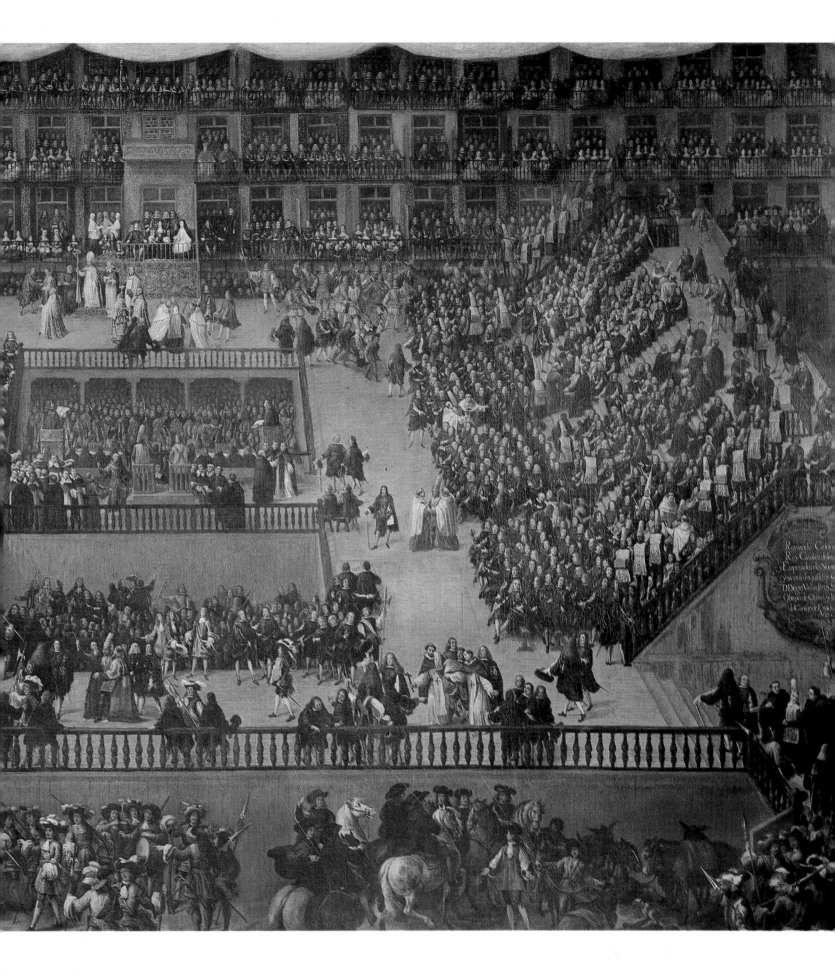

62 The monument to Philip II (1556–1598).
Sculpture by Pompeo Leoni.

63 Spanish King Philip III (1598–1621). The portrait by an unknown artist from the Středočeská Gallery, Nelahozeves, originally was part of the gallery owned by the aristocratic Lobkowitz family.

64 The complex religious conditions obtaining in the Habsburg lands attracted the attention of both the Curia in Rome and of the Spaniards to the Habsburg Court. Permanent consultants to the secret council of Emperor Rudolph (1576–1611) were the papal nuncio and the Spanish ambassador. Guillén de San Clemente, ambassador of the Spanish king to the Court of Emperor Rudolph II in Prague (1581–1608).
Středočeská galerie, Nelahozeves.

65 Archduke Albrecht VII (1559–1621), son of Emperor Maximilian II, was in 1584 Archbishop of Toledo, and after 1596 Spanish viceroy in the Netherlands. He used moderate policies to achieve the Counter-Reformation without violence in the southern Netherlands. Painting by Peter Paul Rubens, left wing of the Ildefonso Altar. Kunsthistorisches Museum, Vienna.

When they felt the time was right, the inquisitors summoned the accused for the first stage of questioning. The accused was supposed to be treated humanely and in accordance with his status; he was not to be intimidated, and was to be questioned sitting down and in a friendly manner. At the first stage of the hearing, the inquisitors asked for personal details: who had brought the prisoner up, where he had studied and whether he had ever been abroad. He had to talk about his background and his family. He was asked whether he knew the reason for his arrest, and was told to tell the truth. The inquisitors had to be very alert at this first session of questioning, and were told to expect the prisoner to try to trick them. During the interrogation sessions the accused was only to discuss the details of his trial. After the first session of questioning, the prosecutor made the charge, with details of the category of heresy involved. After the charge was read, the prosecutor could threaten torture. The charge was read in the presence of the accused and of the inquisitors; the accused then swore to tell the truth at all times. The prosecutor then withdrew from the proceedings and the accused was allowed to answer the individual points of the charge. All his statements were recorded, even if he gave the simple answer "no" to all the questions he was asked.

The accused was allowed the services of one or more lawyers with whom he could consult in the presence of an inquisitor. The duty of the lawyer was, first and foremost, to ensure that the accused told the truth. After the statements, the witnesses' evidence was read. The prosecutor read the statements without identifying the witnesses. If the accused demanded a hearing, he was to be granted one. The witnesses' statements were written down by a notary who also testified on the general condition of each witness when he or she made the statement. Even if the accused agreed to the statements being read, he still had to sit through the reading of the evidence so that he knew his arrest was not a matter of whim. The lawyer was not allowed to speak to his client in private. If the accused requested paper to enable him to construct his defense, he was to be given it, but a tally was kept of how much he was given, and the same number of sheets were to be handed in. The inquisitors had to assess the extent of the guilt or innocence of the accused. When all the documentary evidence had been gathered, the inquisitors could proceed to a vote on the guilt of the accused and on the sentence. The consultors negotiated independently over the guilt of the accused and had an advisory function.

Those who had made a full confession were given a pardon but were stripped of all their assets, and had to wear the so-called *sanbenito* robes, either for a fixed period or indefinitely. They were also imprisoned temporarily or for life, depending on the gravity of the offense. Recidivists had to be surrendered to the secular

powers. If the accused refused stubbornly to confess and had been brought before the Inquisition only on grounds of evidence, then he was an obstinate heretic and also had to be turned over to the secular arm. Care then had to be taken, however, that he had a change of heart and died in the true faith. It often happened that recidivists repented only at their place of execution. It was wrong, said the instructions, that they were then reconciled with the Church and the execution of their sentence was stayed, for many a heretic repented simply out of fear rather than real remorse. The execution order, said the instructions, should only be stayed for those who repented in the night before their execution. If the accused denied everything and refused to implicate others, and if he was therefore to be surrendered to the secular authorities, then he could be subjected to questioning with torture and made to be a witness in other cases. If he could not satisfactorily be proved to have engaged in heretical activities so that neither acquittal nor conviction was possible, he was to recant. Because this was a way of frightening the suspect for the rest of his life rather than punishing him for his past sins, such prisoners had to be made to pay fines and were warned that if they committed any future offenses, they would be treated as recidivists.

Torture, although used frequently, was regarded as a very unreliable method of interrogation, for human character and the resistance of individuals varied enormously. Statements induced by torture always had to be made in the presence of all the inquisitors, who could not ask deputies to represent them. Before the torture began, the accused was told why he was being

Heretics dressed in *sanbenito* robes are taken to their trials under the banner of the Inquisition.

tortured. After the hearing, no commentary was to be made on his statements. Twenty-four hours after the hearing at which torture had been used, the accused was asked to confirm the statements he had made by signing them. If he confessed everything under torture and showed repentance, then he could be reconciled with the Church. If he resisted torture, on the other hand, and if there was no suspicion that the torture had been carried out too mildly so as to spare him, then he was acquitted of the major charge and the Inquisition had to content itself with repentance and a fine. The inquisitors could, however, decide that a hearing with torture was to be repeated.

If anyone was released from prison, the inquisitors were to ask him whether he had noticed anything untoward there, such as contacts among the prisoners, the passing of information and so on. If the accused died in prison, the trial was to continue; if, on the other hand, he suffered mental illness, a guardian was to be appointed and the trial then proceeded as normal. Statements by witnesses related to the accused were not to be treated like other evidence, but were to be checked carefully. If someone sentenced to repentance was unable to pay his fine, he was not to suffer corporal punishment, which could be regarded as blackmail in such a case. If there were differences of opinion among the inquisitors, these were to be submitted to the *Suprema*.

The sick were to be given the services of a doctor and, if they so wished, a confessor. The accused was not to be confronted with the witnesses against him. The food given to prisoners was to be in accordance with the time of year and the prices in the market. If a prisoner was wealthy, he could eat whatever he chose, but any leftovers were to go to the poor, not to his jailer. If an accused whose assets had been confiscated had a wife and children, they were to be provided for out of the money confiscated.

Once the penalty had been decided on, the inquisitors had to fix on a date—a public holiday—for the auto-da-fé and publicize it in the town, extending invitations to all the civic dignitaries. The procedures of the auto-da-fé were to be carried out so that the sentences were read during the day and the executions could be carried out before nightfall. During the night before the auto-da-fé the only people allowed access to the prisoners were confessors and relatives. Those who had been reconciled with the Church returned to prison after the auto-da-fé.

The inquisitors were required to visit the prison several times a year. The *sanbenito* robe was to be on display in the parish church to which the condemned man officially belonged so that the faithful in the church could keep the memory of the sin of their fellow parishioner in view as a warning.

The Inquisition against the Moriscoes— the Valencia Model

One of the specific tasks of the Inquisition in Valencia was to monitor the orthodoxy of the beliefs of converted Muslims. Despite the bloody and violent persecution around the turn of the century, a large number of the apparently converted Muslims remained true to their own religion, in many cases with the secret agreement of their feudal lords. Under pressure from the Cortes, and in the light of interventions by Rome, the Inquisition had relaxed its actions by the 1560s. The Moriscoes who were committing offenses of faith were not to be regarded as malevolent enemies but as neophytes—new Christians who needed teaching, persuasion and encouragement. This change in concept was reflected in a tangible drop in the number of death penalties to only four percent, of which half were effigy burnings. At the same time, the control of the *Suprema* over the legal procedures and the conditions in prisons improved; the instructions issued in 1561 were generally applied in Valencia.

Repression resumed, however, in the early 1590s when in five years almost eight hundred suspects were arrested, half of them Moriscoes. This proved to be a short-lived phenomenon. In the end the State, in the form of the Royal Council, took steps toward a brutal and extreme solution of the problem by driving out the baptized Moriscoes in 1609, solving at a stroke the problem posed to the Valencia Inquisition of monitoring the orthodoxy of this group within the kingdom of Spain.

Between 1530 and 1609, the Inquisition in Valencia had dealt with more than five thousand cases, an average of sixty a year. About seventy percent of these cases involved baptized Moriscoes or converted Jews, and another twelve percent were those up for serious sexual offenses, such as bigamy, sodomy and so on; a large number of Moriscoes were also included in this latter category. The remaining eighteen percent constituted the core of offenses against the faith—mostly simple blasphemy. In fact, the Inquisition dealt with only one hundred and twenty cases of heresy (usually referred to as Lutheranism), just two percent of the total.

The composition of the court of Inquisition in Valencia reflected the overall development of increasing bureaucratization of the Spanish Inquisition. Secular clergy played an increasingly large part while the number of "classical" inquisitors from the ranks of the Dominican Order had dwindled; of forty-two inquisitors who worked in Valencia between 1530 and 1609, only three were monks. Most of the inquisitors had theological or legal training from a university, and twenty-one of them were licentiates, eighteen had doctor's degrees. Since 1590 the Jesuits had become increasingly involved in the recruitment of inquisitors, much of which was conducted in the universities. Most of the inquisi-

Documentary representations of the courts of Inquisition and their activities date only from the second half of the 17th century. This copperplate engraving by Bernard Picart, dating from 1722, gives a rough impression of the conduct of such a burning in Spain about a hundred years earlier. In the foreground the condemned man is being strangled by the executioner before burning on the fire, which has not yet been lit.
Staatliche Kunstsammlungen Dresden, Kupferstichkabinett.

tors came from outside the region, and only two had been born in Valencia. The trends here are completely in keeping with overall trends in the whole of Spain, although the composition of the Familiari in Valencia had one or two specific features—about forty-four per cent of their ranks were peasants, about one-third were craftsmen, and only six percent were nobles. These figures reflected the specific ethnic make-up of the region where the Moriscoes often dominated the peasantry.

The Growing Self-confidence of the Suprema

When Ferdinand of Aragon gave the Spanish Inquisition its extraordinary status within the State, it was assumed that its legal powers were a mandate from the king that could at any time be revoked or amended by him. The same assumption was made under Charles V. The more the Inquisition took on the form of a regular court of jurisdiction, the more jealously it guarded its privileges. Philip II usually sided with the Inquisition in the increasing number of disputes not only with local authorities but also with royal officials. In 1579 and again in 1583, for example, the Cortes complained that any inhabitant of the kingdom who became involved in any kind of dispute with an Inquisition official ran the risk of being thrown into an Inquisition prison like a heretic. Philip's response to the complaint was to promise to check up on this practice, although nothing changed. In fact, under his rule the Suprema entered into a dispute with the Order of the Jesuits, whose head had been granted a mandate in 1584 by Gregory XIII to acquit suspects of heresy, even in cases of recidivism, when the suspect was a member of the Order. After several years of bitter wrangling, the *Suprema* eventually, in 1592, got the *Sanctum Officium* in Rome to recognize its complete supremacy over the members of the Jesuit Order.

If the *Suprema* respected the authority of Philip II in all disputes and regarded his say as final and acted in accordance with his wishes, the same cannot be said of its relationship to Philip's weaker successors. As it had previously ignored the demands of the Cortes, so, toward the end of the 16th century, it started also to disregard the demands of the Royal Council, even of the king himself. In 1607, for example, there were repeated complaints that the Inquisition was holding suspects in its prisons who were not heretics. When in 1615 King Philip III ruled that the secular courts should deal with

such cases, as the Inquisition had no jurisdiction over them, the ruling was ignored. His successor, Philip IV, issued a ruling in 1630 to the effect that once a charge had been preferred by a court institution it was also to apply to all other courts; whereupon the *Suprema* simply added a rider to the effect that this did *not* apply to the officials of the Inquisition. There was also no response to the castigation of the Inquisition by the Castilian Royal Council in 1631 for excommunicating officials of the Royal Court and refusing appeals to higher authorities against sentences given for offenses other than religious ones. More than once, officials of the Royal Court who aroused the displeasure of the inquisitors were attacked by members of the Inquisition staff who enjoyed immunity and could not be brought before a secular court. The courts also regarded themselves as superior to the clerical courts, claiming that it was difficult to draw a dividing line between a criminal offense committed by a member of the clergy and his offenses in the field of belief or ritual.

The right to excommunicate an opponent became a very effective weapon in the hands of the Inquisition. The case of Palomino, a common criminal, is typical of the Inquisition's increasing self-confidence and aggression; he was sentenced in Granada to six years' imprisonment as a galley slave for a number of crimes and also for blasphemy. The blasphemy charge gave the Inquisition a pretext for intervention and it demanded that the offender should be passed over to the Inquisition for assessment of his heretical leanings. The Royal Court agreed on condition that the sentence that had already been passed should remain in force. The inquisitors, however, did not care to negotiate over this point and dispatched Familiari to the prisoner forthwith. They practically kidnapped him against the wishes of the court. In a short trial he was condemned by the Inquisition to hear Mass and to do penance, and then returned to the royal prison. The conflict arose over the unilateral seizure of a prisoner of the State. The inquisitors then excommunicated the judge for arresting their two stewards and the notary who had seized Palomino from prison. They then published an interdictum throughout the city. The dispute was settled after a while, but the Inquisition summoned the judge and accused him of heresy. The judges appealed to Philip IV to intervene, but in vain, for the king sided with the Inquisition.

The Inquisition's growing self-confidence at the time of Philip IV can also be illustrated by the example of the so-called war over coaches in Lograño—a dispute which really belongs in the annals of historical follies. Prompted by an apparent desire to encourage the breeding of horses, Philip IV imposed a ban on using mules to draw coaches or carriages. The inquisitors in Lograño paid no attention, even when the royal corregidor told them to. He dared not take any direct ac-

A. L'Etendart de l'Inquisition.
B. Les Dominicains.
C. Les Criminels qui ont évité le feu par la confession.
D. Les Criminels qui ont évité le feu par la confession après leur condamnation.

La PROCESSION de L'INQUISITION, a GOA.

E. Crusifix qui tourne le dos à ceux qui doivent être brulez.
F. Criminels qui doivent être brulez.
G. Effigies de ceux qui sont morts en prison.
H. Le Grand Inquisiteur.

B. Picart sculp. direxit 1723.

tion but did manage to get the Castilian Royal Council to issue a general ban on the driving of coaches. The inquisitors again paid no attention and appealed to the *Suprema* for help. The *Suprema* intervened and appealed to the king on the grounds that the inquisitors were too old to ride horses. The king agreed to the appeal but the council, to preserve face, at least wanted the inquisitors themselves to apply for a special dispensation. The *Suprema* refused to allow this, and so the inquisitors simply continued to drive their coaches and when the commander of the police tried to prevent them, they had him excommunicated. The king recommended lifting the excommunication order, the Inquisition refused, and so it went on until 1635 when the tug-of-war finally came to an end with the Royal Council agreeing to let the inquisitors ride around in coaches drawn by mules.

In spite of this dispute and other similar cases, it cannot be claimed that the Spanish Inquisition supplanted the power of the State. Its controversies and its struggle for its own prestige as well as its daily workings enabled this centralized institution to help abolish local peculiarities and weakened the position of the estate powers.

It also played its part in the conquest of the historical borders and differences between the individual Spanish territories in the 17th century. Even at the time when its powers were greatest, it was arguably the tool of a modern State and its attempts at centralization. It is interesting that the self-confidence of the *Suprema* and of the local tribunals grew particularly when Spain's international status was foundering. The country had lost its position overseas in favor of England and the revolutionary Netherlands, and had been ruined by its altogether unsuccessful participation in the Thirty Years' War, and if it was to maintain its own internal stability, it needed extraordinary and specific means.

During the early years of the 17th century there was also a change in the subject matter of investigations carried out by the Inquisition. Once the Lutherans had been wiped out and the baptized Moriscoes expelled, only the Judaists remained to be persecuted. The increasing need to combat mortal sin and minor deviations from the faith such as those of the *alumbrados*, the mystics, and various exorcists became central. The number of witchcraft trials grew, although not to the same level and intensity as the trials within the empire.

More than once, the tribunals also settled theological disputes within the general context of orthodoxy. Parallel to this, the penalty system changed, too. The number of death sentences dwindled to around one percent of all sentences by the 17th century. Gradually, manipulation and balancing of human spirituality won out over the penal function of the Inquisition, and monitoring took the place of repression. The Inquisition played a large part in forming the absolutist Spanish State on the basis of specific religious conformity.

The Struggle against the Inquisition in Spain—the Catalonian Model

The Catalonians had already been reproached by the Inquisition in the first half of the 16th century. Inspectors from the *Suprema* discovered in 1544 that all the Inquisition officials in Barcelona were taking bribes, that all but two were indulging in illicit sexual intercourse and that they were not paying their debts. Moreover, the prosecutor himself was accused of making arbitrary charges. In 1549 a further inspection revealed that nothing had been done to rectify these faults and, moreover, an inquisitor had been selling indulgences for the crusade and putting the proceeds into his own pocket. The inquisitor in question was suspended for a time, and a notary and the prosecutor were also suspended for six months. Again, though, nothing changed as a result. On the contrary, new offenses were committed. A third inspection in 1566 revealed that the inquisitors would, if paid a suitable sum, conduct a trial against anyone, make arrests arbitrarily, and impose unreasonable fines so as to make money for themselves. The inquisitors paid a small fine in this instance and were transferred elsewhere.

Under the circumstances, it is hardly surprising that there are documents from the 1560s that speak of the deep hatred of the people of Barcelona toward the Inquisition. On more than one occasion there were attacks on Inquisition officials, and heretics who had been imprisoned were set free. Even Pius V himself was concerned about developments in Catalonia and advised Philip II in 1570 to get the Inquisition to make some concessions. Philip refused because he was frightened that this could increase the self-confidence of the estates. The Inquisition persisted in Catalonia and was more than once the victim of attempts at repression by the regional administration; for example, in 1585 the officials and stewards of the Inquisition were dismissed from all civic functions.

A new dispute arose in 1599. The Catalonian estates had approached the king and asked him to intervene against the arbitrary powers of the Inquisition. Philip III, however, did not dare to act directly against the Inquisition and referred the people to the pope. When the estates and the municipal council realized that the king would not help them, they decided to help themselves. In 1608 the inquisitors were to be driven out of the region; a ship was prepared, but the inquisitors were bent on assuming the spirituality of the people. They covered the doors of their premises with black velvet and hung a cross there. Priests prayed in front of the cross drawing crowds from among the common people, and the police did not dare to take the crosses away and use force. Thus the dispute was never solved and kept recurring at intervals. These disputes with the Inquisition reached a head in the 1630s when the contradictions were becoming ever deeper, and eventually erupted in the revolt of 1640. In the riots of 7/8 June of that year, the people's anger was directed particularly at the officials of the State and the royal army from Naples. The Inquisition acted as though it were not involved and offered to act as intermediary. The leaders of the Catalonian revolt accepted their offer, for they were anxious

During the Thirty Years' War, villages were often sacked and heretics burned at the same time. This contemporary engraving also shows a satirical poem against the enemies of the true faith.

Ifrael ex. Cum Priuil: Reg.

Ces ennemis du Ciel qui pechent mil fois
Contre les saincts Decrets et les diuines Loix

Font gloire méchamment de piller et d'abattre
Les Temples du vray Dieu d'vne main idolatre;

Mais pour punition de les auoir brulez,
Ils sont eux mesmes enfin aux flammes immolez 13.

not to be fighting on too many fronts at one time. This was clarified by an event that took place toward the end of 1640; at Christmas the rumor had been circulating in Barcelona that the Inquisition had up to two thousand Castilians in its prisons. Under the leadership of a coachman who worked for the Inquisition, the people broke into the Inquisition's premises and hanged some of the officials and murdered others. The treasury was robbed and the sole Castilian prisoner who was awaiting his sentence for heresy was freed. The council of the town asked for pardon, had the heretic brought back and had the coachman who had led the revolt executed. In January 1641 the statute of the Inquisition was revised in Catalonia, and the Inquisition was made independent of the Spanish *Suprema*. Officials of the Inquisition were in future all to be native Catalonians and the legal powers of the Inquisition were to be limited to strictly religious questions.

The arrival of French auxiliary troops then complicated the position of the Inquisition. Many French soldiers were Huguenots who made no secret of their views. Heretical views emerged among the Catalonians. When the Inquisition tried to intervene, this caused new outrage, and twice the people tried to torch the Inquisition building. In 1643 some of the inquisitors fled to Castile, and for some time this impeded the operation of the Inquisition.

When the revolt collapsed and Catalonia capitulated in 1652, the victorious Spanish were magnanimous but refused to make any concessions over the role of the Inquisition. In the summer of 1653 the new Grand Inquisitor was ceremoniously initiated; the Catalonian inquisitors were captured, at least those who had not managed to flee to France, and the Inquisition resumed its former practices, knowing this time that the central power was on its side. It did not become any more popular with the Catalonian people, however, and in 1677, for example, the *Suprema* complained that there was only one man in the whole of Barcelona who was willing to act as a steward for the Inquisition.

The Spanish Inquisition to the North of the Alps—the Franche Comté

The Inquisition headed by the archbishops had been in existence in the Franche Comté since 1247, which fell to the Habsburgs in the struggle for Burgundy. During the 16th century the Archbishop of Besançon appointed two inquisitors, usually from the ranks of the Dominicans. They bore the proud title "Sacrosanctae fidei inquisitor a sede apostolica institutus et delegatus" ("inquisitor of the most holy faith, appointed and sent from the Holy See"), but their work was not very onerous. Neither the Protestants nor witches fell under their jurisdiction.

This situation did not change when the Franche Comté was annexed to the lands of the Spanish Habsburgs in 1558. At the beginning of the 1560s, the correspondence of the leaders shows that the jurisdiction of the Inquisition consisted of the investigation of cases that were borderline instances between witchcraft and heresy. The inquisitors' field of influence and their allowances were dictated by the secular authorities. The push for change came after the Council of Trent—not from Philip II but from Pope Pius V. First came the papal breve in 1567, which ordered the Inquisition to arrest one Gilbert Cousin, a sixty-year-old canon and former assistant to Erasmus. The breve also challenged the officials of the secular authorities to prosecute the man as a *placard* (that is by means of a warrant) within the context of the State's struggle to combat Protestantism. At the same time Pius V ordered the Archbishop of Besançon, the young noble Claude de la Baume, to Rome on charges of acting against the decisions of the Council of Trent in failing to have the higher consecration of a priest nor concerning himself with the affairs of his diocese. For three years the archbishop was tried in Rome and convinced of the necessity to be ordained and to conform to the decisions of the Council of Trent. During his absence from the archbishopric, the direct interventions of the pope began. The Grand Inquisitor appointed two new inquisitors for the Franche Comté—probably on the basis of former agreements with Philip II and the Duke of Alba—and instructed them to persecute heretics of all kinds. Although they, unlike their predecessors, had not been appointed by the archbishop himself, they were nevertheless to be paid out of his funds. The protests of parliament in the capital, Dôle, that the pope's action was in conflict with the laws of the country were in vain, and a year later the change in the Inquisition's powers was confirmed by the king of Spain.

After three years of religious training, Archbishop Claude de la Baume was permitted to return to Besançon. The well-known Jesuit Possevino was chosen to accompany him, and his duty was to remind Claude regularly of the promise he had made in Rome to the pope. In October 1571 the returning archbishop held his first Mass, following which Possevino read the decisions of the Council of Trent aloud in the cathedral. When, however, it came to enforcing these decisions in practice, it turned out that they had to be altered to conform to Spanish customs. The king retained all the rights of patronage, the right to give benefices and the supervision of the Inquisition. All penalties, including those imposed by the Church, were handed over to the secular courts. Thus, for example, excommunication was no longer merely a penalty imposed by the Church, and no Inquisition sentence could be carried out without the consent of the secular authorities.

The powers of the Inquisition had, at least in theory, been extended, but in practice, its activities were still

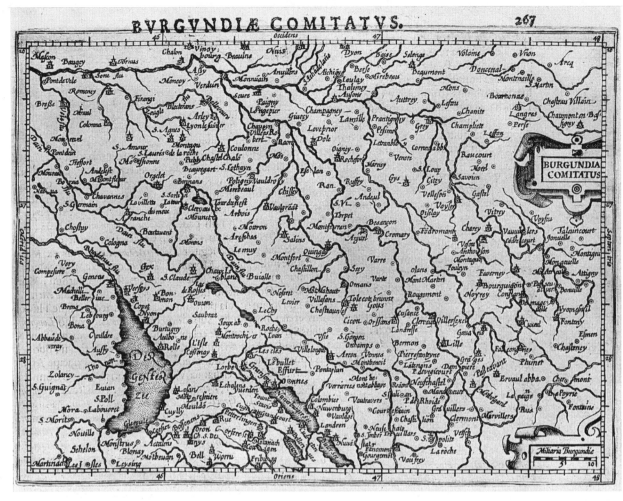

After the abdication of Charles V the Habsburg county Franche Comté became Spanish territory.

under the control of the apparatus of the State. Above all, it was to serve as an instrument in the consolidation of absolutism. In practice, the number of cases examined by the Inquisition had not risen significantly since the time of Philip II. The drastic sentences typical of Spain and of the Spanish parts of the Netherlands were never fully implemented. The struggle against the Reformation was achieved as part of the measures taken by the State in the Franche Comté. The Spanish government respected the developing forms of administration and jurisdiction derived from French principles, but used them for its own purposes. So the Inquisition did not simply undergo changes but was submitted to the decisions and rulings of the Council of Trent.

From Bloody Inquisition to Peaceful Renewal— the Southern Netherlands

The path followed by the southern provinces of the Netherlands back to the bosom of the Catholic Church shows how the Inquisition differed radically from the other methods used by the Catholic Church in its Counter-Reformation strategy. When, in 1567, the Duke of Alba headed the Spanish occupying army and invaded the Netherlands, the Inquisition was given the full public support of the state powers and of the army. Under this direct military protection, the inquisitors began to do their work in the towns of the Netherlands. They made a major, if not decisive, contribution to the total of eight thousand people who fell victim to the Inquisition within a few years. The tragic failure of Alba's methods is well known. Although resistance to the Spanish fiscal system, the *alcabala*, was a far more important factor in the anti-Spanish revolt than hatred for the Spanish Inquisition, the system of inquisitorial terror achieved the exact opposite of what its authors hoped it would.

The region conquered at the beginning of the 1580s by Alexander Farnese presents a quite different picture of Spanish policy; in Flanders and northern Brabant, there were no executions of traitors and heretics, and no mass scale arrests of suspects. When in September 1584 Ghent, the stronghold of the revolution in Flanders, was taken, the Calvinists were given two years to emigrate. The Calvinists in Antwerp even had four years. Only cases of public Calvinist services and any attacks on the Catholic Mass were punished. By no means all followers of Calvin emigrated, many stayed and were tolerated, provided they refrained from making public statements and confessions of a religious na-

The idea that the heretics could physically be stamped out continued to influence Spanish policy under Philip II. The Spanish army caused an appalling blood bath in December 1572 among the inhabitants of the rebel town of Naarden. Engravings by Jan Luyken and Noach van der Meer the Younger.
Národní galerie, Prague.

Scenes of burning and mass executions of Calvinists in the 16th century in the Netherlands were ample material for heroic legends used in anti-Catholic propaganda in the following century. Engraving by J. L. Gottfried in *Historische Kronyk*, Leyden, 1674.

The Spanish reign of terror in the Netherlands around 1570, together with the bloody persecution of those of other faiths as a method of church renewal proved fatal. More than one hundred years later these events were still used as political weapons against Catholicism. The torture of the schoolmistress Ursel in Maastricht. Engraving by Jan Luyken.

At the same time, greater efforts were made to set up Sunday schools. During the 1560s, four Jesuit colleges were founded and by 1584, the Jesuits already had nine, and continued over the next ten years to increase this by another five. By 1625 there were more than 1,500 Jesuits, plus more than 2,100 in neighboring France and about 2,300 in the empire. Other Orders followed them, and the material foundation for their work was provided on the direct instruction of the Spanish estates (especially the Infanta Isabella) of the high nobility.

The courts of Inquisition continued to work, but after 1585 only rarely executed any heretics. The judges mostly had to deal with cases of open hostility to Catholicism and restricted themselves to imposing fines and scourgings. The pyres remained for witches only. If secret heretics were flushed out, they were reported to the bishop or the secular authorities and were assigned a teacher to persuade them to recant and return to orthodox beliefs. If they converted, they were allowed to stay in the country, and they had to send their children for Catholic religious education. If they refused to repent, on the other hand, they were threatened with exile. Gradually, and without bloody violence, the southern Netherlands were "cleansed" of Calvinism and turned into one of the more dependable regions of the Catholic Church.

Anabaptists being hanged in Amsterdam. Water-colored drawing by Barend Dircksz. Stedelijk Museum, Amsterdam.

Duchess Margaret of Parma sought non-violent agreement with the opposition of the Netherlandish estates by means of negotiation and compromise. When this policy failed, the rule of terror of Duke Alba began. Engraving by Karl von Sichem. Former State Library, Wrocław.

ture. During the twelve-year armistice, they were given the opportunity of establishing semi-legal contacts with their fellow-believers in the north. Once the war resumed, of course, the fate of the Calvinists in the southern Netherlands was sealed. The southern provinces became a byword for the new Catholic spirituality.

Under the direct protection of the State, the Church gradually began to implement all the methods of renewal not laid down by the Council of Trent. In the conquered areas, there was an acute shortage of clergy. At the end of the century, between one-third and one-half of all the parishes in the country remained unoccupied, and in 1604 one minister was looking after seven parishes in Antwerp. So steps were taken to found priests' seminaries—in Ypres in 1565, in Arras in 1571, in Bruges in 1571 and again in 1591, in Louvain in 1579, in Antwerp in 1602, in Ghent in 1612 and so on. For the purposes of religious education, a Catechism was published especially for the southern Netherlands in 1607.

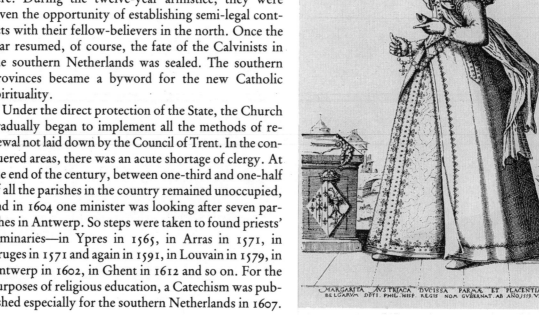

MARGARITA AVSTRIACA DVCISSA PARMÆ ET PLACENTIÆ GENERALIS
BELGARVM DITI. PHIL. HISP. REGIS NOM GVBERNAT. AB ANO 1559. VSQVE. 1567.

NOT EVERYONE WHO COMMITS A SIN OF FAITH CAN IMMEDIATELY BE LABELED A HERETIC, BUT RATHER THOSE WHO SCORN THE AUTHORITY OF THE CHURCH AND WHO STUBBORNLY DEFEND THEIR SINFUL VIEWS.

Catechismus Romanus, I, 10, I

THE DAY-TO-DAY ROUTINE OF THE INQUISITION

There could be no judge without a plaintiff, or any interrogation without a denunciation. The 16th-century inquisitors were dependent upon the denouncers, and this was the major area of difference between the 16th-century Inquisition on the one hand and the 13th- or 14th-century Inquisition on the other. The medieval inquisitor traveling around his parishes to seek out suspects had given way to extensive use of denouncers, whether from the clergy or the lay people. The *Coena Domini* Bull made it the duty of all true believers—underscored by the threat of severe penalties—to inform at Easter time on any cases of heresy of which they might have knowledge. In addition, the inquisitors were busy all year round following up denunciations from rich and poor, famous and simple alike. Confessors encouraged those making confession to report anything suspicious to the *Sanctum Officium*.

Denouncers were generally guaranteed that their identity would not be revealed to the person they had denounced. Unlike the Roman Inquisition, the Spanish Inquisition also accepted anonymous denunciations. Recent research has shown that the importance of this particularly cruel and dangerous form of denunciation grew during the 17th century but that it was far less common during the previous centuries.

So what motivated the denouncers? Simple religious fanaticism is as unsatisfactory an explanation as personal revenge or a desire to impose pain and suffering on others, but these two factors undoubtedly played a part; besides the rules of the Inquisition reckoned with personal hatred and revenge. If the accused could prove that the witnesses against him were biased and were seeking to harm him out of personal hatred, he stood a good chance of escaping with his life. The chance of convincing the Inquisition that this was the case was, however, remote, since the accused were never allowed to know who had denounced them. But other motives also came into play, especially fear of becoming entangled in the heretical views and activities of others. Anyone finding himself in circles where heretical views were being voiced had to worry if his name might be used in a denunciation, even as a witness, and what sort of penalty this might entail for him as an accessory to heresy. When a heretic was discovered, he was likely to confess the names of others in his circle to the inquisitor. Many chose to forestall this eventuality by denouncing the heretic themselves.

Personal hatred or fear was not the only emotion to inspire an act of denunciation. The French historian

Pierre Chaunu has shown that in the records of Inquisition trials in the Spanish colonies of America there is a correlation between the number of denunciations and the level of social tension. In an atmosphere of economic depression behavior becomes not only subconsciously more aggressive but also consciously more competitive. Both these factors would tend to encourage denunciations.

The Inquisition did not depend solely on more or less subjective decisions by individuals to denounce their fellow citizens. Organized groups of accomplices, in particular the Spanish Familiari and the Italian Crocesignati, also played a part. There is no doubt, in fact, that these groups and the criminal elements in society provided most of the Inquisition's spies and *agents provocateurs.*

One very special form of denunciation was self-denunciation. A believer would go to the inquisitor and denounce his own doubts or offenses against the faith. This form of denunciation was both welcomed and supported by the Inquisition because it combined confession with willingness to recant from false teachings and, in some cases, an opportunity to obtain information on other heretics. However, self-denunciation did not by any means guarantee immunity from punishment. The inquisitors proceeded with great caution against those who had denounced themselves, assuming that an attempt to cover up serious offenses could lie behind the apparently ready confession of minor ones, and indeed some self-denunciations did end in

Heretics were very seldom depicted in religious literature. In the initial at the beginning of the chapter "Who is a heretic?" of the *Catalogus hereticorum* by Lutzenburg (Cologne, 1526), a deformed figure of a heretic can be made out.

burnings. But not every denunciation led to arrest and sentencing. The denunciation was merely a first step toward identification of a heretic (yet not always to his successful prosecution). The rules of the Inquisition distinguish in cases of denunciation between accusations, which had to be based on evidence, and mere suspicion, which in itself was not sufficient grounds for arrest. In an accusation, the denouncer himself ran the risk of punishment for false evidence, while in cases of suspicion there was enormous scope for a vivid imagination or malevolence. The Inquisition usually took such cases seriously only when there was a large number of denunciations against the same person. Even then, the suspect was only to be observed and not summoned for questioning, since this would have alerted him to the suspicion of the Inquisition and given him the chance of covering his tracks. The denouncer was protected either way, for even if he formulated his denunciation as mere suspicion, his testimony would suffice as evidence; in the case of a trial the accused had to prove his innocence, which in virtually all cases was practically impossible to do.

Who Was Right?

The Inquisition, unlike a modern court, did not presume its victims innocent until proved guilty. It believed the denouncer more than the accused, especially if the former were a member of the Familiari, the Crocesignati, an Inquisition spy or a member of a religious Order. The instructions of the Inquisition stipulated that if guilt could not be fully proved, the accused should at least repent and pay a fine. This was at least a more humane way of proceeding than the rules under Konrad von Marburg, although it was still very rare for anyone to be completely acquitted. Though undoubtedly an unfair and distasteful procedure, even this aspect of the Inquisition had a "logical" explanation. If the Inquisition had acquitted all those whose guilt could not be fully proved, this would have amounted to an admission that innocent people were being arrested and held for long periods. It would have undermined the authority of the Inquisition and its powers of determent and would also have weakened the denunciation system, since denunciations were only worthwhile if there was a good chance of the accused being sentenced.

Denunciation was, then, a springboard for Inquisition investigations. The ultimate aim of the Inquisition

Juridical manual for the proceedings in Inquisition trials from the year 1584.

66 Torture belt.
Former Historisches Museum,
Dresden.

67 Instruments of torture.
Former Historisches Museum,
Dresden.

68 Stringing up was used as a form
of torture. Drawing by Theodor
Goetz.

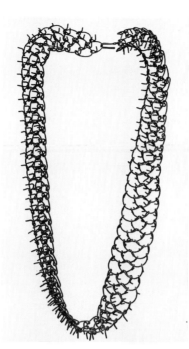

Cock excudebat. 1556.

Bruegel inuen.

69 This engraving by Pieter Brueghel the Elder is an interesting example of the coded polemic against the Spanish Inquisition in the Netherlands. According to the *Legenda aurea*, the Magus Hermogenes was conquered by the Apostle James and sacrificed to his own demons. The saint was able to prevent the demons from tearing him to pieces for the law did not permit conversion with force. Brueghel, however, depicts the scene in such a way that St. James sacrifices the man to the demons. St. James is a national saint in Spain.
Istituto Centrale per il Catalogo e la Documentazione, Rome.

70 "The Massacre of the Innocents in Bethlehem." Painting by Pieter Brueghel the Elder. It is dated at 1567 by some art historians and is interpreted as a critical response to the rule of terror of the newly arrived Spanish troops in the Netherlands.
Kunsthistorisches Museum, Vienna.

71 The practices in the prisons of the
Inquisition also concerned artists of later
generations. Painting by Eugenio Lucas.
Koninklijke Musea voor Schone Kunsten
van Belgie, Brussels.

was to bring people to confess and repent of their offenses, confession being regarded as the most satisfactory proof of guilt. The Church, especially in Italy, was also advising that confessions could be used as an effective instrument of propaganda. The more important the heretic, the greater the publicity surrounding his repentance. If there was any hope or likelihood of public recantation, the *Sanctum Officium* was even willing to delay sentencing or execution. In theory, confession and repentance meant a chance that the victim's life might be spared, although a condition of this was that the inquisitors should accept the motives for the confession and repentance, for only a true confession could guarantee the salvation of the heretic's soul and this—at least in theory—was the Inquisition's overriding concern.

Certainly, not all victims were accused and sentenced on grounds of either false evidence or forced confessions. The fact remains that the majority of inquisitors during the period of the Counter-Reformation, in their zeal to save souls, juggled statements made by the accused to fit in with the denunciation rather than examining all the facts. Their main aim was to extract a confession; evidence and analysis of allegedly heretical writings were factors of secondary importance.

We know that the Inquisition refused to confront the accused directly with witnesses against him, but used two main methods to extract confessions; psychological pressure during questioning and torture. The requirement to make statements under oath formed the basis for the exertion of psychological pressure; in the 16th century, oaths were considered sacred and it was common for eternal condemnation to be passed for lying under oath, a fact the Inquisition exploited for its own ends. The questioning itself was organized so that the accused was not prevented from making a confession when he was ready. To make this easier, the inquisitors were required to treat prisoners in a sympathetic and friendly manner. Other simple but effective tricks, some of them also known to medieval inquisitors, were also used, such as that described in the classic 14th-century work *Directorium inquisitorium* by Nicholas Eymeric. The author writes: "The inquisitor should behave in a friendly manner and act as though he already knows the whole story. He should glance at his papers and say: 'It's quite clear you are not telling the truth' or should pick up a document and look sur-

prised, saying: 'How can you lie to me like this when what I've got written down here contradicts everything you've told me?.' He should then continue: 'Just confess—you can see that I know the whole story already.'" If these small plays failed, Eymeric revealed other ways of exerting pressure. For example, the inquisitor could claim to be going on an urgent journey and tell the prisoner that if he did not confess immediately, he would have to wait lying in chains until the inquisitor returned. Of course, 16th-century inquisitors could hardly pretend to be going off on long journeys all the time, but long intervals between questioning and delays in proceedings were common methods of applying psychological pressure. Theoretically, the prisoners were to be given time in their (often solitary) cells for "examining their conscience," or sharpening up their memory, and visits were arranged for theologians with whom they could talk freely.

Eymeric was also acquainted with *agents provocateurs* being sent into prisons. The inquisitors were to take their spy into the prisoner's cell. The former was to pose as a heretic and prompt the prisoner to make incriminating statements. These were heard by witnesses hiding behind the cell door and taken down by a notary. We know from 16th-century records that this method was especially used in Italy, where fewer prisoners were kept in solitary confinement than in Spain. Some accounts of specific trials tell us that there was another variant of this procedure; one heretic would be put into a cell with another who had already confessed and repented, and the repentant heretic would be questioned after a while on the views of his cellmate.

An examination of the limited way in which prisoners were defended must throw into doubt the desire of the Inquisition to extract the truth. If a witness's statement conflicted with that of the prisoner (both had, of course, sworn an oath), the witness's statement would be given precedence over that of the prisoner. Sometimes, in exceptional situations, the defense was able to turn up subsequent witnesses to contradict the statements of the first ones, but this depended on the court deciding which of the statements it regarded as being more reliable. It was possible, however, to object on the grounds of a witness making a statement on the basis of hearsay *(de auditu alieno)* rather than of his own experience *(autopsie)*. The function of the defense was merely a formality, and its main task was to try to persuade the prisoner to admit guilt.

Torture was one of the ploys commonly used by medieval law courts, and was adopted by the Inquisition, which rapidly incorporated it into its own interrogation procedures. However, the Inquisition did not use all the usual forms; the Church took the hypocritical view that no blood should be shed as a result of torture,

nor should it leave scars on the victim's body. During the 16th century there was a limit on the amount of time for which torture could be applied, and a victim could be tortured only once during a juridical procedure provided the inquisitors were satisfied that he had not in any way been spared; the Spanish Inquisition

**Torture as a Means
of Extracting
the Truth**

was, in fact, less harsh in this respect than the *Sanctum Officium* in Rome. In the Italian provinces torture was rare. It is generally the case that torture applied by the Inquisition in the 16th century was not as harsh as torture applied by the secular authorities. But the torture chambers of the Inquisition have nevertheless acquired a particularly gruesome place in history, not only because of the level of pain experienced by the victims and the variety of torment inflicted, but because of the purpose of the torture—a confession, not of crimes committed, but of religious views and actions or with the result to betray friends.

The 16th-century Inquisition knew very well that torture was a far from dependable way of getting at the truth, so specific rules were formulated governing the conduct of questioning. The victim was not to be asked questions with a possible "yes" or "no" answer because he could be expected to admit to almost anything rather than undergo further suffering. Instead, the inquisitor was to encourage him to tell the truth. Interestingly, the *Sanctum Officium* was aware of abuses of such procedures—for example, to settle old scores or for reasons of personal antipathy—and so it ruled that the decision to resort to torture should come not from one inquisitor alone but from all the members of the court who had to be present during the torture. The following day, once the immediate suffering had sub-

A woodcut by Jacquemin Woeiriot from Milles de Sauvigny's *Praxis criminis persequendi*, Paris, 1541, shows a French variation of the water torture. The victim is not lying on a bench but has been strung up.

sided, the accused was presented with the record of his statements and was asked to confirm them by signing it. In only a very few cases this signature was withheld; the majority of victims signed, evidently out of fear that the torture would be repeated.

Records of some Spanish courts show that torture was used in about one third of cases. Some prisoners made a full and credible confession early on, making torture unnecessary. More than once, however, torture was used even when a confession had been accepted by the Inquisition, usually when the court wanted information about other suspects. This suffering for others—*in caput alienum*—could also be inflicted on a victim who had already been tortured on his own account. Statements extracted in this way were regarded by the Inquisition as completely reliable.

The choice of method was limited by the principles that no blood was to be spilled and that no visible scars were to be left. In Spain and Italy, the *garrucha* was often used; the victim's hands were tied behind his back and he was then pulled off the ground by means of a rope attached to his wrists. This torture could be intensified by first attaching weights to his feet, or by alternate slackening and tightening of the rope. The advantages of this method lay in its simple operation and in its ease of setting up.

A second common method was the so-called *tortura de cordeles*; the victim lay on a rack and straps or ropes were placed around his limbs and tightened with a bold during interrogation. One written account of such questioning records exactly how many turns of the screw the victim withstood and at what point he confessed. The actual tying of the bonds varied from place to place.

The most sophisticated method was the *tortura del' agua,* the water torture common in Spain. The victim was bound to a rack in such a way that his head was lower than his body. His mouth was then forced open and a fine linen filter was placed over it through which water was dripped, putting the victim at risk of suffocation. At intervals the filter was removed to enable the victim to confess. Again, there are detailed records of how much water victims could withstand and of their physical reactions.

Two written records by notaries in Spain and Italy give us some idea of the exact events of a torture session. The first is an account of an interrogation of one Doña Elvira del Campo, the second of the poet and publicist Niccolò Franco; both trials took place in the second half of the 16th century. Elvira del Campo from Toledo was accused of refusing to eat pork and to change her bed linen on a Saturday—both alleged proofs of her being a heretic, a baptized Jew, but clinging to her Jewish customs. During questioning, she admitted her actions but denied being a heretic. In 1568 she was tortured.

"She was taken into the torture chamber and told to speak the truth; she answered merely that she had nothing to say. The inquisitors ordered to have her undressed, she was cautioned again but would not speak. Once her clothes had been removed, she said: 'My Lords, I have done everything that is said about me and am bearing false witness against myself, for I cannot bear to see myself in this state—I swear to God that I have done nothing.' She was told that she was not to lie, but to tell the truth. They began to bind her arms, whereupon she said: 'I have told the truth—what more can I say?' A rope was tied around her arms and she was admonished again to tell the truth, but she still insisted that she had nothing to say. She then screamed, and said: 'I have done everything that is said about me.' Challenged to explain exactly what she had done, she answered: 'I have already told you the truth!' She then screamed and cried: 'Tell me what you want, I don't know what to say!' After a further turn, she said: 'Loose me a little so that I can think about what to say to you. I don't know what I've done; I refused to eat pork because it makes me ill. I've done everything, let me go and I will tell the truth.' She was told to speak and said: 'I didn't eat it, I don't know why.' She was then threatened again, and said: 'Lord, I didn't eat it because I don't like it, let me go and I'll tell you.' She was challenged to admit that she had acted in conflict with the teachings and faith of the Catholic Church. She said: 'Take me away from here and tell me what to say—you're hurting me—on, my arms, my arms . . .' and repeated it over and over again. The ropes were pulled tighter and she said: 'Lords, have you no compassion on a poor sinful woman?' They told her that they would have compassion on her if she only told the truth. She replied: 'Lord, tell me, tell me.' She was told to give details, to which she replied again: 'I don't know what I should say, Lord, I just don't know.' Then the ropes were loosened and counted; there had been sixteen turns of the screw and the rope had broken on the last one." They then used another means of torture on her. "She was told that if she wanted, she could confess before the water torture was inflicted. Then the linen was put in her mouth, and she screamed: 'No, take it away, I'll suffocate, and my stomach hurts.' A jug of water was fetched and she was told to tell the truth. She screamed for the last rites and that she was going to die, but they told her that she would go on being tortured until she told the truth. She failed to answer any questions, and when the inquisitor found she was exhausted, he had the torture stopped."

Four days later, poor Elvira was taken to the torture chamber again and subjected to further suffering (thus breaching the principle that no prisoner could be tortured more than once). Her statements became increasingly desperate, but eventually the inquisitor got a confession of and repentance for secret Judaism.

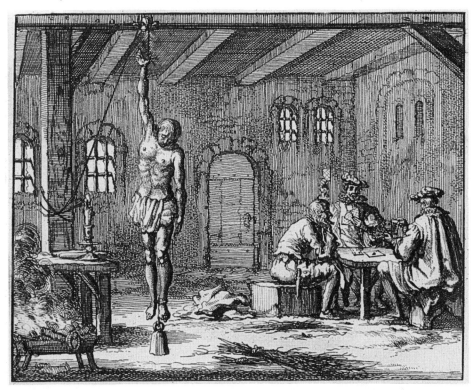

The second example is that of the Italian poet and publicist Niccolò Franco, interrogated in the torture chamber of the Roman Inquisition. Franco had written a pamphlet critical of the pontificate of Pope Paul IV, and the Inquisition tried to persuade him to make incriminating statements about some highly placed individuals—especially Cardinal Morone, whom they suspected of possessing incriminating material.

The first interrogation with torture took place on 1 February 1570, when Franco was suspended in the air with his hands bound for about an hour. He failed to confess, however, and the torture was repeated the following day—again, in clear defiance of the ban on repeated torture.

"Nicolaus Francus was taken into the torture chamber of the *Sanctum Officium* palace in my presence and that of the notary and others. When he had sworn to tell the truth, he was instructed by the Lord (the inquisitor) to tell the whole truth and not to wait till the next torture started. He replied: 'I am, and will continue to be, telling the truth. I have always done so, for although it seems barely credible there was only one copy of the book, no one else besides those I have already named saw it and I had no intention of printing it. I do not wish to add anything, and you cannot make me, whatever you do.' When the inquisitor told him that statements against him showed he was lying, he said: 'What I have said, I have said.' He then began to remove his clothes and the guards were called. They finished undressing him and tied him up. As he stood, naked and bound, he was compassionately encouraged by the inquisitor to tell the whole truth. He merely re-

The etching by Jan Luyken entitled "Torture chamber with torturers playing cards" is an example of later anti-Catholic material.
Staatliche Kunstsammlungen Dresden, Kupferstichkabinett.

Ioh. Dan. Hertz fecit et exc. A.V.   20

plied: 'I do not know what more I can say.' The inquisitor then ordered him to be pulled up so that the torture could begin as ordered. Then he said: 'Oh, Lord Jesus Christ, you know the truth' and repeated it twice more before he fell silent. When the procurator addressed him and said: 'Master Niccolò, do not subject yourself to this suffering, tell the truth,' he remained silent for a while and then said: 'Oh Christ, you knowest the truth,' then again fell silent for some ten minutes, so that they wondered if he had fallen asleep. The procurator asked him: 'Are you asleep, Master Niccolò?' whereupon he answered: 'Oh, Lord, Oh!' and then again fell silent. Another ten minutes passed and then he began to moan, and the procurator said to him: 'Well, Master Niccolò, decide to tell the truth and you can be released immediately.' He answered: 'By the Holy Virgin, I have told you the truth.' He then fell silent again, but then began to vomit, crying: 'O Dio . . . hoimé, hoimé, o gloriosa vergine Maria, hu, hu, hu.' He paused, and somewhat later said: 'My God, is there no end to it?' moaning and crying. After another lengthy silence, the inquisitor again urged him to tell the truth. He answered: 'I don't know any more, my Lord, no more.' That was his last statement, and when the torture had lasted for an hour and a half, the inquisitor ordered him to be released. While they were letting him down, he began to moan, 'O Dio, O Dio, hoimé.'"

Franco was tortured on two further occasions, each time without success. Finally he was surrendered to the secular authorities as a stubborn heretic.

Prison Life

Torture on the rack. Drawing by Johann Daniel Hertz, 1630. Moravská galerie, Brno.

It is not easy to convey a clear picture of the conditions within the Inquisition prisons, for no 16th-century prison building has survived nor have detailed contemporary descriptions been recorded. The best we can do is to use fragments of Spanish inspection reports, which still exist, to reconstruct some aspects of prison life. Even contemporary observers felt that the inquisitorial *cárceles secretas* in Spain were better equipped than those of the bishops' or secular prisons. In fact, it was not unknown for the latter category of prisoner to request transfer to Inquisition prisons.

The Spanish cells were obviously unfurnished, since the 1561 instructions refer to prisoners supplying their own bed and clothing. Food was supplied by the Inquisition itself but at the prisoner's expense (met out of confiscated assets). The food was therefore not too bad—the courts had nothing to gain from making economies; if the imprisoned person was sentenced, his property was confiscated by the State, if he was found to be guiltless, the remainder was returned to the prisoner. Records show prisoners being given meat and the wealthy even being allowed to choose their own menus, although the poor risked starvation and were forced on the Inquisition's charity. In the Spanish—and probably the Italian—prisons, prisoners were allowed to read and write. Conditions in Spain deteriorated, however, between the 16th and 18th centuries. Italian prisons varied enormously. In many smaller towns, prisons were sited in monasteries, while in Rome prisons offered different conditions to different classes of prisoner. The more wealthy ones had rooms with windows, while the poor were locked up in cells in the cellars of the Castel Sant' Angelo.

Although the rules of the Inquisition provided for prisoners to be in solitary confinement, we know from accounts of inspections that there were a number of communal cells. By the latter half of the 16th century, solitary confinement seems to have been the exception rather than the rule. The reason for this was simply lack of space, a frequent complaint of inquisitors. Isolation of the prisoners was restricted to keeping separate those involved in the same trial, to prevent them from corroborating their statements with each other.

As we know from the diaries of jailers and from accounts, a barber regularly attended the prisons of the Roman Inquisition to shave the prisoners and cut their hair—at their own expense, of course. The jailers ensured that clothes and shoes were mended as necessary, and prisoners could even ask for new clothes to be bought, again at their own expense. The prisoners were also allowed to leave their cells, under guard (in the Spanish prisons this was essential, as the toilet facilities were outside the buildings). Their freedom of movement remained restricted, however, by the chains binding their feet.

Although the material conditions in the prisons—at least in Spain—were better than in secular prisons, the *cárceles secretas* nevertheless aroused horror among contemporary observers. The reasons were mostly purely psychological; imprisonment meant total isolation from the outside world, and the Inquisition rules were more stringent in this respect than those of other prisons. Prisoners were forbidden to have any contact with their families, receiving neither letters nor visits, and were also denied contact with each other. They were told nothing of what was going on outside the prison, and the only people they saw were their jailers and the officials of the Inquisition. At intervals, however, prisoners would establish some illicit contact with the outside world, aided and abetted by the guards and prison employees—for a suitable bribe, of course, for the Inquisition itself was not immune to corruption. The isolation of prisoners was more consistent than in the Italian prisons, while in France heretics in custody were permitted visits from family and friends.

If the prisoners were fortunate enough to escape burning or a sentence to galley slavery, their conditions of imprisonment were improved. These prisoners served out their sentence in a normal prison, the *casa de penitencia* in Spain and the *carcer perpetuus* in Italy. Here, prisoners lived in cells or small huts with their family or friends. They enjoyed an only slightly limited contact with the outside world and were allowed to go to market to buy their own food. Accounts of inspections describe the Spanish prisons as enclosed camps with prisoners living in small cabins, moving fairly freely among one another. Those with no money were allowed to seek work in the town, although they were still required to fulfil their religious obligations and to lead exemplary lives. As in prison, the wealthier were more fortunate while the poor suffered. Some albeit unreliable figures show that the number of destitute prisoners began to increase in Spain and Italy toward the end of the 16th century. By 1625, the Milan Inquisition was beginning to pay for prisoners' food, and soon economies became necessary. The more responsibility the State took for its own prisoners (to be followed by the Church), the worse the material conditions in the prisons got until they degenerated into the stinking cells of the 18th century, with piles of straw for beds and only bread and water to eat and drink. Prison thus became the great leveler of rich and poor.

Escapees

Part of any auto-da-fé was the sentencing of heretics not actually present—sometimes they had died in prison but more often they had escaped. The flight of a suspect was regarded as proof of guilt and stubbornness and so such cases fell under the responsibility of the secular authorities. A straw doll or a picture was then executed, representing the mortal "shell" of the person concerned. Such burnings *in effigie* were, however, only a minor part of trials and autos-da-fé, despite the fact that few suspects were taken by surprise when the inquisitor's bailiffs arrived. Most knew in advance the dangers facing them, through hints or direct tip-offs. Sometimes, too, they were alerted by the arrest of a close friend or by a summons for questioning. Most of them made no attempt to flee, even if they had an opportunity to do so. Some even went to the *Sanctum Officium* to denounce themselves, and it does seem today as though any courage and initiative they may have had was stifled by the great power and authority of the Inquisition.

The reasons for such behavior clearly varied from one person to another. Many of those accused did not want to make a new life elsewhere without material security and far from their friends, and the material security argument was a strong one at that time. Flight was easy for those who could take their money across the Alps or the Pyrenees—the burghers and mer-

chants—but was much harder for those whose money was tied up in land or who relied on an income from their work, such as university teachers. Many, too, stayed to face the Inquisition because they were free of guilt and were convinced of their own orthodoxy. This happened particularly often in Spain and during the early years of the Inquisition in Rome. Suspects were anxious to show they were under false suspicion and to clear their own names and those of their children. Those who did flee did so for the most part because they realized they had split completely with the Church and had no intention of being reconciled with it, since they had in any case lost all belief in an effective church reform. It is no coincidence that the Italian emigrés north of the Alps included the followers of those with explicitly reform tendencies—most notably Calvinists—and also of the radical anti-trinitarian movements. For example, the Sozinis had already left Italy before being threatened with arrest, and the Spanish refugees, too, tended to flee and head for Calvinist Geneva.

A certain amount of evidence survives to suggest that there was still a chance to escape even when the arrest warrant had been issued. In 1576, for example, Cardinal di Pisa, a member of the *Sanctum Officium*, asked the Duke of Mantua to arrest the Latin Canon Don Valerian de Cremona, but he escaped, was sentenced *in absentia* and burned in effigy in 1581, along with his

Heretics condemned to death though not present at their trials were burned *in effigie*—that is, one of their belongings or a doll was thrown into the fire in their place. Engraving by Theodor Goetz dating from the 18th century.

books. The Inquisition had also asked for one Giovanni Marsaglio to be summoned for questioning, but he, too, disappeared before he could be arrested. Bernardino Ochino, too, is mentioned as an escapee along with a number of others. Sometimes, entire groups managed to flee; the best-known example is that of a number of burghers from Lucca in the early 1540s when the supervision and persecution of suspects was not yet properly organized. Some Hieronymites also escaped from Seville in groups, although most of their fellow-believers in Seville and, despite warnings, those in Valladolid, remained to await arrest.

There was clearly another reason in not fleeing—their conviction that the Familiari enjoyed excessive power and that flight was, in any case, pointless. The fate of individuals who had tried to flee from Castile would seem to justify their fears. The Italian Don Seso, founder of the Protestant community, tried to escape in disguise with a friend. He was recognized and arrested at a tavern on the Spanish border. Juan Sánchez, a zealous preacher of Lutheran teachings, reached the coast where he managed to stow away on a Dutch ship for Flanders; from there he went to Geneva under a

false name but was discovered by the agents of the Spanish Inquisition who found out that he intended to travel to England via the Spanish Netherlands. They set a trap for him, arrested him and brought him back to Valladolid in chains. It has been calculated that Sánchez's arrest cost the Inquisition more than 4,000 ducats—the cost of a small property. The psychological effect of such efforts did not go unappreciated; Sánchez was burned, thus demonstrating the futility of trying to escape from the power of the Inquisition.

Many escapees paid dearly for their clumsy attempts to remain fugitives. A good example is Giordano Bruno, who was eventually returned to Rome in chains. Another fugitive, Giovanni Paolo delle Agocchie, fled from Bologna to Geneva in 1591, and was sentenced and burned in effigy. When a year later he was arrested in Rome, he got away with five years as a galley slave, a sentence that he was fortunate not to have to serve fully. The story of Jacob Palaiolog was another case where a burning in effigy did not automatically mean that the same fate would befall the suspect once he was actually captured; his story, in fact, shows that it was even possible to escape from an Inquisition prison.

The Material Concerns of the Inquisition

Many heretical ideas in the 16th century were essentially anti-feudal, although there are a number of exceptions to this. Similarly, the argument that the Inquisition was an instrument of the ruling classes against the common people is not wholly accurate. Even a cursory

glance at the composition of the victims during the period of the Counter-Reformation shows that the Inquisition took its victims first and foremost from among the ruling classes and paid only scant attention to heretics among the common people. This can be explained quite simply in terms of the material position and interests of the Inquisition and of its function in the eyes of the Church, that is, of strengthening unity among the ruling strata of society and consolidating power structures in the feudal kingdoms. For this, it was necessary to liquidate ideological leaders and subversive members of the ruling strata—particularly in Italy, but also in Spain under Philip II.

The overwhelming majority of the victims of the Inquisition of Rome came from among wealthy families, nobles, merchants, notaries and, of course, clergy and monks. The urban masses were hardly affected at all, nor were those who lived on the land. The Spanish Inquisition was another story; Moriscoes made up a large segment of the victims if not the majority, among them many small-scale farmers, converted Jews, numerous merchants, and many poor town-dwellers. The *Sanctum Officium* had, however, only a marginal interest in simple, ordinary people.

This relatively modest attention paid to poor heretics was a result of the lack of interest the poor aroused in denouncers; they were usually imprisoned only for involvement in public heresies. Moreover, the courts had no particular advantage to gain from imprisoning the poor, for it would itself have to bear the cost of their interrogation, and here there was no real divergence between the practices in Spain and Italy. For example, from 1565 onwards the Bologna Inquisition received 200 gold scudi a year to finance the interrogation of the poor. In Spain in 1559, the representative of the Grand Inquisitor and the Bishop of Tarragona, Don Juan Gonzales, protested that poor heretics should not be imprisoned but should immediately be surrendered to the secular powers for burning, for they were of low birth, had no shame or remorse and could not even make amends by paying fines. If they were to be imprisoned, the Inquisition would have to bear the costs; if they were released, on the other hand, they would be forced to return to begging to support themselves and would then be able to spread their heretical views.

The poor were not thought worthy of major autos-da-fé, and smaller ones were held for them in churches. An interesting communication from Rome dated 1571 shows that Rome, too, was considering similar arrangements. The *Sanctum Officium* arranged repentance in St. Peter's Cathedral for five heretics of low birth, insignificant people whose autos-da-fé were unpublicized. The attempts of the Inquisition to keep it secret were also motivated by fear of an uprising, as was the case when a large group of poor heretics was arrested in Sicily.

The Spanish and Italian Inquisitions were interested in the powerful and wealthy, not only because they had an influence on society and their sentencing could be expected to have a broader deterrent effect but also because their sentencing represented a valuable source of income for the Inquisition; for while the confiscated property, at least in Spain, went to the Crown, fines and extraordinary court fees all went to the Inquisition, whose officials were not among the better paid.

Even the *Suprema* itself was shocked to discover that inquisitors were particularly diligent in persecuting those who promised a large income. Thus in 1623, for example, it issued a reminder to all courts to speed up the processing of cases. This was aimed at stemming the tide of arrests of wealthy suspects, which incurred unnecessary costs and ate into the victim's income, thus damaging the interests of the State. In Italy, the situation was more complex; in the pontifical state, the property confiscated passed of course to the Church. In some of the city states the Inquisition received a share of the income arising from the confiscation of goods—one third in the case of Milan. The Inquisition in Venice, where law required that all goods confiscated went to the republic, faced severe financial difficulties and had to rely on subsidies from Rome which barely met the cost of paying the various officials. One of the major causes of the dispute between the papal Inquisition and the Spanish Inquisition in Naples was the refusal of the popes to approve the principle (already applicable in Spain) that all property confiscated should pass to the State.

It would be an over-simplification to try to explain the interest of the Inquisition in wealthy and influential heretics merely in terms of the income they represented. After the Council of Trent, heresy in both Spain and Italy lost ground among the lower classes, with the exception of the Waldenses in the alpine valleys. Real heretics were wiped out within a few decades in both

Variant of the *sanbenito* robe worn by heretics.

Heretics shortly before their execution. Etching by Jan Luyken. Moravská galerie, Brno.

countries, and large groups, such as the Muslims, were eventually expelled. It is certainly true that the personal greed and acquisitiveness of the inquisitors was more than once the subject of public criticism, and in Italy the popes were also known to have intervened on the subject. For example, in 1575 Gregory XIII changed the method of financing the Inquisition so as to counter rumors of disloyalty. Inquisitors reserved for them-selves the right to dispose of the monies acquired, but now these no longer passed directly into their purses but instead to so-called depositories—men who were chosen especially for this task. However, this hardly changed things as far as the main goals of the *Sanctum Officium* were concerned, that is, acquiring as much money as possible to use in the struggle of combatting heresy.

Guilt and Innocence

In the broad publicity given to the history of the Inquisition since the 19th century, the concept of "innocent victims" often arises: those who fell victim to the procedures of the Inquisition. These cases of innocent victims are the most frequent and most emotionally charged argument used by opponents of the Inquisition, citing victims who had in fact remained true to the Catholic Church and its teachings but who were wrongly convicted of heresy. This conjures up a disturbing picture of men and women standing before the inquisitor and although free of sin and offense, they try in vain to convince the court of their innocence.

As difficult as it may be to dispute the effect of publicity, this kind of distinction between the innocent and guilty is not particularly appropriate. It implies justification of at least some of the trials, those of genuine and proven heretics, and results from the same idea as that of the apologists for the Catholic Church, for example, Ludwig von Pastor. In his interpretation of the history of the papacy and the papal Inquisition, heretics were

The burnings by the Inquisition in the Netherlands were only later depicted in anti-Catholic publications. These illustrations show clearly the atmosphere of the places of execution. Etching by Jan Luyken.
Moravská galerie, Brno.

to blame for their own tragic fate because they had dared to express their own non-conformist views. Their sentences were entirely justified, he argued, because they were guilty.

The question of guilt is, of course, one that has to be asked not only with respect to the guardians of religious orthodoxy in the 16th century but also from a general historical viewpoint. Most of those sentenced, regardless of membership of any specific group, were victims of brutal repression and unfettered fanaticism. It is, therefore, fundamentally irrelevant whether the "innocent" were pressured into admitting offenses they had not committed or whether the "guilty" recanted; each was waging a private battle with the

Inquisition, which varied according to his own conscience, his physical state and his mental abilities.

The question of guilt and innocence takes on a different aspect, however, when considered from the viewpoint of the struggle for progress and human emancipation. Those who were persecuted by the Inquisition for genuine deviation from the faith—whether followers and supporters of the Reformation or independent free thinkers of the status of Giordano Bruno or Galilei—engage our sympathy more from this angle, and their religious offenses become a point of honor. We must pity those who, as true sons and daughters of the Church, fell into the clutches of the Inquisition by mistake and through no fault of their own. Their human fate is particularly moving and has remained so to this present day. These people could not understand how unfair the system was that passed unjust sentences on them and decided their fate and that of their families. They persisted in their view that Mother Church could not be wrong in fundamental questions of faith and had right and truth on her side. The Inquisition quite deliberately wrung a statement from those sentenced, whether guilty or innocent, to the effect that they agreed with the death penalty for heretics.

The question of guilt can also be posed at a different level altogether: who was guilty of the monstrous Inquisition trials during the Counter-Reformation? The Church, as an institution? Or the State which made the Inquisition its tool? Or, as Catholic apologists argue, was it a necessary if drastic solution to a major social, intellectual and moral crisis that threatened to destroy the existing order and a solution that stemmed the spread of the theological conflicts and the religious wars that had wrought such havoc in France and the Netherlands in the latter half of the 16th century? We may find it hard today to accept the argument that Pius V saved Italy from civil war, but we must at least pay passing attention to the debate over the nature of the Spanish Inquisition that has continued since the early 19th century.

The major critic of the Spanish Inquisition and author of important controversial revelations, Juan Antonio Llorente, saw the Inquisition first and foremost as an institution answerable to the Catholic Church. In the 1830s, Joseph Marie de Maistre put forward the argument that the Inquisition was in fact a royal court, answerable only to the king, for whose inhumanity the secular powers were responsible. Many other Catholic authors subsequently supported this view, and they, unlike De Maistre, marshaled a range of factual evidence. It is worthy of note that the Protestant historian Leopold von Ranke also lent support to this view and commented that the inquisitors were in fact officials of the king who confiscated goods passed to the Crown, and that the Spanish State had not assumed its definite form until the Inquisition had become established. Opponents of this view argued primarily that the right to appoint the Grand Inquisitor had passed to the king from the pope and that the power of the Inquisition was actually based on church law. The fact that the State used the Inquisition for its own ends did not make it any less an institution of the Church.

Many of these arguments are no longer politically or ideologically current, and even the Catholic Church has meanwhile distanced itself from the methods of the Inquisition.

SO IT HAS PROVED ADVISABLE AND NECESSARY TO ORDER PARENTS, LANDLORDS AND MOTHERS… WITH ALL EARNESTNESS AND UNDER THREAT OF FINE OR IMPRISONMENT TO SEND THEIR CHILDREN AND OTHER MEMBERS OF THE HOUSEHOLD OVER FIVE YEARS OF AGE TO CHILDREN'S CATECHISM EVERY SUNDAY AND EVERY HOLIDAY, AND TO INSIST ON THEIR ATTENDANCE.

Decree of Ferdinand, Prince-Bishop of Münster, 14 November 1624

THE MOVE
TO A DENOMINATIONALIZED
SOCIETY

Although infamous and powerful, the 16th-century Inquisition remained an institution with limited geographical and social scope. Spain and Italy were a small, though important, part of the Catholic world, but even there it was not the Inquisition that determined the success of the Church's efforts at reform after the Council of Trent. If the Counter-Reformation had any success in halting the progress of the Reformation, the Inquisition had an even smaller part to play. And while it should not, of course, be underestimated, it was nevertheless only one element in a developing system of manipulation and unification of social awareness. In seeking an answer to the question of the measures and institutions that really determined the success of reform and Counter-Reformation, we must take at least a brief look at the methods used by the Church after the Council of Trent.

Its methods were effective and well thought-out, based on the experience not only of the preceding decades but also, in a more general sense, of the entire century. The first area that deserves closer scrutiny is the methods of trial, which formed a counterweight to those of the Inquisition. Order had to be restored and discipline in the Church had to be strengthened. The role of the sacraments had to be stressed and, in some cases, re-formulated. The believers were involved in new forms of community and social interaction. The system of worship of saints also had to be strengthened and re-formulated. Above all the Counter-Reformation was becoming a new instrument of the increasingly strong and centralized absolutist State. The development of absolutism was not, of course, peculiar to Catholicism, but represented a general trend in the development of European society at that time.

The Bishops' Concern for the Church

The Council of Trent had stressed the responsibility borne by the bishops for the standing of religion. The practice of giving episcopal honors such as profitable prebendaries to aristocrats who had neither been ordained nor possessed the requisite personal qualities was to be abolished. The new ideal of a bishop—as a Good Shepherd—was developed, and Cardinal Carlo Borromeo, Archbishop of Milan, served as a model. His asceticism and abstinence from material pleasure, his selfless care of his diocese, his consistency in implementing church reform, his exemplary execution of administrative tasks and his courage in fighting for the interests of the Church against the secular authorities all became exemplary qualities. The idealized picture of Borromeo served as subject matter for many booklets and other religious publications, and it was not by chance that he was the first theologian of the Counter-Reformation period to be canonized.

Some orders and instructions will serve here to illustrate the eight basic qualities adopted by Cardinal Bellarmine as the Church's picture of an exemplary bishop. First, he had to reside in his own diocese; second, he had to preach there regularly, even though the ruling of the Council of Trent did not include this instruction; third, he was to strive for moral perfection in his life and his faith; fourth, he was entitled to appoint suitable priests and was to take responsibility for them, and to ensure that no unworthy person took office as a priest in his diocese; fifth, he was to give up all benefices except his diocese (the pope himself was to approve any exceptions to this rule); sixth, he was to deal cautiously with the secular powers in defending the Church's interests and was to use methods that would not arouse the anger of the secular powers; seventh, he was not to make payments to his parents or other members of his own family out of his income; finally, he was to use his income for education. The bishops were to seek inspiration for their own lives from the lives of the holy bishops.

This description was no abstract ideal but rather a set of pragmatic principles whose aim was clearly to consolidate and strengthen the influence of the Church and to revive its inner life. The most important element in this was the episcopal control over the orthodoxy of the priests at diocese level. This control and oversight was to be exercised mostly through visitation by the bishop—in itself no innovation, since the early medieval Church in the 5th century had also organized such visits, but the bishops had gradually delegated the task to their archdeacons who in turn delegated further, so that the whole practice fell into disrepute and was neglected.

The Council of Trent restored order and discipline in this respect. The office of archdeacon remained, but the bishop became the central figure in visitation. It was his duty to visit each parish and congregation in his diocese at least once every year. On these visits, he was to oversee the orthodoxy of the priests, identify any malpractice and eliminate it, and help to teach the people fear and awe. The bishops themselves had specially appointed officials—*oculi episcopi*—who also took special responsibility for the spiritual health of the churches. Particular attention was paid to the content of the sermons; they had to be clear and readily understandable and given in the language of the people. Carlo Borromeo, for example, accused one bishop in Bologna of preaching in Latin. Sermons also had to conform to the Tridentine Catechism.

The bishop was to examine on the spot any shortcomings and do what he could to rectify them. His tasks in the diocese were considerable, and he bore overall responsibility for its well-being. Morone's Tridentine reform of the Church, in which the local bishop was a key figure, had proved completely workable.

Conditions in France and in the Habsburg inheritance were the most complex anywhere at this time. Rome was very concerned to maintain its influence and authority here. One can say that this was an almost existential concern of the Catholic Church, for both regions had been penetrated by the most diverse forms of heresy. In addition, there was an old-established tradition of reform that was used in political struggles. But Rome's hope of bringing both regions back under the Church's influence was eventually fulfilled, as events in the 17th century show. The support of the Catholic Habsburg rulers for Rome was not, however, always unequivocal. Neither Emperor Maximilian II nor Rudolph II was willing or politically able to meet the Curia's demands. No less complex and sometimes less pleasant and hopeful was the situation in France at the end of the 16th century. With the help of the bishops the Curia had, however, managed to implement the reforms of the Council of Trent, apparently without acquiring the contemporary political complexion of the century.

Successful reform demanded that suitably qualified candidates be assigned to all the bishoprics, and this was where the problems started. For example, it proved impossible to find a suitable Italian bishop for the imperial lands. The Curia had to respect the rights and customs of the countries concerned, implying all kinds of compromise. During the Council of Trent, under very difficult circumstances verging on an infringement of canon law, and after a vacancy of one hundred and forty years, the bishopric of Prague was eventually filled. The compromise reached represented approval both of the concept of Communion being given by the laity and of the secularization of the Church's lands,

which thus remained in the possession of the secular feudal lords, some of whom were not even Catholic. These and other compromises proved very useful to the Church, however, and the Prague archbishopric was extraordinarily valuable in implementing the Counter-Reformation in the imperial lands and in combating the Reformation throughout Central Europe.

The selection and training of a bishop was not simple. There was a shortage of good bishops, especially in the countries north of the Alps. Carlo Borromeo was a valuable supporter of the Church in this field. He educated the first generation of post-Tridentine bishops who worked well in their own dioceses. The Curia was willing to release them from their residence duty and use their talents elsewhere. For example, we could cite here Francesco Bonhomini, Bishop of Vercelli, and Cesare Speciani, Bishop of Cremona, who served as nuncios at the Habsburg imperial court and were able to steer Rome's Counter-Reformation course without difficulty. As experienced bishops, they maintained excellent control over the local bishops.

Visits were one of the major methods of consolidating ecclesiastical power, both in basically Catholic areas and in the regions that had been penetrated by the Reformation. The records of these visits are a remarkable testimony to the standing of the faith, the people and their way of life. Even in those areas where Catholic visitation was allowed, the visiting bishop was only permitted to visit the rulers and the clergy who were subordinate to the Catholic authority. This was the case, for example, in the imperial inheritance lands where the visiting bishops were accused of spreading the Inquisition and its methods. In the imperial countries, they did not dare to use inquisitorial methods against the secular and clerical powers. This is illustrated, for example, by the bishop visiting the bishopric of Regensburg in 1574 who complained about the dean of the chapter. He made a list of all the offenses of which the dean, as a Catholic priest, was guilty—twenty-three in all, some of them serious. Apart from the fact that the dean was not fulfilling all his clerical duties, he was neglecting his parishes and, as a native Saxon, had been raised a Lutheran. He read forbidden books and, to the general displeasure of the congregations, was living with a very arrogant woman who even dared to ride in his carriage. If this was the dean, what was going on among mere junior priests?

The Seminaries

One of the most important episcopal duties was to supervise reform of the clergy and, in particular, that of the secular local clergy. The visits undertaken by the bishops had shown that the standing of clergy in the parishes was not only unsatisfactory but verged on disastrous. It was clearly necessary to reform these old corrupted priests and replace them by new, well-

trained and well-prepared young men, grounded in the teachings of the Roman Church and loyal to Rome. The Council of Trent demanded that every local bishop should have a seminary in his diocese for the training of priests, but this ruling was not always easy to implement; in 1568, one of the German archbishops complained to the nuncio at the imperial court, Biglia, that the pope knew perfectly well that there were no seminaries in the empire. This was not, in fact, entirely true for, according to Jedin, there had been one in Eichstätt since 1564. And while it was difficult to set up seminaries in individual bishoprics, there were centers for the training of priests in "exile," mostly in Italy. The Jesuits, too, were able to give the local clergy the training it required. There were a number of obstacles to the establishment of seminaries. The vocation of a priest was not a particularly attractive one and so it was not easy to recruit the necessary number of young boys. The trainees also, of course, had to speak the national language fluently, without which their work would have been pointless. There were financial problems, too; in particular, the secular authorities were not willing to finance the training institutions, which could not hope to survive without financial support. Thus it was not until the 17th century that seminaries were finally es-

tablished north of the Alps. It was a different story on the Appenine Peninsula, where Rome made greater direct efforts to implement the rulings. In Spain there was a seminary in Granada by 1492, one in Tortosa since 1544 and another in Valencia since 1550. In post-Tridentine years, between 1565 and 1616, twenty-six institutions for the training of priests were opened.

The situation in France was complicated by the religious wars. In the early part of the 17th century there were nine seminaries, including those in Rheims, Avignon, Toulouse, Rouen, Metz, and Lyons. Gradually, they began to spring up in other areas threatened by Protestantism but ruled by Catholic sovereigns, such as, for example, in Ypres in 1565, Bruges in 1571 and 1591 and in Louvain in 1579. From the outset, however, other ways had to be found to replace the secular clergy, and one of these was to make greater use of clergy from monasteries.

Priests from the Religious Orders

By the middle of the 16th century, the situation in the old institutions of the religious Orders was critical and the Council of Trent had made its improvement one of its priorities. There had even been some support on the council for the idea to close some of the Orders and less-useful convents. That this did not happen was more a result of the efforts of the representatives of the Orders than of the usefulness of the Orders themselves. The large monastic Orders as well as the mendicant Orders were facing a serious crisis, illustrated, for

example, by the case of the Cistercians whose French head was feeling the effects of the unsatisfactory standing of the Catholic Church throughout France. The Benedictines and their congregations found themselves caught up in the situation in their homelands and were not receptive to change. The role of the individual bishops who were taking responsibility for changes in monastic life was also problematic, for the majority of Orders had until now escaped episcopal jurisdiction. However, some of the bishops soon received powers

Two Dominicans and a Paulician illustrated in 1645 by Wenceslaus Hollar, a Czech emigrant living in England.

Patres Dominicani.

Patres Dominicani.

Patres Minores. F. de Paula.

from the pope enabling them to visit individual monasteries in their dioceses and to reform them. Although a number of convents had until then enjoyed considerable land ownership, life in the monasteries was often of a lower standard than that of the local clergy. The Curia took drastic action to re-establish order. First of all, an overall picture had to be obtained of the actual situation and of the usefulness of the monastic clergy. Between 1573 and 1577 the Dominican, Felicián Ninquarda, traveled on behalf of the pope round the mendicant Orders in Bavaria and the imperial lands. He used the opportunity to talk to the local bishops and to study the activities of the congregations he was unable to visit. His first task was to inspect and reform the three mendicant Orders—the Dominicans, the Minorites and the Augustinian hermits—including both the male and female Orders. In this whole area—Germany and the Slav regions—the majority of those in the monasteries were Italians living under conditions worse than the visiting Dominican could have imagined. Their customs and practices were certainly not in accordance with church regulations. Ninquarda managed to remedy matters in those cases where the monks were still in the monasteries and had not fled before his arrival, but as soon as he was gone, they resumed their old sacreligious ways. One of the least serious and most easily remediable offenses was that of having young women in the convent with them. To remedy this, the Dominican suggested that if it was really necessary for the convent or the priest to have a female cook (and it would be very difficult to have a man doing the job) then she should be at least forty-six years of age.

During these visitations, Emperor Maximilian II expressed a desire that Germans, not Italians, should live in the mendicant convents in Vienna, since the Italians were unable to fulfil their preaching obligations if for no other reason than that of linguistic difficulties. Ninquarda had tried long and hard—but in vain—to implement this, and finally he managed to track down one German in a monastery of the Augustinian Order who had spent his time by making salve. He eventually became prior of a monastery in Vienna.

**Education
and Schools**

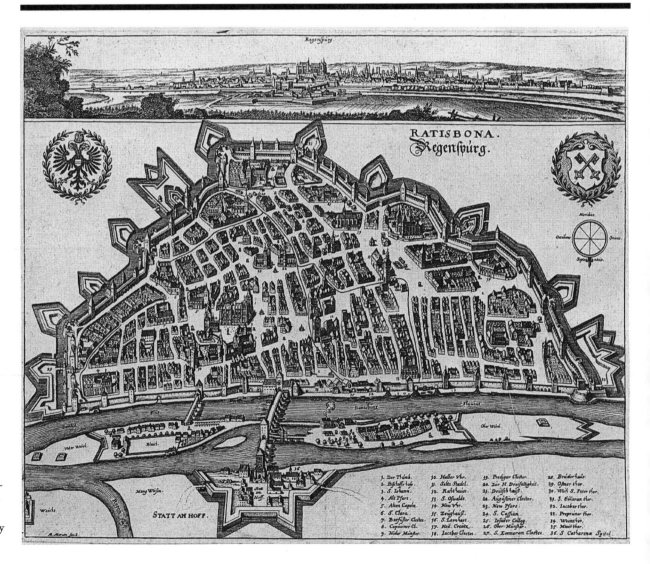

It was difficult for the town of Regensburg to maintain its Protestant faith in the face of the aggressive policies of the Bavarian dukes. Copperplate engraving by Matthäus Merian the Elder.

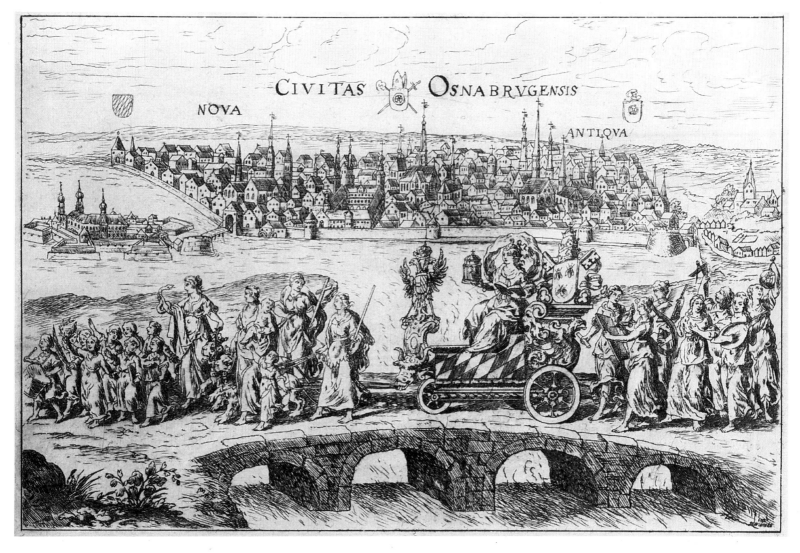

In the CIVITAS OSNABRVGENSIS NOVA ANTIQVA

In the mid-16th century the Church in Rome had another very serious problem. As a result of social developments and great social upheaval, educational questions—education of the clergy and also of the secular population—had become prominent. The basic school education and also higher education, including university courses, was no longer the preserve of the élite, as a result of the social changes that were taking place. Training had in the meantime become a necessity for a large section of the population who required education to enable them to pursue their professions. Acquiring an education was, however, often the occasion for acquiring at the same time dangerous anti-clerical views. The Church was faced with the urgent need to maintain control over schools and education in general.

The Council of Trent had, therefore, also turned its attention to the question of education in schools. Its attitudes toward the universities, which could preserve their rights and privileges, was also very interesting. However, these old freedoms and privileges were beneficial to neither the Church nor the State, which had an even greater interest in controlling education,

since it wanted both educated and controllable subjects.

The attitude of the Church toward the nature of the universities was expressed aptly by Pope Pius IV in a bull dated 13 November 1564. In a number of points, the bull laid down the conditions under which students at Catholic universities were to pursue their education. Only those confessing the Tridentine Creed were to be entitled to apply for a place at a Catholic university, an important point since it meant that all students with unorthodox beliefs would in future be excluded from Catholic universities. Of course, initially it was not easy to implement this ruling fully. The Church itself was using Catholic education in areas with a more or less significant Catholic population as a means of winning over non-Catholics, especially children from non-Catholic families.

An equally serious problem was that of finding suitable teachers for the existing universities and of founding new universities while converting the old ones into modern centers of Catholic education. The Jesuit Order had concerned itself particularly with educa-

The Order of the Jesuits and its colleges were most effective instruments for the Catholic Counter-Reformation north of the Alps. When the University of Osnabrück was opened, the Jesuits instigated a triumphal procession that was depicted by an unknown artist. Kulturgeschichtliches Museum, Osnabrück.

tional methods at universities, and proved to be of immense use in this. Their direct interest was in faculties of theology and philosophy. By the mid-17th century they had been able to acquire control of the majority of Catholic universities—a testimony not so much to their methods as to the success of their militant political means. They even opposed the interests of the papacy to meet the demands of the Catholic State.

Papal Nuncios and Congregations

The daily routine of church life in the regions north of the Alps was difficult and multi-faceted. It is, then, all the more surprising that the Church should have maintained its position there and should eventually have been victorious. The reasons are difficult to explain in more detail, but in essence, the State had given the Catholic Church priority over the reformed churches. In the most problematic areas, such as the Bohemian kingdom, non-Catholic resistance was eventually broken by the military means used by the Catholic State. The Thirty Years' War opened up other, deeper conflicts than just religious questions in the lands where the Catholic Church stood the best chance of strengthening its position—France and the lands of the imperial Habsburgs. Then, with judicious timing, it gave its whole-hearted support to the victorious political powers of the Catholic State. Although the Council of Trent had not explicitly confirmed the overall primacy of papal power, this monarchist principle was implemented in the Church and in the Curia authorities. Local priests were, obviously, also subject to the Curia; it observed their work and they were wholly accountable to it. Every bishop had regularly to give a personal account of his activities and of the fulfilment of his diocesan duties. The *Romanus Pontifex* Bull of 20 December 1585 contained the definitive rules laid down by Pope Sixtus V for visits by bishops to Rome—the so-called *Visitatio liminum ss. Apostolorum* rules.

The Curia was, however, still not satisfied with its control and supervision of the episcopal activities, especially in cases where the Roman Inquisition had no influence and where orthodoxy was the sole responsibility of the local bishops, and devised a range of methods for systematic supervision and control of the local bishops. First of all, it set up papal nunciatures that were basically bodies representing the Curia at the courts of the sovereigns or in areas where Rome was keen and able to maintain a political presence. In post-Tridentine times, there were some twenty permanent nuncios. The nuncio was not only a legate of the Curia in a country or region but also took responsibility for overseeing the local bishop or helping him. So it was hardly surprising that at about the year 1600 the most important nunciatures were at the courts of the imperial Habsburgs, in France and in Spain. The nuncio or his deputy sent regular reports to Rome, sometimes several times a week, and addressed them either to the Vatican secretariat or to the pope himself. These reports included reports on the fulfilment or non-fulfilment of the duties of the individual local bishops. Rome would then instruct the bishops to assist the nuncio and obey all the wishes and instructions of new nuncios. Thus the bishops were under the permanent and direct control of the Curia. As the examples of Bonhomini and Speciani show, the nuncios were often men who were highly qualified to judge the dealings of bishops. In addition, Jesuits, those critical and frequent visitors, and others also filed reports that were read and assessed in Rome; instructions, along with criticism or praise, then came directly from Rome.

Other institutions were also set up by the Roman Curia that were of special importance in countries where the Inquisition's powers were limited. These included local congregations that intervened in the work of the bishops, some directly, others indirectly. The German congregation came under suspicion of planning a St. Bartholomew's Day for the empire. The congregation was made up of real experts, former nuncios and, later, Curia cardinals who not only assessed the nuncios' reports but also determined papal policy toward the individual princes and tried to intervene

This decree gives an example of papal power politics. Pope Gregory XIII instructs the Archbishop of Prague to obey the papal nuncio who is on his way. Státní ústřední archiv, Prague.

72 In the central portico of St. Peter's Cathedral in Rome, Christ gives care of his flock over to St. Peter with the words, "Pasce oves meas," ("take my sheep to the pasture"). This underlines the primacy of the pope. Relief from the Bernini School, Rome.

73 An exemplary bishop was to be abstinent
in eating and modest in his life-style. Crespi
painted the saint Carlo Borromeo very much
in this light. The bishop has only bread and
water on his table; he is concerning himself
with scholarliness even during his meal.
Painting by Daniele Crespi.
S. Maria della Passione,
Milan.

74 The Apostle Peter is depicted sitting on the papal throne with the tiara. Painted wooden statue by an unknown Master, dating from the 16th century. Středočeská galerie, Nelahozeves.

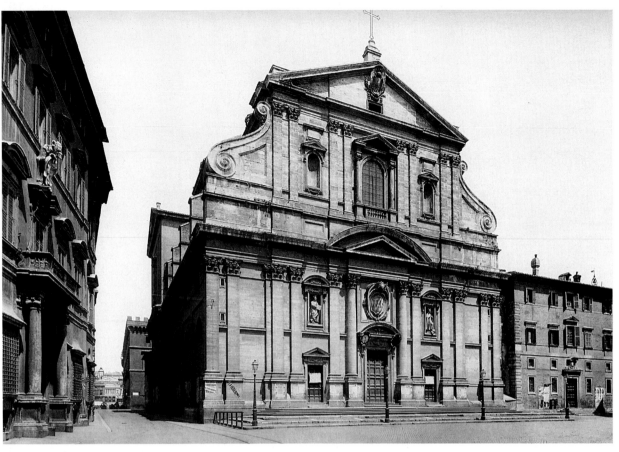

75 The unadorned and severe monumentality of the Chiesa del Gesù in Rome was the model for most of the Jesuit churches in Europe.

76 The Collegium urbanum de propaganda fide in Rome was erected by Giovanni Lorenzo Bernini. This college was an important institution in the spreading of Catholic teachings in non-Catholic regions.

77 A sermon by the papal nuncio Cornelius Musso in the Church of St. Augustine in Vienna before Emperor Ferdinand I. Painting by Jakob Seisenegger. Family collection of Duke Harrach. Schloss Rohrau.

168

82 The pilgrimage church, Nuestra Señora del Pilar, in Saragossa was one of the most famous of all Spanish places of pilgrimage.

83 The climax of a pilgrimage to Rome was the papal blessing in St. Peter's Square. Pius V was the pope responsible for making this ceremony popular again. Engraving by Etienne Dupérac dating from 1567.
Gabinetto Nazionale delle Stampe, Rome.

AREAE ET PALATII PONTIFICII VATICANI TOPOGRAPHIA · PONTIFICISQVE POPVLVM SOLEMNI RITV BENEDICENTIS IMAGO
ACCVRATISSIME DELINEATA

85 Saint Filippo Neri. Bust
by Alessandro Algardi.
Vatican Museum, Rome.

86 Even the angels were involved in the struggle against heresy. An engraving dating from the 17th century by Jean Lenfant shows angles driving out heretics in the presence of the true sons of the Church.
Gabinetto Nazionale delle Stampe, Rome.

87 Immediately after his canonization, Ignatius of Loyola was commemorated in many paintings and other works of art. "The Miracle of St. Ignatius." Altarpiece by Peter Paul Rubens. Kunsthistorisches Museum, Vienna.

88 The victory of the Catholic troops in the Battle of the White Mountain near Prague in November 1620 marked the end of the revolt by the Bohemian—and mostly Protestant—estates against the Habsburgs. The rejoicing reached Madrid and Prague, and to express his joy and gratitude the pope had the Chiesa di S. Maria della Vittoria built in Rome.

89 The Roman church Trinità de' Monti was designed in thanks for the destruction of the French Huguenots by Louis XIV. Engraving by Pietro Santi Bartoli. Gabinetto Nazionale delle Stampe, Rome.

VENITE ET VIDETE OPERA DOMINI QVÆ POSVIT PRODIGIA SVPER TERRA PS XXXXV

LÆTETVR MONS SION PS XXXXVII

Prospetto della facciata della Reale Chiesa della S.ma Trinita de Monti in occasione delle sontuoss feste celebrate dall Em.mo
Sig. Card. Destrees Titolare di essa in rendimento di grazie per l'estirpa.ne dell'Eresia in francia

90 Duke Albrecht V of Bavaria (1550–1579) played an important part in the implementation of the Counter-Reformation in Bavaria. He broke the resistance of the Protestant nobility there and drove the Protestant minority from the towns. Portrait by an unknown artist.
Středočeská galerie, Nelahozeves.

91 Theological disputes persisted even after the full victories of the Catholic religion in Bavaria and the Lutheran in Saxony. One debate—probably held in Regensburg—is depicted in a colored engraving dating from 1601.
Municipal Museum, Regensburg.

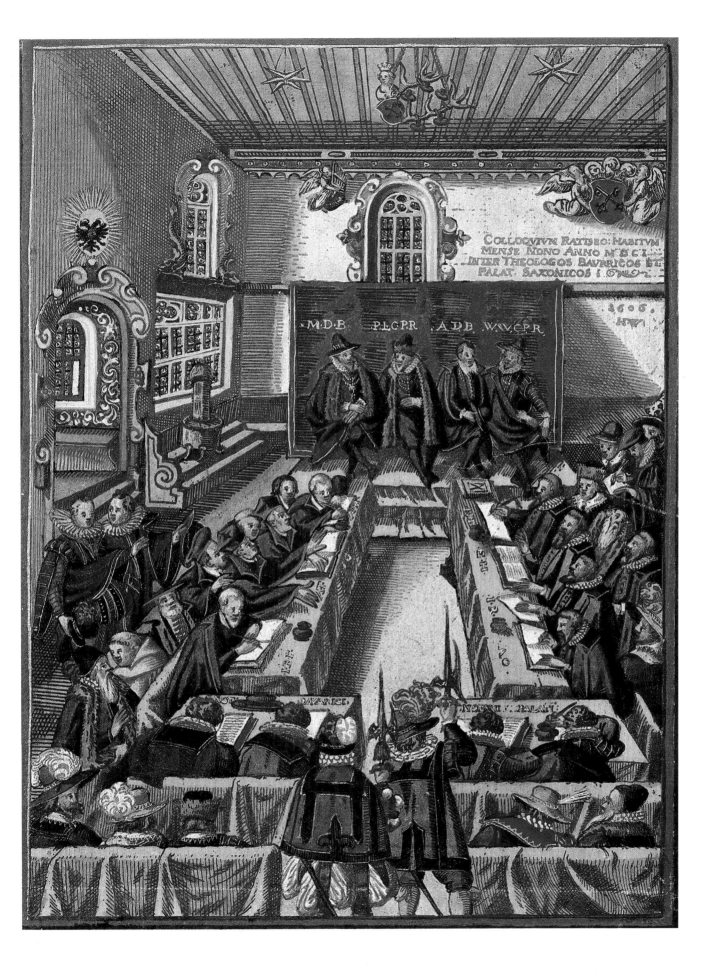

92 In two countries of Europe—Bohemia and France—the secular powers sought to create religious peace by means of enlightened tolerance. In France this was achieved by the Edict of Nantes in 1598. Ninety years later the edict was repealed by the absolutist King Louis XIV and denominational unity based on Catholicism was imposed. In protest Jan Luyken issued an engraving in which Henry IV is depicted issuing the edict.

93 On 25 July 1593 Henry IV (1589–1610) was officially introduced into the Church of St. Dionysius by Cardinal de Bourbon in the name of the pope. This marked the end of the period of religious strife in France, though Henry's intention to create a State with two denominations remained without much hope of success. Engraving by Franz Hogenberg. Staatliche Museen zu Berlin, Kupferstich-kabinett.

SANCTI DIONISII

Episcopus à Bourges

Anno Domini 1593, 25 Julij. Cardinalis Bourbonius

Vff sanct Iacobs tag ist geschehn, | Des Konings neff, geleitt in frei, | Ins Chor, die Meß wirdt da verricht, | Zwey tausent kronen strewen ließ,
Konig Heinrich der viert theil gehm | Mehr ander Herrn warn auch dabei. | An Music, Orgeln nichts gebricht, | Vier tausent brodt, austheilen ließ
Nach Sanct Dionisi Kirche schon, | Der Ertzbischof von Bourges In | Der Meßen gheimnuß lernt er mit | Den armen. Darnach sahe man vil
Der Cardinal genant Bourbon | Herlich entfengt, und furet hin | Vergaß darnach der gsangnen nit, | Fewrwerck, geschutz vnd frewdenspil.

94 After considerable delay, Pope Clement VIII decided to recognize Henry IV's conversion to Catholicism. The peace between France and Spain, mediated by the pope, also formed part of the overall reconciliation. Ippolito Buzzi represented the settlement of the peace between the two kings as a success for papal policy on the sarcophagus of Clement VIII in the Church of S. Maria Maggiore in Rome.

95 The marriage between French King Henry IV and Maria Medici was destined to put an end once and for all to the religious wars and to strengthen the alliance between the king and the Catholic Church. Painting by Peter Paul Rubens. Louvre, Paris.

96 Under Cardinal Richelieu France took the first step toward denominationalization without losing its independence from intervention by the pope. Richelieu medallion by Jean-Baptiste Varin.
Louvre, Paris.

97 The heart of Paris at the time of Richelieu—La Place Royale in 1639.
Bibliothèque Nationale, Paris.

in the internal affairs of countries penetrated by the Reformation. Their experts included men like Morone and Delfino.

The Curia's strong principle of centralization was motivated by a desire to increase its power against the individual bishops and, with their help, apply and implement the principles laid down by the Council of Trent at a time when not even the secular authorities could use power against non-Catholics with immunity, having to content itself with political means.

The Council of Trent also shaped and inspired religious debate. It had finally put an end to the religious debates in which supporters of the Reformation were bombarded with arguments in an attempt to persuade them of their errors.

A new Catholic publicity was addressed to the believers, with the aim of revealing to the Catholics the blasphemous views of the reformers and to face them with telling arguments for a confrontation with holders of views opposed to those of the Church. The Church also sought to expose the Reformation and its supporters in the eyes of both rich and poor and humiliate it as well as to provide a response to the avalanche of the Reformation literature. The growing demand for literature of a religious nature showed that the polemical pamphlets were being widely read and that its publication had been merited. For example, during the fifty years after the Council of Trent, the amount of Catholic literature available more than doubled, while interest in classical Antiquity and in philosophical writings waned. Religious literature even came close to competing with secular literature. In Venice in the 1550s, religious literature accounted for only fourteen percent of all literature printed; by the 1580s it was thirty percent and in the early 1590s, thirty-five percent.

Distinctions must be made here between the different categories of religious literature. There were two main types, serving different functions: scholarly and controversial literature to stimulate debate; and popular literature in the form of religious pamphlets for the lay people. Scholarly polemics against the theology of the Reformation was a fairly new phenomenon. It had its roots in the Jesuits' teachings and in Canisius's Catechism, but the first proper systematic confrontation with Reformation teachings was provided by the scholarly Jesuit professor from Louvain, Robert Bellarmine. Called to Rome on the basis of his fame, he founded the Chair of Controversial Theology at the Jesuit College Gregoriana in 1576. In the 1580s he published his fundamental writing, *Disputationes de controversiis christianae fidei adversus huius temporis haereticos* (Debates on the Christian controversies of faith against contemporary heresy). Evidence of the atmosphere of dilettante zeal was the placing by Pope Sixtus V, a former inquisitor, of Bellarmine's book on the Index of Forbidden Books in 1590. His pretext was that Bellarmine had not advanced any arguments in his book in favor of the power of the pope over all the world. No one on the College of Cardinals responsible for the index dared to oppose the pope's wishes, al-

Polemics against Heretical Views

A treatise that was published in Venice against the false teachings of the heretics, dating from 1562.

Title page of a treatise written by the eminent papal nuncio, Carlo Caraffa. It describes the religious situation in the imperial lands during the reign of Ferdinand II.

Title page of a polemic theological treatise by the famous historian and humanist Matthäus Dresser against Cardinal Bellarmine.

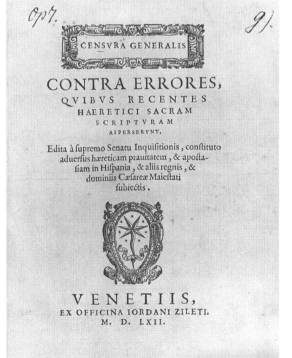

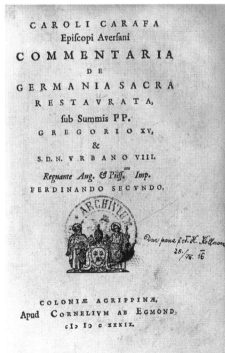

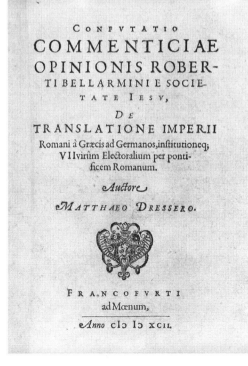

The simple but impressive portrayal of the Last Judgment comes from the *Katholisches Lesebuch für das Volk* by Jacob Zeter, dated 1617.

An instantly recognizable, though unnamed, caricature of Calvin in the same book is followed by the admonition: "When gnats get into a glass, they buzz around . . . and so with a heretic, when he looks into the Bible he starts to rave. Neither gnat nor heretic do any good, they poison the good instead. Poison ends the life of a gnat, while a heretic's fit for burning."

There is also a warning about excessive education. "Playing the lute and reading books is good pleasure, but don't pluck the strings too hard and watch out for falsehood."

though the book was removed from the list immediately after the pope's death. A further attack on Bellarmine followed in the early 1590s, this time from the Jesuit College in Vienna. The Jesuits accused Bellarmine of propagating the views of the heretics by describing them in detail. They were also concerned that he had ignored some traditional Catholic arguments (clearly because he did not find them worthy of defending). Bellarmine defended himself against the criticisms and the next generation of theological scholars vindicated him. His book became a classic and prompted his appointment as a cardinal in 1599. Three hundred years after his death, he was canonized and elevated to one of the major teachers of the Church.

Although Bellarmine's work is a systematic polemic, there is unevenness in the debate. According to Bellarmine, the most dangerous of the Protestants' views were those concerning the Eucharist and the Mass. He was less interested in the teachings on the sacraments, the position of the pope and punishment for sins, and paid only scant attention to the question of the person of Christ and the Holy Trinity. The views of the antitrinitarians and other radical groups, he argued, were not as dangerous as those of the Lutherans and Calvinists.

Since the Council of Trent had again stressed ecclesiastical traditions, history once more became an impor-

A contemporary engraving depicts the struggle between the "Church of Christ" and the "hordes of the Antichrist" using theological theses and antitheses.

tant weapon in scholarly polemics. The supporters of the Reformation described the tradition of the Church as a summary of falsification cast as a veil over original religious truths, and so it had become necessary to demonstrate the truth of the traditions, to defend the legends and to justify the old ways of the struggle against heresy. Many legends concerning saints were examined critically, fantastic stories were revised and some were withdrawn, or, more frequently, simply passed over. Bolland came to the fore with his critical school, while the famous scholar and compiler Cesare Baronio was the force behind the criticism and the formation of a new official line within the Church toward its own history. In his multi-volume work *Annales ecclesiasticae* he described the function of the Church as not merely a teaching institution but also as *ecclesia militans*, in its struggle against heresy. The struggles of the Counter-Reformation and the methods of the Inquisition were thus shown against their historical background and given the formal seal of approval. The ticklish problems of the Reformation and post-Reformation were passed, on Baronio's death, to the Polish theologian Bzovius, who unfortunately did not always manage to find the sources that best served the interests of the Church. In some cases his compilations even included information that did not correspond to the official views of the Church in the first half of the 17th century, and so the last few volumes of his work met with severe criticism from the Inquisition of Rome and had to be revised.

Scholarly works of controversial theology were not aimed at the general public simply because they were written in Latin and so their direct impact on society was limited. For example, when Baronio's history of the Church was published, eight hundred copies were printed and took a long time to sell. An attempt to translate the work into German failed, moreover, through lack of interest.

The tendentious literature in the form of polemical propaganda and pamphlets, on the other hand, was aimed at the masses. It was not, of course, concerned with countering heretical views by means of theological arguments except in the case of the Catechism of Canisius. The fundamental role of these works was to parody the thoughts and practices of religious opponents and to slander them personally. Reformers were to be made the enemies not only of the Catholic faith but also of the family and of society. Every heretic was to be stamped as a threefold deviant, harmful to the Church, the State, and the human soul. Such a man deserved, of course, the harshest penalties. In French Catholic defamatory literature, for example, attacks were made against the Huguenots. These enemies of mankind were to be eliminated from the face of the earth, for good. Reformation pamphlets had condemned the followers of the pope as allies of the devil and so in Catholic pamphlets heretics were increasingly accused of demonic characteristics.

Church propaganda often put forward different arguments depending on the social group to which it was addressing itself. For example, there is the extensive and well-researched Polish material—the defamatory literature destined for the ruling classes accused heretics of trying to destroy the existing social order. The hertics were, according to this literature, seeking to set the lower nobility against the king and the subjects against the sovereigns and the administration, hence virtually all popular revolts were the work of heretics.

The pamphlets aimed at the middle classes, on the other hand, did not stress the interests of the State but the more general social threat posed by the Reformation. The heretics were accused not only of setting subjects against their sovereigns, but of setting farmhands against peasants, apprentices against artisans, children against parents and wives against husbands. The pamphlets frequently contained vivid descriptions of the specter of sexual misconduct—the heretics were alleged to share women and to hold mass orgies. Another powerful accusation was that they destroyed pictures of saints, particularly of the Virgin Mary. In the 17th century, literature for both poor and rich identified heretics as foreigners or as agents of a foreign power. The Catholic faith was linked with the nation, to which all good, loyal Poles should remain faithful.

Catechisms

Tridentine Catechism.

Southern Slav Catechism dating from 1564.

Even in the 18th century Catechisms were still printed in Latin for priests.

In drawing up its plans for the effective and uniform spread of the true Catholic faith, the Curia did not want to rely solely on the personal abilities and knowledge of the bishops and priests belonging to an Order. Even the most frequent visitation was no substitute for the reliable and practical manuals that were to help the Catholic clergy to uncover false views, defend Catholic teachings against the Reformation and protect the simple believers against the influence of the heretics. The clergy had to know their standing exactly and were not permitted to teach; so in 1555 the new Emperor, Ferdi-

nand I, commissioned the Jesuit Petrus Canisius to write a handbook to explain all the Catholic Church's teachings in a question and answer form. Canisius did this by writing the *Summa doctrine christianae* in which he expounded Catholic dogma through 213 questions and answers. This was the first of many famous Catechisms by him and became especially popular in the German countries once it had been translated into German. The Catechisms by Canisius had a polemic and apologetic character, entirely in keeping with the difficult religious confrontations in the empire. The

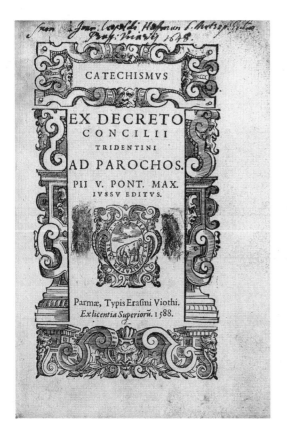

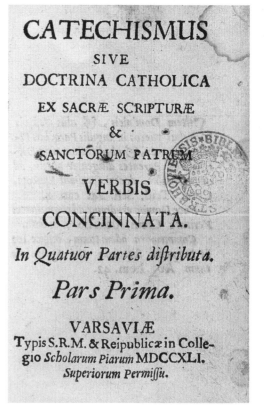

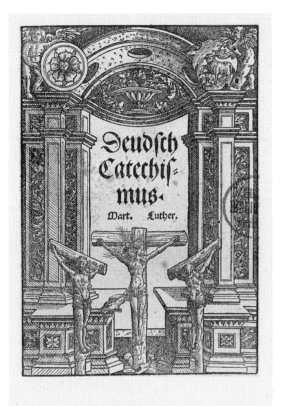

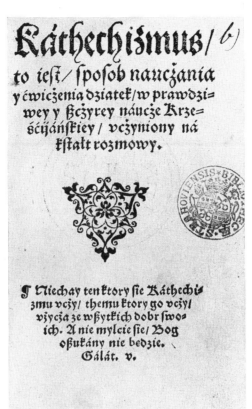

main area of difference from pre-Reformation Catechisms was that it gave instructions on how to oppose heretical views—in particular, Lutheran views.

The French parallel were the Catechisms of the Jesuit Augerius. The major Catechism, designed for adults, was published in 1563 (the year the open conflict with the Huguenots began), while the minor one, for children, appeared in 1568. Unlike Canisius's Catechism, these argued specifically against Calvin.

During the final deliberations of the Council of Trent, Canisius tried to persuade the council fathers to make his Catechism the basis of the new, official council Catechism to be used for the whole Catholic Church. He had a number of supporters, including the Archbishop of Prague, Brus of Müglitz, who recommended the council to adopt large portions of Canisius's text. The attempts were in vain.

The council decided to write a Catechism of its own, to be made generally applicable, but in fact it was not until 1566, after the council's work was completed and under the pontificate of Pius V, that work was finished on a new Catechism, a new standardized breviary (finished in 1568) and a revised missal (1570). Although contemporaries recognized this new *Catechismus ex decreto Concilii Tridentini ad parocho* (also known later as the *Catechismus Romanus*) as a major new weapon in the struggle against the advances of the Reformation, it lacked the polemic ardor of Canisius's. It was quieter in tone, without invective or controversy, and comprised mainly a systematic account of the Catholic faith and its teachings, taking no account of the attitude of Protestantism toward certain questions. Many zealous Catholics at the time made no secret of their disappointment at its insufficiently militant tone, and saw little in it that could be used in polemic against the Reformation, while the priests from the monastic Orders found it too scholarly. It is, then, hardly surprising that Canisius's Catechism remained the most popular one north of the Alps.

During the 1560s, Canisius also wrote two further popular versions of his work. By the 1570s, two hundred editions of three Catechisms by Canisius were in existence, and the so-called major Catechism was published in Cologne in 1566 as an extended version of the original *Summa doctrine christianae* aimed especially at students. The minor Catechism was aimed at older children while for very young children there was the so-called Small Catechism.

This need for a variety of Catechisms arose out of the rulings of the Council of Trent. The council had instructed the clergy to give religious education on Sunday afternoons and public holidays, and was particularly concerned about the religious education of children. Carlo Borromeo himself instructed the clergymen of his diocese to give children catechismal lessons every Sunday and stressed the duty of parents to send their children along regularly. However, it was not until much later that Sunday religious education caught on generally throughout the Catholic world. In Italy and France, it did not do so until the 17th century; in the

Martin Luther's *Deudsch Catechismus.*

Polish Catechism dating from the 16th century.

Calvinist Catechism used in the Palatinate.

German lands, threatened by the Reformation, it had already been introduced by the end of the 16th century. In general, it was easier to introduce catechismal lessons in the towns than in the countryside. Outside the empire, too, simpler Catechisms for children were introduced along the lines of those of Canisius. As printing techniques became more developed, woodcuts and copperplate engravings were used as illustrations in Catechisms as a means of helping to teach illiterate children. Of course children learned the questions and answers by heart.

The translation of the Catechisms into the various national languages was a matter of great cultural importance. During the Tridentine Council, many legates had been dismissive of such translations, arguing that it would indirectly assist the heretics. Yet finally, the dispute was settled by Pope Pius V who put his authority behind the translation of the Catechisms into the various national languages. If the Church were to confront the Reformation, he said, it had to speak the language of the people not only in sermons but also in Catechisms.

Parishes and Religious Brotherhoods

Religious education for children on Sundays was only one of many tasks entrusted to the parishes by the Council of Trent. They also had a general responsibility for spiritual welfare and counseling. It was the duty of every parishioner to attend Mass every Sunday in his local church. His baptism and marriage were the responsibility of the local priest who also took his confession at least once every year, gave him the last rites and buried him. None of this was new, but what was innovative was the control and consistency with which these duties were to be observed and supervised. The efforts made to give the subjects a real awareness of their communion and fellowship within the parish was also new. There were new administrative tasks, too: the priest had to enter details of all baptisms, marriages and deaths in the parish register, keep a list of those attending confession, and keep general control of the number of his parishioners. Membership of a parish gradually became a basic social relationship that took precedence over the previously dominant blood and family ties.

There were also new regulations relating to baptism. The Church ruled that all new-born babies had to be baptized within three days of birth (within twenty-four hours in France), leaving the parents little time or opportunity to invite their relatives to the ceremony to fulfil their social responsibilities by giving gifts. For similar reasons, the number of godparents of a child was limited to one or two (at that time, a child's godfather or godmother was regarded as a full member of the family). Marriage rules, too, were revised so as to remove the validity of arrangements made between families for the future marriage of their young children. The aim was both to remove excessive family ties and to eliminate disputes between the sexes. Families in dispute had to attend Sunday services in their local church together.

Another threat perceived by the revived Catholic Church in many areas was that of the traditions linking inhabitants of villages. The Church saw obstacles to discipline here and incitement to immorality. A new religious, disciplined form of sociability was encouraged, based on the model of the resurrected religious brotherhoods that, under the patronage of the Church, began successfully to dominate the social and religious life of the Catholic towns. These urban religious brotherhoods were, in fact, no new invention as they had existed since the late Middle Ages as associations with firm religious functions including, for example, the collection of indulgences or the organization of religious ceremonies and celebrations. These too, however, did not escape the grave internal crisis faced by the Church; they degenerated or declined or became involved in new activities as spokesmen for political or social movements (the Spanish Hermandades, for example, took part in the stormy events of the Comuneros revolt in the early 1520s). Some rulers, such as Charles V in Spain and Henry II in France, banned the brotherhoods precisely for this reason. The Council of Trent made provision for them to continue, but underlined the general recommendation that the bishops should keep a close watch on them during visits.

In situations of open conflict and tension, the religious brotherhoods even proved to be belligerent and, in some cases, armed units—the vanguards of the *ecclesia militans*—especially in France, where they organized a number of Huguenot massacres in the 1560s. In the 1570s and 1580s they appeared not as armed units but as closed societies with influence over the political life of many cities in the interests of the Catholic league. After Henry of Navarre's victory and his accession to the throne, the brotherhoods, too, faced a serious crisis and a number of them finally were dissolved.

The foundation for the revival of the religious brotherhoods in the Catholic world was laid by Pope Clement VIII in 1604 when he announced his reforms. The reconstituted brotherhoods were to be subject to the bishops who would have to approve their statutes. The aim was to intensify the quality of religious life in the cities. In the 17th century, female Orders were originally open to women from the circles of local dignitaries, but later they were also opened to women from lower classes. Women were to be educated and trained for the spirituality the Church demanded of them—passive, obedient reverence.

Reformation, the questioning of the primacy of the pope and the general criticism made of the Church. The success of the publicity to renew interest in pilgrimages surprised even the Curia, which in 1575 designated another Holy Year and saw an unprecedented number of pilgrims making their way to Rome. This success could be viewed as a test case for the renewed vitality of the Church or evidence of the effective linking of the center in Rome with the provinces. The success of the Holy Year also prompted the broad popularization of pilgrimages to local centers of worship. This also helped to restore the authority and popularity of indulgences that had been so shaken as a result of the Reformation. At the same time, Rome gave pilgrims and their clerical companions the opportunity of familiarizing themselves with excellent preachers, as Rome once more became the model for preaching in the Catholic world.

Pilgrimage Church Zur Schönen Maria (The Glorious Virgin Mary) in Regensburg. Woodcut by Michael Ostendorfer, 1529. Germanisches Nationalmuseum, Nuremberg.

Confession and Forgiveness of Sins

The dispute over the sacraments came to occupy a central role in the Catholic Church's struggles against the Reformation. It was no mere accident that Luther's efforts to secure reform had begun with a campaign against the sale of indulgences. Catholic theologians were unable to agree at all over the complex questions arising over the issue, and the Council of Trent had to consider the role of the sacraments in the life of believers and make them once more an effective instrument of renewal of the Church. In this regard, confession and penances took on special significance. It cannot be said that the council brought in any major changes; it merely reiterated the adherence to the old principles of regular confession and Communion at least once a year, and returned to a more scholastic and psychological view of sins. Not only were tried and tested principles and standards strengthened, but focuses were shifted, and the implementation of the rules was closely monitored.

The principle of compulsory confession all through the year may not have been new, but only when the Church understood how to use the new social progress for its own ends was it able to implement the principle effectively.

The rules included written records of the fulfilment of ecclesiastical duties and obligations (particularly the famous list of sins) and the use of force by both the Church and the secular powers. For example in Beauvais in France a whole range of measures was laid down for use against those who failed to come to confession and Communion at Easter.

First, the priest called those concerned to an interview at which the episcopal rulings were read to them. If this failed to bring the desired results, the renegades were brought before the secular authorities. In particularly stubborn cases the priest could refuse infant baptism and burial in consecrated ground. The Prince-Bishop of Münster, in the mid-17th century, called for a list of all those who had not attended Communion and imposed fines or other penalties on them.

The urgency with which the Council of Trent stressed the observation of the last two commandments, which condemned conscious, deliberate sin, was an attempt to intensify the psychological impact of the sacraments in general and of sin in particular. The confessors of the new, revived Church were to take a greater interest than before in the sins that their parishioners had committed in their private life in deed or even in thought. This gave them an opportunity to penetrate their parishioners' bedrooms and question them on their clandestine practices—mostly unapproved use of contraception and unusual forms of sex-

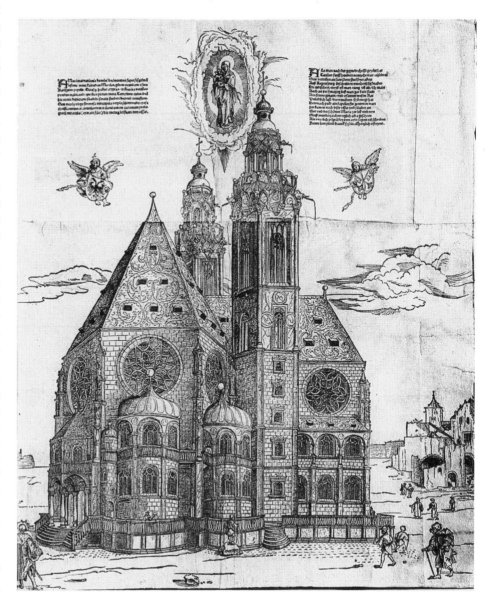

ual intercourse. The priests also reserved the right to check up on the religious observance and doubts of their parishioners in question of faith. In this way they were able to detect any nascent heresy and nip it in the bud without in any way breaching the confidentiality of the confessional. (Indeed confession had been the ma-

One method of influencing opinion was to make a very realistic portrayal of the punishment of sinners in Hell.

jor factor in the exposure of the Lutheran community in Valladolid.) If the confessor was a good judge of human psychology—and the Jesuits in particular made great efforts in this field—he was able to influence the spiritual life and conduct of the parishioner making confession to him.

This also explains another significant change in the form of confession, probably originating from Carlo Borromeo—the introduction of the confessional. Until the mid-16th century, Catholic believers had made their confession directly to the priest in a designated area of the church.

Carlo Borromeo felt that the priests should be in a wooden cubicle that separated them from their parishioner by means of a grille. The idea behind this was to prevent any physical contact between the priest and the parishioner, especially female parishioners. The confessional was introduced, in the *Rituale Romanum* in 1614, initially only for women but later for men, too. At the same time another, more important feature of the confessional emerged; it created an extraordinary intimate milieu of absolute solitude, an atmosphere in which the believer was able to speak not only of his own sins but also those of others.

The renewed Church would not countenance the compromising practice of dealing in indulgences, although even such an authoritarian pope as Pius V could no longer forbid their sale altogether, even in compliance with the rulings of the Council of Trent. The Spanish king, in particular, had pressed for approval of indulgences to be paid for at the time of confession, since indulgences represented an important source of income for the royal treasury. Of greater significance for the Church was the move toward making indulgences more concrete by embodying them in holy objects. The possession of a holy cross, a holy candle or medallion or similar object not only paved the way to indulgence but also brought with it the direct protection of God.

The origins of the worship of holy objects dated to pre-Tridentine times when Clement VIII issued a bull in 1536 relating to holy candles. It reached its peak after the council when Popes Pius V and Sixtus V recommended use of holy objects. They were easy to obtain. A simple ceremony of blessing by a pope or bishop was all that was required, and their popularity grew across Catholic Europe over the next one hundred years. Thus, for example, pilgrims in Rome purchased some 100,000 holy medallions in 1625, depicting five saints of the Catholic Church who had been canonized only a short while before, in 1622. These medallions, along with other holy objects, served as talismans for believers and were thought to protect them not only against sin but also against illness and accident. The common people's spirituality in this respect verged on superstition, but the cult of holy objects made it possible for the Church to use it to its own advantage. Pictures represented another form of holy object for the people. These were not completely new, as even in the late Middle Ages all rulers and magnates had small works of art depicting biblical scenes, small statuettes or small altars. This time the Church made a radical change in the practice. New printing techniques made it possible to reproduce thousands of copies of woodcuts or copperplate engravings with religious motifs.

This form of printing first cropped up in Antwerp, then in Cologne and Augsburg, but also in France and Italy. The rapid spread of such pictures was evidence of the way in which the Church learned to use technical progress to its own advantage. The pictures first depicted mystical motifs (sacred hearts, Christ and the soul in adoration), but gradually, the subject matter became more concrete so that it could more readily be understood by the common people.

The dominant themes which were depicted in these pictures were the Virgin Mary, scenes from the life of Christ and pictures of saints. They had several functions: They served not only as a holy object or a talisman, but also as a sort of visual aid in religious education, and so became an important instrument in ecclesiastical renewal, and in the manipulation of mass spirituality—the worship of saints.

Jan Sarkander was tortured as a faithful Catholic and supporter of the Habsburgs by the rebellious Moravians. The torture was not as inhumane as is depicted in this illustration by Samuel Dworžák. Jan Sarkander was later beatified as a local patron saint. Národní galerie, Prague.

Saints Old and New

The reformers were very critical of miracles and the worship of saints, although it seems that their refusal to accept the worship of saints also affected the Curia, since the Renaissance popes were already far more reticent in the matter of canonization. One exception to this was the short pontificate of Hadrian VI, the first pope to be favorably disposed toward renewal of the Church. In 1523 he canonized the late Bishop of Florence, Antonio, who had died in 1459. Antonio's main virtue had been his exemplary life and his concern for his diocese. After Hadrian there was something of a hiatus until almost the end of the century. Although the Council of Trent had confirmed the worship of saints, it took a while for the Church to begin canonizing new saints. It was not until the beginning of the 17th century that a liberal policy of canonization emerged that was farsighted and wise.

In 1604 the Curia began the process of canonizing an extraordinarily popular Roman lady, Francesca Romana. Four years later the negotiations had been completed and Pope Paul V fixed the date for the canonization for the anniversary of his pontificate. Francesca's life was made up of several exemplary and remarkable stages: She was an exemplary virgin, and a no-less exemplary wife, she bore the trials of widowhood with patience, and then spent the last few years of her life before her death in 1440 in isolation in a convent. The scholarly

The Guardian Angel. Engraving by Petrus de Iode after a design by Domenichino. Moravská galerie, Brno.

Saint Francis Xavier. Engraving by B. Thiboust dating from 1698.
Národní galerie, Prague.

Saint Francis of Sales. Engraving by De Larmessin, 1665.
Národní galerie, Prague.

Cardinal Bellarmine praised her as a model of virtue for people of all ages and all strata of society.

When the canonization process begann, a delegation from Milan traveled to Rome and asked the pope also to include in the deliberations Carlo Borromeo, former Archbishop of Milan, an exemplary official, a model diocesan administrator and zealous church reformer. Pope Paul V had his case examined; this delayed the process until 1610. The fact that following his canonization three churches were consecrated to him in Rome alone, along with others throughout the Catholic countries, was evidence of the popularity of this saint. These two saints were followed by many others.

At the time of these canonizations, there were also a number of beatifications in Rome. Thus the Curia took the first step toward increasing the number of saints. In late 1609, Ignatius of Loyola was beatified, followed by Theresa of Avila in 1614 and Aloysius Gonzaga, another Spaniard, in 1618 and finally the Basque Jesuit, Francis Xavier (Franciscus Xaverius), in 1619. Of the trailblazers of Catholic renewal in Rome, Filippo Neri, was beatified in 1615. These people were canonized

soon after their beatification, at a solemn Mass in 1622. Those saints all embodied a certain ideal: They were models and examples, and were to become protectors of and intercessors for the people who for one reason or another felt an affinity with them.

Four of the five had already achieved fame as fighters for ecclesiastical renewal, although in differing ways and at differing levels of social life. The church official and administrator, Carlo Borromeo, found himself in the company of the main founder of the Jesuit Order, Ignatius of Loyola, and of the simple priest, confessor and representative of orthodoxy, Filippo Neri, popular for his jolly spirituality and social responsibility. Another level of spirituality was represented by Theresa of Avila, an exemplary nun and reformer of the Carmelite Order but also authoress of mystical contemplative writings that testify to a talent for poetry as well as to an extraordinary education. Saint Francis Xavier, one of the seven co-founders of the Jesuit Order, represented the saint of the newly revitalized activity of mission. The fifth saint, Isidore, was a simple farmhand around the end of the 11th century or the beginning of the 12th, working near Madrid, and was said to have been an exemplary, zealous and devoted subject. Aloysius Gonzaga, along with the Pole Stanislaw Kostka and the Belgian Johan Berchmans, embodied another type. Gonzaga was initially only beatified, not canonized for almost another hundred years. He was the "exemplary student" who besides following his studies obeyed his superiors and tried to help those in need.

In the heated debate on the teachings of the Reformation, the Catholic Church stressed good works as a pre-condition for salvation and redemption. It followed that among the recently canonized persons there would be those who had merited their canonization for their care of the poor and sick. The most visible of Carlo Borromeo's attributes in this respect (and those of Filippo Neri, too) was his charitable work. Many other models of neighborly love were in the first instance only beatified, such as Thomas of Villanova who, as Bishop of Valencia , had made a major contribution to the conversion of the Muslims and was an exemplary dignitary of the Church, leading a simple life and giving all his income to the poor. Among others who cared for the poor and needy were John of God, Vincent de Paul and Camillus de Lellis—all beatified. Care of the poor and needy was one of the primary virtues of the

Portuguese Queen Isabella, who lived in the early 14th century. The decisive factor in her canonization in 1626 was her success in resolving disputes and in mediating in belligerent conflicts. This virtue was also shared by the Bishop Andreas Corsini, who had died in 1373 and was canonized in 1629. These two saints stressed the peacemaking role of the Church, at a time of severe destruction because of the Thirty Years' War. One particular type of the new spirituality was practiced in the high nobility, the milieu of one Francis of Sales who was a scholarly man and very sociable, capable of combining cultivated mysticism with true service to the Catholic Church in France. It is interesting that the victims of Reformation zeal, the Catholic martyrs from the disputes and wars of the 16th century, had no particular part to play in the rise of these new saints. Some of them were canonized much later, such as the victims of Henry VIII, Thomas More and John of Rochester (canonized in 1935). Others attained honor in their own country or were merely beatified, such as Fidelis of Sigmaringen, initially an advocate but later a Capuchin monk, who was murdered while taking the gospel to Calvinist peasants in Graubünden or the Moravian priest Jan Sarkander who was one of the victims of the Moravians' stand against Ferdinand II.

Angelus Custos.

L'Immaculée Conception.

The worship of the Guardian Angel was particularly stressed by the revived Catholic Church. Engraving by François de Poilly. Moravská galerie, Brno.

One of the many popular illustrations of the Immaculata glorifies the immaculate conception of the Mother of God. Engraving by François de Poilly. Moravská galerie, Brno.

Attributa Beatæ Mariæ.
Callot fecit   Israel excud.

patron saints against epidemic diseases; in France, for example, these included St. Louis and St. Geneviève, in Italy St. Rosalie and St. Januarius, in Spain St. Nicholas of Tolentino, and in Bohemia St. Wenceslas.

Hand in hand with re-awakened worship of saints was worship of the archangels. Pope Pius V supported attempts to increase the number of archangels from the original three (Michael, Raphael and Gabriel) to seven when he had one of the chapels of the newly built church upon the former thermal springs of Diocletian consecrated to the seven archangels. He was not successful and in post-Tridentine times the number remained at three, the militant Michael becoming the new symbol of the *ecclesia militans*. His victory over the dragon symbolized the victory of the Church over heresy. The worship of patron saints grew more popular, however, gaining enormous popularity by the 17th century when it became one of the most effective instruments of the Church for influencing the spirituality of the people.

The Holy Family and the cult of Mary occupied a central place. While the humanists kept an ironic dis-

Pour la feste de tous les Saints.
Que de saints rassemblex c'est sur ces grands Modeles.
Qu'un Chretien doit jetter les yeux;
Pour joüir du bonheur qu'ils goutent dans les Cieux,
Soyons de leurs vertus imitateurs fideles.   Poilly ex.

The worship of Mary was extended and promoted by didactic portrayals of the attributes of the Virgin Mary. Engraving by Jacques Callot.
Národní galerie, Prague.

An All Saints representation could be linked with the Holy Trinity. Engraving by François de Poilly.

Saints of the early times of Christendom had not been forgotten either—in fact, the Church gave pre-eminence to three categories. The first included those who had been martyred when the Christian faith was being propagated and defended; examples are St. Sebastian, St. Agnes and St. Cecilia. The second group was constituted by patron saints against the plague and other sudden catastrophes, such as St. Rochus and St. Anthony. The third group comprised local national heroes who were in many cases martyrs of the faith and

tance from it and the Reformation refuted it, it gained enormous popularity in Spain as early as the first half of the 16th century. The exalted piety often took on pathological proportions, with manifestations of ecstatic visions, love songs and love poems, dubious miracles and wonders, and suspicious apparitions. Theologians resumed debate on the Immaculate Conception, and although the Jesuits accepted the teachings, the Dominicans rejected them. The Jesuits were, in any case, among the more passionate proponents of the cult of Mary, for it should be remembered that the Virgin had played a key role in the conversion of Ignatius of Loyola. Philip III intervened personally in the dispute, which elevated the dogma of the Immaculate Conception to the rank of a matter of state.

For the Catholic Church as a whole, the rulings of the Council of Trent that pictures of Mary were to be set up in all churches and that Marian worship was to be given priority, were of great importance. Mary soon showed herself to her followers; the victory of the Spanish and the papal fleet over the Turks at Lepanto was linked directly with her intervention, and the link was further consolidated by Pius V. This spread of the cult was not independent of the Counter-Reformation; on the contrary, it represented the main thrust of the fight against heresy. Mary personified triumph over heresy, and the passus "Gaude Maria Virgo, auae auc-

tas haereses sola intermisti" was incorporated into the rosary. The Mother of God crushing the serpent (the symbol of heresy) into the dust became one of the more popular themes in art. Mary herself was often involved directly in the struggle for true and orthodox faith, for example in the Chapel of Pius V in the Church of Maria Maggiore in Rome. Close on the heels of Marian worship followed the cult of Joseph, Christ's earthly father, who in the Middle Ages had been only a peripheral figure in the life of Christ. He was acknowledged as a saint, but was paid no great attention by the hagiographers and was seldom chosen as a patron saint. The basis for this cult began with Theresa of Avila, who "discovered" in him the protector of Christ, someone particularly near and dear to Christ. From Spain, this movement spread rapidly throughout the world. He became the symbolic head of the Holy Family and was for contemporary observers the example of the Christian family idyl. This was above all a social cult; Joseph as a simple carpenter was an obvious candidate for the role of patron saint of craftsmen and the champion of the manual workers. It explains his firm and unmistakable role in the hierarchy of saints, which was revised not only to express the changing structure of society on the threshold of capitalism but also to express the growing self-confidence of this stratum of the population.

State Power and Its Contribution to Denominationalization

The Council of Trent had no powers to enforce its reforms, and not even the best-formulated and developed methods could be reliably implemented if there were no support from the State. Success depended on a grand scale on the attitude of the individual states or their rulers toward the council and its rulings. In the bastions of Catholicism, in Spain and Italy, the rulings gained a foothold rapidly, though not always smoothly. One of the special concessions obtained by the Spanish king was the preservation of the Spanish Inquisition. The last vestiges of the major heretical groups had been stamped out in the lands of the Spanish king before the end of the council session—the Lutherans in Seville and Valladolid at the end of the 1550s and the Waldenses in Calabria at the beginning of the 1560s. The Inquisition was to focus its attention on the suspicious Moriscoes and the clandestine Judaists. In Italy, only a few individuals remained who were discovered by the Inquisition.

The situation north of the Alps was more complex, where larger or smaller numbers of non-Catholic minorities professing Luther or Calvin sprang up in virtually all the Catholic states. The rulers here endeavored to stem the tide of the Reformation with force. Charles V tried in vain to subdue the Protestant princes and the free imperial towns in the empire, but succeeded in preventing further expansion by means of his victory in the Schmalkaldic War. Henry II of France wanted the Cal-

vinist groups to be exterminated or expelled, and Mary Tudor used all the means at her disposal to stamp out what her father—King Henry VIII—had done for the Reformation in England. Persecution of unorthodox believers in the Netherlands assumed brutal proportions under Philip II and culminated in the terror of the Duke of Alba. Yet Charles V was forced to accept the Peace of Augsburg in 1556. The persecution of the Huguenots prompted the outbreak of the religious wars in France. In the Netherlands the revolt against the Spanish took the form of an anti-feudal revolt. The attempt to return England to the bosom of the Catholic Church ended with the death of Mary Tudor and ensured her a place in history as "Bloody Mary."

North of the Alps, the Catholic rulers were having only sporadic and isolated success in the latter half of the 16th century; in some smaller areas in which they were in a majority, they were able to use a combination of Tridentine reforms and religious oversight by the State. Considerably later revived Catholicism was consolidated in France and Poland. The overt attack by armed force was successful only in the southern Netherlands, the Bohemian lands after the quelling of the revolt from 1618 to 1620 and, for a time, in the Palatinate after 1622. Here, the gains of Catholicism were based on military occupation combined with the methods of the post-Tridentine Catholicism.

The Persecution of Unorthodox Believers in the Countries of the Reformation

The famous Capuchin monk Pater Joseph successfully carried out several secret missions in the service of the French State without taking account of the Church's interests.
Bibliothèque Nationale, Paris.

Vraye effigie du R.P. Ioseph de Paris predicateur Capucin, Prouincial de Touraine, superieur de missions és trangeres et de Poitou, fondateur de Religieuses de Caluaire. A rendu l'esprit entre les mains de ses superieus le 18. decembre. 1638.
Pet. de Iode exe.

The renewal of the unity of faith was implemented not only by the Catholic states but also in those lands where the Reformation had been successful and where the State was at pains to achieve unity of belief among all the inhabitants. It was no coincidence that about the time when the legates of the Council of Trent were deliberating, official, binding Catechisms were published in a number of non-Catholic countries. These were the Anglican Catechism, the Calvinist Heidelberg Catechism and various Lutheran variations. Religious control could be effective only if it were based on an orthodox, standard interpretation and exposition of faith. Denominationalization was achieved in most of the non-Catholic regions by the second half of the 16th century, but the principle of intolerance toward those of other faiths was soon represented by most of the great reformers: Zwingli, Calvin and Beza all advocated the use of force against the enemies of the true faith (as did the successors of Luther—and their definition was not merely restricted to Catholics).

The pioneers of the Reformation took different views on the question of judgment of orthodoxy in a Church that rejected papal infallibility. In the states that had adopted the Lutheran Reformation, rulers had a greater or lesser degree of sovereignty, and the first to exercise it was Henry VIII of England. In the Habsburg empire, the Lutheran princes faced the dilemma of how to position themselves among all the debating factions of Lutheranism. The basic form of religious control was regular visitation undertaken by commissions comprising both clerical and secular officials. The princes of the empire regarded these commissions increasingly as part of their national right to sovereignty. For example, visitations in Saxe-Weimar focused primarily on the exposure and elimination of Calvinists and Zwinglians. When, in the 1560s, Duke John William turned to the teachings of Flacius, a commission was dispatched to expose him and other followers of Melanchthon and moderate Lutherans. After the duke's death in the 1570s, the elector of Saxony ruled for a while and had the Flacians persecuted. Twice a year the superintendent called all the pastors together for a "synod" at which they were tested with the Augsburg Confession.

In England, visitation was even more visibly under the control of the State. It was carried out by bishops, but the real power was reserved for organs of the State. In the second half of the 16th century, they affected mostly the clergy, but by the eve of the revolution they also impinged on suspicious lay people from the ranks of the nobility, burghers and peasants. The growth of state surveillance by the police was a parallel development. Following Elizabeth's open conflict with Spain, a special commission was set up and given powers to open a trial against any suspect, to use the clergy and special spies to obtain the names of clandestine Catholics, to search their homes and to question them.

Not only the Lutherans but also Zwingli and his followers laid the control of orthodoxy in the hand of the State and of the police. Calvin, however, refuted the State's intervention and demanded the exposure and punishment of the heretics by an independent consistory—the Church itself. This was how supervision was achieved in Geneva. These principles led to an interesting conflict when in 1563 the decision of Elector Palatine Frederick III made Calvinism the official religion of the Palatinate. Frederick transferred religious oversight to a church council that was actually a state institution. Superintendents served as instruments of the council and had complete control over the clergy and the schools in their areas. Jurisdiction was in the hands of the state authorities, and ultimately rested with the elector himself. At the end of the 1560s, orthodox Calvinists opposed this secularization of religious control and demanded that the Church should have the oversight. The ecclesiastical discipline regulations of 1570 represented a compromise in the dispute, for it left the oversight in the hands of the church council but ruled that the clergy should have equal representation on the council. It was not long, however, before the members of the Church dominated the council and kept at least purely theoretical disputes away from the secular powers. Persecution was directed first and foremost against the Anabaptists and the anti-trinitarians. When they had been expelled from the Palatinate, the spirit of visitation became more moderate, with interest focused instead on the morals and theological knowledge of the clergy and on superstition and apostasy among the common people.

Sanctions against the unorthodox in non-Catholic countries were implemented as part of the struggle for religious control on two fronts; on the one hand, against the last vestiges of Catholicism and the influence of the Catholic Church, and on the other, against the competing movements within the Reformation and denominations. This dual-front struggle assumed a classic form in England where renewed Catholicism was the result of infiltration and direct intervention by foreign countries. This meant that the same sanctions could be taken against it as against other acts of treason. The Jesuits and other emissaries trained in special seminaries on the continent were regarded as spies. Their fate was as gruesome as that of the Protestant emissaries who fell into the clutches of the papal Inquisition. Elizabethan England provided Catholicism with many famous martyrs. The English legal system did not order burnings, but death by quartering or by being broken on the wheel was no more merciful than burning. Torture was an integral part of the trials, for in England, too, the aim was to extract the names of other suspects and it was regarded as a triumph if the condemned person recanted of his papist misbeliefs before his death or under torture. In many countries the procedure of the interrogation commission was different from that of the central authorities; they were more tolerant, especially to the local Catholic believers. Often the commission recognized anything the suspect said as being orthodox. Many judges did not regard Catholics as heretics in the sense of the English law. One specific component of English religious policy was the persecution of Catholicism in conquered Ireland.

Attitudes toward the persecution of the Puritans —those who had espoused radical Reformation teachings, especially Calvinism—were also ambivalent in England. The officials were often hesitant when they had to punish those who had agreed with the Anglican Church in the fight against Catholicism and had helped in the struggle against the common enemy. Thus in Elizabethan England, the sanctions against the Puritans were often milder than those against the Catholics. They were frequently punished merely with warnings or fines, and only in very exceptional cases were they expelled. A similar ambivalence also existed in the proceedings of the Scandinavian states against unorthodox beliefs. During the conflicts with the Catholic Church the practice was to punish Catholic emissaries with imprisonment or death. At a time when efforts were being

The Bavarian duke Maximilian was the most important ally of the Habsburgs among the imperial princes during the Thirty Years' War. When Frederick V was expelled from Bohemia in 1620 and from the Palatinate in 1622 he was rewarded with the electorship of the Palatinate. This engraving from 1623 shows him in his new role.

SERENISSIMUS ET POTENTISSIMUS PRINCEPS AC DOMINUS, DN: MAXIMILIANUS, DEI GRATIA COMES PALATINUS AD RHENUM, UTRIUSQ, BOIARIÆ DUX, S.R. IMP. ARCHI-DAPIFER ET PRINCEPS ELECTOR. ETC:
M.DC.XXIII.

Although the Inquisition was not re-introduced into France, the state authorities nevertheless kept a close watch on all unauthorized religious movements. This distaste for those of suspicious faith and learning was expressed in the form of accusations of witchcraft and involvement in Satanic deeds. In 1632 the famous and dubious theologian Urban Grandier was accused of abusing his position as confessor to corrupt the nuns in the Convent of S. Ursula by means of exorcism involving the devil. After a trial he was condemned to death and burned in 1634. Etching by Jan Luyken, 1718.

After the defeat of the resurrection of the estates against the Habsburgs, twenty-seven leaders were given death sentences. A contemporary engraving shows the execution on 27 June 1621 in front of Prague Town Hall.

The Calvinist churches and services were very different from Catholic ones. Interior of the church Kirche in Stein near Nuremberg. Copperplate engraving.
Germanisches Nationalmuseum, Nuremberg.

The Communion of the Calvinists. Engraving by Bernard Picart, 1732.
Národní galerie, Prague.

B. Picart invenit et del. 1732.

The vain attempt to re-Catholicize England under Mary Tudor (1553–1558) gave the Protestants ample propaganda material. Even a hundred years later Fox's *Book of Martyrs* played a significant part in the propaganda of the English revolution.

Title page of an anti-Catholic treatise from 1666 (2nd edition).

made to achieve reconciliation with the pope—under John III in Sweden—the Catholics were tolerated regardless of the views of the Lutheran clergy.

Expulsion from the country was the most common form of persecution in all the German Lutheran lands. This affected especially the clergy and teachers. Members of all strata who were Calvinists or Anabaptists were exiled and sometimes their property was confiscated. The exiles in general did not move to an area where they did not understand the language, and hence the clergy in particular was usually able to continue to earn a living. The princes imposed harsher sentences on the agitators of radical heretical movements. Executions were not common, though, and were largely restricted to the anti-trinitarians. Extreme procedures were

more common where Calvinists were in power. Calvin himself set the tone, and often led the hearings and passed sentences himself, also death sentences. Among the most famous examples was the fate of the physician Serveta who had come to Geneva to find refuge with Calvin, whom he considered a friend. Instead, he met his death. A number of Italian anti-trinitarians also came before the courts and were sometimes put to death in Geneva or other Swiss towns. The numbers affected were usually fairly small. Overall, the number of sentences imposed in the Swiss courts for religious crimes cannot have been more than five percent of all sentences passed in 1562, for example.

The Palatinate followed the example of Calvin. The Elector Frederick III set up a trial in 1570 against two well-known anti-trinitarians who had initially found refuge with, and a friendly reception from, one of the elector's councillors. The trial ended in the passing of a death sentence, but this was carried out in only one of the cases, for the other prisoner managed to escape. The decisive factor in this harsh sentencing was a political one. Frederick III wanted to demonstrate his religious zeal in the struggle against heretics, and so take the wind out of the sails of his Lutheran critics.

In the northern provinces of the Netherlands, too, the authorities of the State gained precedence over the theocratic regiment of the Calvinist clergy. In the 1580s attempts to restrict the appointment of clergy and teachers to orthodox Calvinists failed. In the ensuing debate, one politician said that he rejected the Calvinist Inquisition as much as the Catholic one. This argument flared up again in a public debate that was started in 1595 when the theologian Philipp Marnix published a short pamphlet. Therein he called for the States General of the Netherlands to be merciless with all unorthodox people. His opponents accused him of seeking to establish a Protestant Inquisition in the Netherlands and to eliminate "with fire and with the sword" all those who did not follow orthodox Calvinism. They even accused him of wanting to become "our master

and inquisitor haereticae pravitatis." It is particularly interesting that Marnix found it necessary in his own defense to distance himself from the Inquisition policies of Charles V and Philip II although, theoretically, he still represented the position that heretics merited their deaths a hundredfold.

Theological debate took on more extreme forms later, in the struggle between Arminianism and the followers of Gomarus. This had originally been a theological debate on the exposition of Calvin's teachings on predestination. The move away from theological disputes toward violent intervention came when the difference of opinion became the ideological expression of political conflicts between the aggressively anti-Spanish followers of Maurice, Prince of Orange, and the followers of the compromising politician, Jan Olden-

More than hundred years later, Queen Catherine Medici was still considered to be a pioneer of the renewal of the Church and of Jesuit domination. A caricature dating from 1710 shows her in front of a miraculous mirror which portrays not only her three successors but also three Jesuit priests who have stolen the French crown. The policies of the French kings, which were based on denominationalization, were often interpreted as being the product of Jesuit intrigues.

barnevelt. When the latter's party, which had adopted some of Arminius's ideas, was defeated, its leader was executed and a number of adherents were arrested. However, the Calvinist consistory clearly failed to gain overall exclusive control of religion throughout the country.

Religious persecution, therefore, in the form of enforcement of one denomination was not unknown in the non-Catholic countries; on the contrary, it became an integral part of the emerging state power. The Protestant state, like the Catholic, was seeking religious unity, and while its methods were not as drastic as those of the Spanish or papal Inquisitions, they nevertheless stand comparison with the violent means used by the Counter-Reformation in Catholic countries. As in the Catholic states, it was in most cases *not* the Church that took the decisive part in the organization of control over religious orthodoxy.

. . . they shall be cast into the fire, so that no monument may be erected to them or to the opinions of the author . . .

. . . IN IGNEM CONJICERENT, QUO NEQUE IPSIUS, NEQUE OPINIONIS CUJUS AUCTOR FUERAT, ULLUM MONUMENTUM EXTARET. . .

Constantine the Great

INDEX LIBRORUM PROHIBITORUM

Men have always found it easy to destroy fellow human beings. It has been much more difficult to eliminate the thoughts and ideas for which such people gave their lives. The inquisitors were well aware of this, and felt a deep revulsion for and hatred of books that contained unorthodox ideas. The books were destroyed along with their authors in the mistaken belief that the ideas embodied in those books could as easily be destroyed and permanently eliminated—a conviction that characterized not only the Inquisition.

The Church's Control over the Written Word in the Middle Ages

Since the compilation of the Index of Forbidden Books in the 16th century—the *Index librorum prohibitorum*—history focused on the destruction of the written and printed word. Yet this violent revenge on human thought was not the brainchild of the Inquisition. The burning of books had been associated with Christianity since its establishment as an official state religion. The very first church council—the Council of Nicaea in A.D. 325—laid the foundations. It condemned and sentenced the teachings of Arius who was exiled by Constantine the Great after the latter had had Arius's teachings explained to him by the orthodox clergy. The emperor also banned all Arius's teachings and ordered his books to be burned, so that they could not constitute any kind of monument to their author and his false teachings.

This highly effective means of early Christianity was adopted in the Middle Ages even before the courts of Inquisition came into being. Although pre-13th-century Europe widely lacked original concepts and individually stamped ideas and written documents, books and their authors were burned, including the works of Erigena and Peter Abelard, the well-known French philosopher who was ordered by the Soissons Synod in 1120 to burn his own books. Indeed some heretics were burned at the stake with their writings.

In fact, in the Middle Ages heretical thought did not enjoy easy and unhindered access to broad sections of the populace. It was not until the universities were founded and the towns provided new opportunities for education that this picture changed. After its experiences with large-scale persecution of the Cathari and the Waldenses, the Church in the 14th century grew increasingly vigilant with regard to books. For example, the Italians Segarelli and Fra Dolcino were burned around this time. The Church also condemned the works of Marsilius of Padua, John of Jandun, Michael of Cesena and William of Ockham in the first half of the 14th century. Until then there had been no need to publish a major Index of Forbidden Books; the names of the heretics were listed in papal bulls and published. However, in the latter half of the 14th century the Church was facing a more complex situation. The generally critical situation of the Roman Church, culminating in the Papal Schism, was in large measure the result of scholarly criticism of the Church. The universities—whose faculties of divinity also monitored orthodoxy and the purity of dogma—welcomed into their midst men whose writings advocated ecclesiastical reform, scholars who were excluded by the Church and whose writings were to be found on the Index of Forbidden Books for many hundreds of years.

The famous English scholar John Wycliffe, a member of the University of Oxford, was among the front-line heretics. Not so well known, though more characteristic of the attitude of the Church toward such books, was the struggle of the University of Prague against the burning of Wycliffe's writings. Scholarly disputes over reform within the University of Prague had taken the form of a struggle for the teachings of Wycliffe at the end of the 14th century. In the early 15th century this struggle, led by Magister John Hus, passed beyond the lecture halls of the university and reached out into the Bohemian kingdom and beyond. Following an archiepiscopal commission of inquiry, the verdict was that the books should be burned. The assembly of the university opposed the ruling and asked the king for help. The archiepiscopal decision aroused strong and determined opposition in Prague. Hus himself hastened to write his own small work, *De libris hereticorum legendis*, in which he countered theoretically and based on legal principles the idea that heretical books should be burned. Hus himself and the majority of the masters of the Czech universities refused to hand in the banned books, and although the archbishop had a bonfire lit in the courtyard of his palace on 16 July 1410 and had two hundred works by Wycliffe burned, most of his works were saved throughout Bohemia. When, centuries later, there was renewed interest in Wycliffe's writings, the publishers found a large number of his manuscripts preserved in Czech libraries.

The struggle in Prague against the burning of Wycliffe's books must be viewed against a greater international background. The protests against the burning of books sent by Hus to Rome was passed on by the pope

Wherever the Franciscan John of
Capistrano (1386–1456)
preached, the flames blazed up to
the sky soon after. He burned all
"beautiful" and "non-essential"
things, such as books.

to four cardinals. They in turn asked the masters of Bologna University to give their comments. In August 1410 professors of divinity from the universities of Bologna, Paris and Oxford met the Dean of the faculty of divinity in Bologna, Thomas of Utina, and after debate decided by a majority that the books should not be burned. However, the Curia ignored their advice. In early February 1413 the council met in Rome and condemned the works of Wycliffe. On 10 February, his books were burned in Rome as well. The Czech reformers condemned the papal bulls on the banning of Wycliffe's work. The commentary on the bulls by Master Jan of Jesenice is bitterly satirical on the lack of education and sophistication of the Curia. But it was to

be a long slow process before more enlightened ways of thinking were embraced by the masses.

The Inquisition had ways of making this process more difficult. For example, one of the tasks and responsibilities of the tribunals was to watch over "those who read, possessed or distributed books which had been condemned for their heretical content." When the net of the Inquisition tribunals was cast wider in the 14th century, it was not at all hard to track down the owners and readers of such books since almost all were written in Latin. The majority of the people in the German, Slav or Romanic countries were unable to understand this language of the educated Europeans in the Middle Ages. The real problem for the Church came

toward the end of the 14th century when some of these publications began to be translated into national languages and when priests backing the reforms began to use their contents in sermons. An obstacle to a broader readership of these books critical of the Church was their rarity. These manuscripts were difficult to obtain and very expensive. For the most part the church institutions were able to track down and eliminate these books.

There was one book (or rather, a collection of books) that was more dangerous than all the rest because of its heterogeneous content and the possibilities of exposition—the Bible. The Latin translation was used in Europe. The Bible was the basis and the starting point for scholarly as well as heretical lay criticism of the Church. The Church soon recognized the danger of this bedrock of the Christian faith with its multi-faceted content that was regarded as being the incorruptible, once and for all revelation of the truth of God. Expounding the Bible was then permitted only for the clergy. The Church also resolutely forbade all translations of the Bible or any part of it into national languages. The first major threat resulting from this faced the Church in the 13th century when it was persecuting the Waldenses. Official bans on Bible translations from synods in Toulouse (1229) and Béziers (1246) date from this time, and there were similar bans repeated later on. In 1369 Charles IV ordered, with the consent of Pope Urban V, that lay people of either sex should not be permitted to use books that were translations of the Holy Scriptures into the national languages. But these proscriptions failed. By the end of the 14th century, there were translations of the Bible or of major parts of it in Provençal, French, Catalan, Italian, German and Czech. The texts were predominantly

those that had been written and used by the Waldenses. Of special significance was the translation of the Bible into Czech. Despite his own ban, Emperor Charles IV promoted this translation that proceeded under his control and that of the Dominicans. He hoped his own Catholic translation of the texts into Czech would preempt that done by the Waldenses. However, the Bohemian kingdom in the first half of the 14th century with its violent Inquisitorial trials of heretics represented a second Languedoc. Without a translation of the Bible into Czech, the revolutionary and anti-clerical Hussite ideology would never have come about. Similarly, later European reformers—such as Luther—had the Bible translated and then declared their own versions binding.

By the mid-15th century the Church was still able to meet the challenge of controlling new books, but Gutenberg's invention of printing represented the real turning point and was very uncomfortable for the Church in many ways. Printing arrived on the scene at a time when the Renaissance was reviving the wealth of philosophical ideas from antiquity and spreading and expounding this knowledge. Consciously and unconsciously, the conceptions of the Renaissance led European society away from God toward the immanence. This also coincided with the time when the Church had just recovered from the crisis of the great Papal Schism without having regained its internal unity and formulated an attitude toward the demands of the secular powers, despite two councils, those of Constance and Basle. The Czech Hussite reform was also not without influence. At the end of the century reform efforts in all regions had gained a foothold, and printing helped directly to spread critical thinking among the educated classes.

State Censorship after the Invention of Printing

In the early 15th century, the Church could still fairly easily control the production of handwritten books. By the beginning of the 16th century the discovery of printing had complicated the situation enormously. While in the mid-15th century Cardinal Nicholas of Cusa called printing a "holy art," the Church was quick to see that it served its enemies' ends just as well as its own.

In 1501, Pope Alexander VI issued a bull addressed to the archbishops of Cologne, Trier, Mainz and Magdeburg—dioceses where numerous heretical books and tractates circulated. The pope gave the archbishops and their officials instructions on more effective control of the publication of printed material and on the way they were to exercise their control over printers, the owners of books and those who read them. All confiscated books were to be burned. In 1515 Pope Leo X, in agreement with the Fifth Lateran Council, issued another bull relating to book censorship, and this in-

tensified the measures further. No book was to be published without the approved signature of the local bishop or of a person authorized by him or of the local inquisitor. There were heavy penalties for publishing and owning or reading heretical literature. The *Coena Domini* Bull was to intimidate the masses. In 1524, Pope Hadrian VI was the first to use this bull to persecute those who printed, read or even possessed works by Martin Luther. In the *Coena Domini* Bulls issued by subsequent popes, this was extended to writing, printing, possession, distribution and reading of any work that represented a threat to the Church.

This famous papal bull soon proved inadequate, however. The Church had to find new ways and means of restricting the influence of the printed word. By the mid-16th century, thanks to the Inquisition, the conditions had been created for the publication of the Index of Forbidden Books, the *Index librorum prohibitorum*. But before the Curia itself acted, intervention

IMPRESSIO LIBRORVM.

Poteſt vt vna vox capi aure plurima: Linunt ita vna ſcripta mille paginas.

A printing workshop of the 16th century. Copperplate engraving by Galle after Jan van der Straet (Stradano). From: *Nova reperta*, c. 1580.
Bibliothèque Nationale, Paris.

came from the State, which feared the hostile influence of printing as much as the Church, and from the universities, which were directly commissioned by the Church to exercise censorship.

In 1521 the Edict of Worms was promulgated by Charles V. Under the threat of severest penalties, the publication of all works written by Luther—whether in Latin, German or other national languages—was banned. This edict was subsequently defined and specified with the help of the papal nuncios. Luther's writings represented a threat to both Church and State, particularly because his reformational views appeared in printed form in the national languages and were thus accessible even to the less nominally educated. Publication of a book required the consent not only of the local bishop but also inclusion of the name of the printer, the

place of publication and the author's name. This applied not just to academic books but to belles-lettres and poetry, too.

Any anonymous books—and there were more and more of them, especially pamphlets—were to be destroyed and anyone found in possession of them would be fined heavily. Other secular authorities took similar steps. In the empire, the publication of literature was the responsibility of the emperor, a position consolidated and strengthened after the Peace of Augsburg in 1555; there was no alternative to adherence to the terms of the religious peace. Individual free imperial towns and states in the empire, kept control within their own boundaries and retained powers of censorship over printing and the distribution, sale and reading of printed material. England and France were moving toward state control, and surveillance was stepped up in Spain. Of interest here was the way control was exercised over book publishing in the Netherlands, at that time dominated by Spain. The growing interest of the State and its uncompromising and punitive action against Reformation thinking increased as its writings became available in printed form in national languages. The ideas even formed the subject of brochures and booklets which were illustrated with satirical drawings and were, readily understandable even by the illiterate—another new dimension for the new art of printing and its rapid distribution.

The universities were the first institutions to have lists of forbidden books before the index was published. In conjunction with the Inquisition, these were extended to cover the names and writings of heretics from the Middle Ages as well as of contemporary opponents and critics of the Roman Church. In 1542 and 1543, the faculty of divinity at the Sorbonne published a Directory of Forbidden Books that was later clarified by a royal edict and published as a definitive index. Recognized and endorsed by the State, it was exactly what the Curia wanted. It focused on contemporary Reformation thinkers as well as on medieval scholars, and was based on the assumed danger of translating the Bible into national languages. The new, extended and comprehensive index compiled by the faculty of divinity of the University of Louvain in 1546 and published in 1550, occupied a special place among such indexes, for it prompted the publication of others throughout Europe. One could even argue that it formed the basis of the Roman indexes. Initially, however, the Spanish State Inquisition, headed by Fernandez Valdés, Archbishop of Seville, and the Spanish Grand Inquisitor, adapted the index enthusiastically. Emperor Charles V, who approved the publication of the Louvain index, sent it to the Grand Inquisitor as early as 1550 so that it could be published in Spain. This was done in 1551 after some minor additions.

Fernandez Valdés was rather special among the Spanish Grand Inquisitors, for his name is linked to the trial of the Archbishop of Toledo, Carranza. Indexes of Forbidden Books in Spain fell under Valdes's jurisdiction, and in 1559 he published a revised index which was to form the basis of subsequent Spanish indexes. It is interesting, too, that these indexes, which were recognized only for Spain and were compiled along its proper lines, influenced also the Roman indexes and in this way the whole of Europe. The 1550 Louvain index itself was one of the major sources used by Pope Paul IV to compile his own index. The Curia itself did not publish its own official index until the mid-16th century; instead, it relied on publication of the *Coena Domini* Bull and on bulls relating to bans of a more general nature addressed to individual bishops, universities or inquisitors. The initiative was left to them or to the State, a fact explained by the situation within the Curia and by its inability to take a more active and systematic line in the struggles of contemporary society before the Council of Trent.

The Council of Trent and the "S. Congregatio indicis librorum prohibitorum"

Before we look at the attitude of the Council of Trent to book publishing and its own compilation of an Index of Forbidden Books, we must turn our attention to the first papal or Roman index, and its author, Pope Paul IV. In drawing up his plans for ecclesiastical reform, he, too, compiled an Index of Forbidden Books. This was meant to be revised and corrected by the Index Commission during the third session of the Council of Trent.

During the last years of his reign, Paul IV took on the task of compiling a new, central Index of Forbidden Books. It was published in Rome in 1559 and re-printed in Bologna, Venice, Genoa and Avignon in the same year. One of the collaborators, the head of the Augustinian Order, Christopher of Padua, later commented that it took account of all the previous known lists of forbidden books, including the Louvain index. Paul's index aroused hostility and ironic debate among non-Catholics, undoubtedly because it originated from the Curia and was to be universally applicable.

As already indicated, the deliberations of the third and final session of the Council of Trent were allowed to proceed without direct intervention by the Roman and Spanish Inquisitions. It was, however, impossible for the council to exclude some elements falling within their purview, including the Index of Forbidden Books, the reading and other use of such books, and the rulings on attitudes toward heretical authors and their works. So, at the general assembly of the council at the beginning of 1562, the question of the index came up for debate, because Paul IV's reform achievements had to be reviewed. Top of the list of priorities was revision of the Index of Forbidden Books, the drawing up of a new index and the establishment of guidelines for the Church to follow in future deliberations on this subject. Thus the council began debating an area which had previously been the concern of the *Sanctum Officium*. At the beginning of the council session, the papal legates appointed a special Index Commission, headed not surprisingly by one of the few representatives of the empire, the Archbishop of Prague, Brus of Müglitz, who was attending the council as the official representative of Emperor Ferdinand I. Debate on the index was scheduled for January and February 1562, and apart from Brus of Müglitz, the commission comprised three other archbishops, nine bishops, and a large number of friars, especially from the Dominican and the Augustinian Orders and of the Observants.

Veüe et Perspectiue de la Chapelle et Maison de Sorbonne; œuure singulier, et l'vn de ceux, que le grand Cardinal Duc de Richelieu a faict bastir par Monsieur le Mercier Architecte du Roy. A Paris Chez Israel rue de l'arbre sec au logis de Monsieur le Mercier Orfeure de la Reyne proche la croix du Tiroir. Auec priuil. du Roy.

The University of Paris, the Sorbonne, was commissioned in the 16th century to preserve the purity of the Catholic faith and took an active part in the persecution of unorthodox believers. Their own Index of Forbidden Books preceded the papal ones. In return for its services to the process of denominationalization, the Sorbonne was granted new premises.
Bibliothèque Nationale, Paris.

Our knowledge of the deliberations of the Index Commission derives mostly from correspondence sent by Brus to the emperor or to friends, which shows that he was not pleased at being appointed chairman. Not only did he resent the responsibility placed on his shoulders but he also realized that his own views on certain individual authors and their works were, in many cases, not shared by the commission, dominated as it was by Spaniards and Italians. Understandably, Brus complained to the emperor about lack of understanding on the commission, "for there are few who know anything about the heresies or customs of the Germans." On several occasions he even urged the emperor to release him from this responsibility. He also asked the papal legates to discharge him, arguing that as a representative of the emperor he was taken up with other matters. But neither the legates nor the emperor would allow Brus to resign. The emperor, in fact, encouraged him to use his position as the only German to plead for liberality and to ensure that some well-known authors and their works escaped condemnation. The emperor also demonstrated his disapproval of, for example, the inclusion in the index of the decisions of the imperial diets. Brus further criticized the attitudes of the Spanish and Italian prelates to the severe index of Paul IV, which banned authors and books that were of great significance and had nothing to do with religion or faith, such as the work of Leonhard Fuchs. He was at pains to salvage the works of Erasmus of Rotterdam, Boccaccio and others and to clear them of suspicion of heresy.

He pored over the originals of Erasmus's letters to prove his innocence and to show Erasmus's own service to the Church as a true Catholic. He refused to endorse even an amendment and revision of Erasmus's work, and wrote in a letter to the emperor on 3 February 1563 that if Erasmus were to be alive now, he would barely recognize his own work. King Philip II of Spain, however, took a quite different view.

The Trent index was published in Rome by Pius IV in late March 1564, immediately following the conclusion of the council. The Index Commission continued its work, however; it amended and revised a number of books and also drew up a list of ten rules for the assessment and publication of books. These were published along with the index of Pius IV, and were subsequently tightened up further. They are extremely interesting, and we shall discuss some of them here.

For example, any books and authors banned before 1515 by the pope or the church councils were not to appear in the index, but their ban was still in force and they remained condemned in perpetuity. They included the work of Hus and Marsilius of Padua. This principle was often not observed, however, and the names did frequently re-appear, particularly on diocesan indexes, to avoid any doubt or confusion.

98 John Wycliffe (died 1384), an early English reformer. Copperplate engraving by Hendrik Hondius the Elder. Staatliche Kunstsammlungen Dresden, Kupferstichkabinett.

99 Presumably a double page of Wycliffe's Bible translation. British and Foreign Bible Society, London.

Following double page:
100 A copperplate engraving by Jacques Callot depicts inferno—hell. In the center of the spiral is the deepest part of hell where heretics are burned along with their books. Istituto Centrale per il Catalogo e la Documentazione, Rome.

101 The Spanish Inquisition always remained independent in compiling its Index of Forbidden Books.

INDEX LIBRORVM
PROHIBITORVM
ET
EXPVRGANDORVM
NOVISSIMVS.

PRO CATHOLICIS HISPANIARVM
Regnis PHILIPPI IV, *Regis Cathol.*

ILL. AC R. D. D. ANTONII A SOTOMAIOR
Supremi Præsidis, & in Regnis Hispaniarum, Siciliæ, & Indiarum
Generalis Inquisitoris, *&c.* juſſu ac ſtudiis, luculenter &
vigilantiſſimè recognitus:

DE CONSILIO SVPREMI SENATVS INQVISITIONIS GENERALIS.

Iuxta Exemplar excuſum

Catalogo   *Bibliotheca*

Strahouiensis   *Inscriptus*

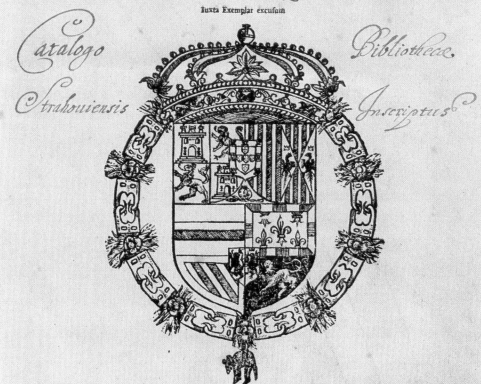

MADRITI,
EX TYPOGRAPHÆO DIDACI DIAZ.

Subſignatum LL.do HVERTA.

M. DC. LXVII.

102 "St. Hieronymus translating the Bible." Painting by an unknown painter. Národní galerie, Nelahozeves.

Moreover, the names of all major representatives of the Reformation in the 16th century appeared on the index without exception. These included Luther, Zwingli and Calvin. The principles applied to Bible translations as well. There was a clear statement to the effect that, as experience had shown, reading the Bible in a national language led to unclear exposition. Strict guidelines were, therefore, laid down for Bible translation and for authorization to read the Bible, which could be obtained only from the *Sanctum Officium* itself. There was a similarly stringent rule on the reading of books in the vernacular that touched on controversial religious topics debated by Catholics and non-Catholics (the latter being called heretics). It was stressed that all books with a controversial content would be persecuted by the bishops and were under no circumstances to be used to educate young people. (This related mainly to the writings of authors from antiquity.) Books with a generally positive content that did not touch on religious questions had to be purged of any immoral or similarly unacceptable passages and prefaced with a good Catholic commentary or foreword. Any writings that touched on, or could be linked in any way with magic were condemned. All books not approved by a local bishop, a prelate designated by him or an inquisitor were not to be printed at all, not even those from other dioceses unless they had been authorized. All books were subject to diocesan censorship, and the bishop or the inquisitor would regularly visit and search printing presses and bookshops. Finally, the import and sale of books from abroad needed official authorization. Anyone in breach of these rules was not only punished but had all his books seized and destroyed. Believers caught in possession of, or reading or distributing, books on the index, or failing in other ways to adhere to the rulings of the Council of Trent were excommunicated. The local bishop was responsible for ensuring the observance of all these rules. It was not long, however, before a special congregation was summoned to take responsibility for ensuring observ-

ance of the ten principles. (The Trent Index of Forbidden Books was divided into three main categories, depending on the degree of threat posed by the author and the content of his books.)

Clearly the Index Commission had devised very detailed censorship principles whose observance was precisely laid down and closely monitored. They could be used for any aspect of control over the publication and distribution of literature. The Church was not, however, content with these measures. The Trent index was supplemented and there were special editions for dioceses where persons or works deemed particularly dangerous were involved. Special indexes based on the Trent index were extended and published by subsequent popes and also used in individual states with individual guidelines. Even this, however, was not felt to be enough to cope with the growing ideological and political splits and the growing threat posed to the Church by the development of scientific knowledge. Printed books represented a very simple means of communication capable of rapid dissemination of material hostile to the Church.

Not even the omnipotent *Sanctum Officium* could gain complete control over book publication, and Pius V, based on his experience as an inquisitor, summoned a special independent congregation of cardinals to concern itself with censorship of written material. It was called the *S. Congregatio indicis librorum prohibitorum*, and its function was further refined by Pope Sixtus V and later popes. Its members were required to have specific qualifications; they were cardinals, and had a secretary and a number of advisers, particularly Dominican friars and theologians. Despite the fact that this body was independent of the *Sanctum Officium*, there was close collaboration with it. The congregation's primary task was to decide whether books were a threat to the faith and the Church or were immoral. It also gave dispensations that enabled certain persons to read forbidden books; without this, the clergy themselves would have faced severe penalties for possessing

"Fortitudo mea et laus mea dominus et factus est mihi in salutem" ("The Lord, who is my fortress, whom I praise has entered the world to redeem me"): this was the motto of the President of the Index Commission for Forbidden Books at the Council of Trent, Antonin Brus of Müglitz, entered by him in his own hand into the books he himself owned as well as in those forbidden by the index.
Kapitulní knihovna, Prague.

222

or reading books of this kind. Even such dispensations were normally valid for only three years. In exceptional circumstances, they were also granted to secular or lay people, such as princes, in the case of poetry or the works of authors from antiquity or the Renaissance.

Owners of forbidden books were instructed to keep them separate from the rest of their books and well away from all unauthorized persons. These guidelines and the efforts made to ensure their observance enabled the Church to be effective as a brake on progress.

In the mid-16th century, however, the situation was not all that clear. The chairman of the Trent Index Commission, Archbishop Brus of Müglitz, and his li-

brary are an interesting illustration. After the death of the archbishop, the Prague imperial commission compiled a list of all the books of the archiepiscopal library in 1580 that did not at all correspond to the regulations of the Council of Trent. From 1562 till 1580 Brus had been archbishop and had a library of more than 1,200 volumes. Heretical books and banned works were kept together with the others. The works of Erasmus, Canisius, Zwingli and Luther were placed among Catholic literature, regardless of theological or dogmatic considerations—an unusual occurrence, since the archbishop must have been well aware of the principles to be observed.

No images are to be exhibited that symbolize false dogmas and might lead the unexperienced into dangerous errors . . . everything lascivious is to be removed.
It is allowed to no one to place an indecent picture in a church or in any other place or have it placed there by others, without the permission of the bishop, not even in exceptional cases.

NULLAE FALSI DOGMATIS IMAGINES ET RUDIBUS PERICULOSI ERRORIS OCCASIONEM PRAEBENTES STA-TUANTUR ...OMNIS DENIQUE LAS-CIVIA VITETUR.

NEMINI LICERE ULLO IN LOCO VEL ECCLESIA ETIAM QUOMODOLIBET EXEMPTA, ULLAM INSOLITAM PO-NERE VEL PONENDAM CURARE IM-AGINEM NISI AB EPISCOPO APPRO-BATA FUERIT.

(Extracts from the rulings of the Council of Trent)

ART AS AN INSTRUMENT OF CATHOLIC RENEWAL

The Council of Trent made the general demand that art should support the Church, that the themes represented in pictures and wall paintings in churches had to conform with ecclesiastical teachings. It fell to the bishops to monitor the religious purity of art. Church fathers had a clearer concept of how art should *not* look than of how it should. It was not until after the council that theologians began to turn their attention to the creative principles that would serve as guidelines for fine arts to be effective in serving the renewal of the Church.

Shortly after the completion of the council's work, Giovanni Andrea Gilio published two tracts on the role of art. He argued that it should play its part in the striving after religious truth and that artists should stick more closely to the acknowledged sources—the Holy Scriptures, tradition and legend. Artists were to have as broad an education as possible in the spirit of the Catholic Church. Content was to take precedence over form in their work, and art was to be released from external features that would only confuse the believers. It was to be clean and simple, with no portrayal of human nudity. The bulk of Gilio's ideas were taken up about twenty-five years later by the renowned Jesuit theologian, Antonio Possevino. Around the same time, Raffaello Borghini was recommending in a tract for artists that they should observe three principles: They should restrict themselves to topics recognized by the Church; they should exercise restrain in expressing their own imagination; and they should keep away from immoral subjects.

It was to be some time, however, before the Church had taken complete control over preventive authority in art. Initially, its intervention bore the stamp of censorship of art that was already on display in the churches. The debates over the immorality of nudity in Michelangelo's "Last Judgment" are well known, but another less celebrated example is the trial against the painter Paolo Veronese. In 1573 he was summoned before the Inquisition and questioned as to his intentions in depicting soldiers, dwarves and various animals in the picture entitled "Feast in Levi's House." The armed soldiers reminded the Inquisition of the German—and thus Lutheran—mercenaries, while the dwarves, drunkards and dogs seemed to them to be a desecration of the presence of Christ. Veronese insisted in vain that an artist had a right to use his own imagination in depicting biblical stories, and finally saved himself only by agreeing to repaint the picture.

In 1582 the sculptor Ammanati wrote a semi-open letter to the Academy of Florence expressing his deep regret at having painted nudes and urging other artists to follow his example and mend their ways. His letter gained some publicity for the Church, notably because he also suggested a sort of preventive censorship of art. Indeed, such a form of censorship was phased in, starting in Rome with an edict from Cardinal Camillo Borghese in November 1603. The edict stipulated that all works of art for display in churches in Rome should first be submitted to the cardinal for approval. Invoking the Council of Trent, it was recommended that artists should submit preliminary sketches of all planned art works. The edict forbade indecent sculptures destined for display in public places in Rome. Pope Urban VIII later consolidated the edict, to be followed not only in Italy but also north of the Alps.

The New Iconography

The iconographical content of works of art had been considerably modified by the Church after the Council of Trent. Selection of motifs was, to an extent, determined by the secret and sometimes open debate against various elements of Reformation teachings. All major articles of faith that were questioned or attacked by the Reformation were to be celebrated in works of art, to spread their influence among the masses. The Church took on a commissioning role as the representative of "social demand" and, as such, determined the subject of all works of art in churches. In areas more severely threatened by the Reformation, this kind of artistic creativity was a weapon in the Curia's struggle for power, while in areas that had remained true to the Catholic faith it had a more prophylactic role, aimed at preventing the spread of heretical ideas and teachings.

It became necessary to defend and stress the primacy of the papacy, and so many paintings were commissioned to depict episodes from the life of St. Peter and in particular the episode in which Christ told Peter to look after his Church. An even more common theme was the Holy Virgin, including defense of the teaching of the Immaculate Conception. The Marian cult also served as a direct attack on the heretics; the Mother of Christ had received the command to crush the head of the serpent, which was symbolizing heresy. We most commonly find Mary in pictures depicting intercession for souls in purgatory, a defense of the belief in purgatory, which had come under attack in Reformation teaching.

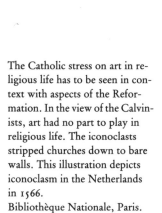

The Catholic stress on art in religious life has to be seen in context with aspects of the Reformation. In the view of the Calvinists, art had no part to play in religious life. The iconoclasts stripped churches down to bare walls. This illustration depicts iconoclasm in the Netherlands in 1566.
Bibliothèque Nationale, Paris.

Differences of opinion frequently arose over the sacraments. Glorification of the sacraments was one of the most common themes in art—primarily, celebration and defense of the Eucharist expressed, for example, in a new artistic portrayal of Holy Communion. Medieval artists preferred to portray the foretelling by Christ of his betrayal by one of the disciples, whereas from the time of Tintoretto and Barocci, the element of Christ giving bread and wine to his disciples took precedence —the main, underlying argument of the teachings on the Eucharist. The Communion of the saints was another common element, as was the death of Hieronymus and St. Francis of Assisi, among others. As in churches, so in art, too, the cult of the Eucharist gradually culminated in the replacement of the host by an elaborate monstrance.

The renewed worship of saints was reflected in sculpture, too. It embraced all the recently canonized saints, and not only were scenes from their lives depicted but also their solemn canonization. Interest in the early saints was clearly differentiated. Among the most popular and most frequently requested saints were Hieronymus, hermit and translator of the Vulgate, the official translation of the Bible refuted by Erasmus and

the Reformation; Mary Magdalene, the exemplary penitent; and John the Baptist. The Baptism of Christ, moreover, was a chance to portray the presence in one scene of the entire Trinity—Father, Son and Holy Spirit, symbolized by a dove. Here, the Church was reacting to the doubts and constant criticisms of the antitrinitarians.

Closely connected with the worship of saints was the worship of holy relics, and sculptors and other craftsmen had a chance to become involved in the processing of innumerable relics.

Hand in hand with these developments went the glorification of miracles. Their depiction opened up opportunities for direct influence over the masses. The Jesuits rapidly grasped the significance of miracles, and surrounded their new saints—starting with Loyola —with supernatural events. Particularly popular were pictures in which defenders of the faith were shown involved in miracles. Glorification of miracles served two purposes—a general religious purpose, as evidence of God's intervention in human life, and a more specific Counter-Reformation purpose, as evidence that God was on the side of those who defended the Catholic Church.

Glorification of works of charity was also reflected in iconography, especially in the honoring of the distribution of alms and the nursing of the sick. This category also includes pictures portraying a good, modest and abstinent way of life. Deeper, more philosophical and ethical aspects were developed within the framework of the iconography of the Last Judgment, where reflection on the way to salvation was the central idea. Paintings here included Michelangelo's famous picture "The Last Judgment."

For the purposes of this book it is actually immaterial whether post-Tridentine art is categorized as Mannerism and Baroque or simply as Baroque, nor, indeed, is the distinction central to our consideration of the social impact of Counter-Reformation art whether we regard the Baroque as the decline of good taste (as Benedetto Croce did) or as a great artistic era. Our task is not to assess whether Spanish and Italian art declined in the 17th century or merely changed focus, but more specifically to assess the means used in art after the Council of Trent to influence the thinking of believers.

The well-known painter Federico Zuccari observed in the early 1690s that the Church wanted to influence not only believers' hearing but also their sight. The Jesuits, too, stressed that in religious experience man should be able to picture in full detail the secret world of the Scriptures and the saints, primarily by having his thoughts focused on art. In 1652 the theologian Ottonetti and the painter Pietro de Cortona published a keynote tract on the educative function of art. They attached great importance to the influence of paintings and tried to categorize works of art by their educational impact at one of three levels of aesthetic experience: sensual pleasure (*diletto sensitivo*); intellectual pleasure (*diletto intellettuale*), which enables the content of the work to be evaluated; and supernatural experience (*diletto spirituale*), the highest level of response. The second level could be reached only through the first, and the third only through the second.

Once the Church accepted its loss of monopoly over ideology, new methods of influencing the masses had to be found. In art, it meant primarily that artistic expression had to be simpler and more accessible to the people. This gave rise to the Baroque naturalism—the accurate portrayal not only of human bodies, gestures and movements but also of the everyday objects surrounding them. Ease of comprehension was seen as a means rather than as an end in itself. Counter-Reformation art also sought to satisfy excessive curiosity and its exploitation, a heritage from the Renaissance. At a time when secular power was legitimized through pomp and splendor, the Church also had to resort to greater decorativeness and look to its outward appearance if it was to gain influence over believers. The church buildings themselves became wonderfully ornate palaces, glinting and sparkling with precious stones and materials—or at least imitations of them. Sophisticated interior design and lighting, the unity of architecture, the art of sculpture and painting, the increasing importance of the altars, in particular the domination of the ever larger High Altar—all these details combined to form an effective framework for religious experience. This experience was heightened by effects created through optical illusions with perspective, creating an effect of a transcendent sphere. A believer gazing up to a domed ceiling had the vision of a heavenly world with the throne of God and its hosts of angels and saints—a picture that also symbolized the secular feudal hierarchy.

Artistic expression of mysticism and heroism are part of this framework. Painters depicted the praying and mystic devotion of saints whose faces conveyed visionary sight. Gradually, a standard attitude of piety emerged, usually with an upward gaze. There also emerged a new type of heroism, to be distinguished from that of antiquity or the Renaissance by its martyrdom and asceticism rather than by physical or psychical strength. This heroism or strength, in fact, was maintained only for a few isolated defenders of orthodoxy against the unfaithful. A new representation of martyrdom was also formulated. A picture of a martyr no longer merely illustrated a legend but portrayed instead the real-life sufferings of men and women—complete with realistic detail such as blood and portrayal of torture. The disgusting faces of the torturers are always in stark contrast to the dignity of their victims. Despite their sufferings, most martyrs are represented in idealized form as being of great beauty and heroism; pain suffered for the sake of the Church was pleasure.

We cannot consider here all the categories and forms of art that came under the supervision of the Church; all we can do is to point out that the Council of Trent concerned itself also with music, especially the role of music in religious services. The episcopal duties included supervising music from educational aspects.

But the Church did not assume all this subtle and sophisticated control immediately after the Council of Trent. It was to take almost fifty years before the principles of art in the service of the Church were established and widely accepted. Another fifty years were to pass before art became the instrument of the Church in the Catholic states.

Emperor Charles V had used a variety of means and expended much effort in seeking to break the Reformation in Germany, yet all his political and military actions failed. He regretted the fact that the Inquisition could no longer exercise its power in the empire, and that Luther could not be burned to end the nightmare. As Spanish ruler, he was able to assess the exact value to him of the Spanish *Suprema*. Pope Paul III was undoubtedly thinking along the same lines when, in 1542, he revived the Roman Inquisition on a slightly different basis. Certainly he, too, bemoaned the fact that in the wake of the political ambitions of the Renaissance papacy, the Church had allowed the Inquisition to take a more background role.

Nostalgia for the activities of the Inquisition was justified on both sides. History shows that the courts of Inquisition had served both monarchy and Church well since the 13th century in stamping out the Cathari, the Waldenses and other overt or covert sects and in burning many heretics, famous and obscure. But

would it be possible to repeat the success at the beginning of the 16th century? At that time relations between Church and State had undergone a fundamental change, as had also the role of the Church in the individual states. In the changing feudal society, heretical teachings were increasingly becoming the expression of interests of new groups and classes—the middle classes, the knights or magnates—and their interaction. Moreover, each new heresy was likewise an expression of resistance to the existing feudal system. The same is true of the Reformation, which already had the support of large and powerful social groups that it used to draw up its political programs. Neither the Church itself nor any of its institutions was able to put up an effective resistance to the advance of the Reformation, lacking both adequate power and the necessary resources. Paradoxical as it may sound, even true Catholic rulers resorted to controlling the property of the Church in order to enforce state interests, and it is no coincidence that the view that heresies posed a threat to the State,

Cesare Ripa designed allegories in such a way in his highly popular handbook of iconology that they bore characteristic traits of Counter-Reformation concepts. The ugly allegory of "Heresia" was not, however, included until later editions of the work in the 17th century.

H E R E S I A.

103 This painting by Frans Floris shows the
"Last Judgment" as a response to the famous
work by Michelangelo.
Kunsthistorisches Museum, Vienna.

104/105 The fate of the human soul after death was reflected in many ways in art —here as an individualistic juxtaposition of a lost soul and a redeemed one. Busts by Giovanni Lorenzo Bernini in the Chiesa di S. Maria di Montserrat, Rome.

106 The Virgin Mary played a special role in the struggle against heretical teachings. In the famous painting "Madonna delle Palafrenieri" by Michelangelo da Caravaggio (Galleria Borghese in Rome) the head of the serpent—a symbol of heresy—is crushed by Mary and the Christ child.

107/108 Two examples of the renewed cult of Mary at the time of the Counter-Reformation: Federico Barocci, "La Madonna del Popolo." Galleria degli Uffizi, Florence; Bartolomé Esteban Murillo, "Immaculada." Prado, Madrid.

109 "Guardian angels praying to Christ and the Mother of God for the souls in purgatory." Wall painting by Federico Zuccari. Chiesa del Gesù, Rome.

Page 235:
110 "Saint Dominic."
Painting by Titian. Villa Borghese, Rome.

Following double page:
111 "The Last Supper." Painting by Jacopo Tintoretto.
Chiesa di S. Giorgio Maggiore, Venice.

112 "The Last Supper." Painting by Bonifacio Veronese.
Galleria dell'Accademia, Venice.

113 The motif of the Last Supper aroused the interest of many painters—Catholics and non-Catholics alike. Lucas Cranach the Younger depicted all the reformers in his version.
Village church near Dessau.

114 Mary Magdalene is one of the most popular saints of the early times of Christianity, especially as a symbol of the conversion of sinners. Painting by Jusepe de Ribera.
Prado, Madrid.

115 The famous painting "St. Theresa in Ecstasy" by Giovanni Lorenzo Bernini in the Church of S. Maria della Vittoria in Rome is one of the works of art commemorating saints who were canonized in the time of the Counter-Reformation.

116 It was hoped that miracles would help to revive the worship of saints. A well-preserved corpse found in Trastevere at the end of the 16th century was held to be St. Cecilia. She is commemorated in Maderna's sculpture in the Chiesa di S. Cecilia in Rome.

Page 241:
117 Bernini also participated in the struggle against heresy by creating for the altar of Saint Ignatius of Loyola in the Jesuit church Il Gesù an allegory of the victory of true faith over heresy.

Following double page:
118 On the ceiling of the nave of the Church of S. Maria della Vittoria in Rome, Giovanni Domenico Cerrini portrayed the triumph of Mary over the heretics. The painting has a motto: "Tu sola omnes haereses intermisti."

119 The painting by Andrea Pozzo, an impressive illustration of the "Acceptance of St. Ignatius into Paradise," adorns the ceiling of the church dedicated to the saint in Rome. On the edges the falling figures of the conquered heretics are depicted.

120 The teachings on purgatory were refuted by the Protestants and therefore were one of the most hotly contested points of faith at the time of the Counter-Reformation. Even before the Reformation, the teachings frequently had to be defended. "The angels free redeemed souls from purgatory." Illumination from a Netherlandish prayer book of the 15th century. Formerly Deutsche Staatsbibliothek, Berlin (West).

121 An initial with an illustration of purgatory. Detail from a page in an illuminated manuscript of the Missale Ms. A III. Christian-Weise-Bibliothek, Zittau.

122 Peter Paul Rubens celebrated the "Triumph of the Eucharist" in a series of tapestries bearing that title. One of the works shows the conquered heretics: one is under the wheels of the triumphal chariot, another is blinded by the shining light of the golden monstrance.
Prado, Madrid.

123 Another tapestry from the same series shows the triumph of the love of God, symbolized by the figure of the Madonna. Prado, Madrid.

966

124 Even before the Reformation, processions were major occasions for stately pomp and national festivities. A procession on the Piazza San Marco in Venice on the feast of Corpus Christi was painted by Gentile Bellini.
Galleria dell' Accademia, Venice.

DEMOCRATIA.

Significantly, the artist of the allegory of "Democratia" and "Heresia" has given democracy the same attributes as heresy—the serpent and the apple.

necessitating religious unity, was gaining currency. So it was that the State—represented by its ruler—had a keen interest in eliminating heresy. In many cases, these people even worked towards reviving or strengthening the Inquisition, as, for example, in France, in the Netherlands at the time of Charles V and in the Italian states. The Inquisition acquired a new status in the power structures of the State, depending directly on it rather than being a mere tool of it. In theory, the State also set the boundaries for the Inquisition's sphere of operation. The Spanish Inquisition, whose inception had been dictated not by the struggle against the Reformation but by the fight against unorthodoxy, and which served the expansive ambitions of the Spanish kingdom, also fell into this category. This did not change the fact, however, that the Spanish *Suprema* later proved to be an effective barrier to the advance of the Reformation in Spain. This struggle was led directly by the king, and Philip II must take most of the credit for using—and misusing—the Inquisition for his own political ends and making it dependent of the State's insti-

tutions, without allowing intervention from Rome to influence his conception of the Spanish function of the courts. This special status—which remained outside Rome's control—eventually brought about a situation where, in the following centuries, the Inquisition in Spain was able to escape the control of the State and was also able on more than one occasion to oppose not only the pope but also the wishes of the ruler.

In some regions of Catholic Europe, the courts of Inquisition were revived in varying forms and at different levels of power. The question remains, however, of why attempts after the Council of Trent to extend their work to the regions north of the Alps and the Pyrenees were unsuccessful. The only clue lies in the national traditions of the Spaniards and Italians. Certainly the resistance of civilized people in central Europe to the drastic methods of the Inquisition is not the only explanation. The Inquisition methods and witches' trials particularly in Germany were no less cruel—the Reformation as well as the Counter-Reformation knew how to carry out burnings of ideological opponents.

"Fallacy" is not nearly so repugnant as "Sin." To err was considered human, but not persistent and deliberate fallacy.

It was always possible to convert to the true Catholic faith and was so earnestly desired that "Conversion" was included here among the positive allegories.

The reasons for the failure of the Inquisitions are to be found in the social situation. The Reformation was not limited to certain groups or to educated individuals and critics of contemporary events, but it also enjoyed a mass base among the peasants. In many countries the non-Catholics did not hide but publicly acknowledged the new religion. Groups of the lower classes protected by the political interests of the higher classes even formed military defense organizations—the Calvinists in Poland and France and the Lutherans in the empire. The State Inquisition in pre-Tridentine times as, for example, in France and in the Netherlands, had not needed to spy these out; on the contrary, it strengthened the opposition and provoked it to open revolt.

It should also be borne in mind that in the majority of countries north of the Alps there was no mass persecution of unorthodox believers as, for example, of the Muslims and Jews in Spain. The argument that frequent changes in beliefs or insufficient demarcation allowed a certain religious uncertainty or even indifference to arise was justified up to a point. During visitations in those countries, it was invariably the case that not only many lay people but also clergy were not sure of the rites and procedures to be followed. In areas where the victorious Catholic states oppressed the non-Catholic population for political reasons, its methods of religious control and persecution differed little from those of the Inquisition, even though the Inquisition as an institution did not exist. Finally, the Church itself had not been keen to secure the existence of the courts and their constitution, precisely for political reasons.

There could be no suggestion either that the same methods could be used everywhere. Religious persecu-

tion in the lands of the Bohemian Crown and in the Upper Palatinate was complex, with the military repressing political resistance stamped with religious ideology. Yet at this time the Church was able to offer the Catholic states more established methods, which were as reliable, yet less provocative, as those of the Inquisition, and included visitation, censorship and control of education. The methods were definitely more effective and, as it subsequently proved, very successful, although they certainly owed their success to neither the perception and innovation of the church dignitaries at Trent nor the fanaticism typified by Pius V. Instead, they simply used the progress being made in means of communication, and state administration and the generally better level of education. These, together with further progress in the cultural sphere, were for their part a reflection of major social and economic change that in turn mirrored the complex problems of the Reformation.

It is striking that the struggle against heresy, manifested in the Inquisition or other institutions, was at its most powerful at a time when social intercourse and social mobility were both on the increase—people traveled more frequently, especially to the towns where there were opportunities for social advancement. This was a de-stabilizing factor and created the necessary conditions for damage to be done to the ideological unity of the State. Greater vigilance and sharp reactions were needed to any threat of destruction of religious unity—not only in Spain when foreign continents were discovered but also in England when arable land was turned into pastures for sheep breeding and thousands of tenant farmers were expropriated and flooded the towns. The elimination of heresy and the creation of one single religion became one

PECCATO.

TOLERANZA.

of the most important instruments of the absolutist State, regardless of whether it was based on reactionary magnates or a progressive bourgeoisie.

The Inquisition, that particularly brutal court to which we have devoted most of our attention, was, however, only one of the methods used by the State to seek unity of religious belief. Its role within the framework of the Counter-Reformation can be seen from various angles: the structure of the objectives pursued by the State and the Church; the means used to achieve those objectives; the extent to which heresy was stamped out and religious unity achieved; and, in a broader sense, the effects on the development in individual regions.

Although we would categorize the Inquisition as part of the panoply of methods used during the Counter-Reformation—and not one of its most effective ones—its horror is not to be excused nor is its significance for social awareness and religious beliefs to be underestimated. The Inquisition inspired fear and terror in people even at a time when it had already lost its real political effectiveness, and it will remain forever a symbol of ideological repression and intolerance.

"Sin," one of the negative allegorical figures, is represented as the impure heart being eaten by snakes.

"Tolerance" found no sympathy in the renewed Church. The commentary reads: "I serve insignificant interests."

APPENDIX

General History		Religious and Ecclesiastical History		Cultural History	
					1200
		1198–1216	Pope Innocent III		
				1203	Wolfram von Eschenbach, *Perceval*
1206	Peter Waldo died				
1212–1250	Emperor Frederick II	1215	Fourth Lateran Council		
		1216–1260	Dominican Order founded		
				1222–1224	*Sachsenspiegel* (Saxon Mirror)
1226–1270	Louis IX, king of France	1226	Francis of Assisi, founder of the Minorites, died		
		1227–1241	Pope Gregory IX		
				1228–1253	Assisi Cathedral built
1229	Successful completion of the crusades against heretics in southern France				
				1230–1298	Jacobus de Voragine, *Legenda aurea*
1237–1240	Mongol invasion of central Europe				
		1243–1254	Pope Innocent IV		
				1260	Niccolò Pisano, chancel for the Pisa Baptistery
1263–1265	English Civil War				
		1274	Thomas Aquinas died		
1285–1314	Philip IV, le Bel, king of France				
					1300
		1305–1314	Pope Clement V		
		1309	Papacy brought to Avignon		
		1311–1312	Vienne Council		
		1312	Order of the Knights Templars dissolved, Inquisition trials	1312–1314	Dante Alighieri, *Divina Commedia*, Part 1
				1324	Marsilius of Padua, *Defensor Pacis*
1337	Hundred Years' War began				
		1342–1352	Pope Clement VI		

General History	Religious and Ecclesiastical History	Cultural History
1346–1378 Emperor Charles IV		
		1353 Giovanni Boccaccio's *Decameron* completed
1356 Battle of Poitiers		
		1374 Francesco Petrarch died
	1384 John Wycliffe died	

1400

General History	Religious and Ecclesiastical History	Cultural History
		1400 Geoffrey Chaucer died
	1414–1418 Council of Constance	
	1415 John Hus burned as a heretic	
1419–1434 Hussite movement		
		1420 Filippo Brunelleschi started the dome of Florence Cathedral
1428–1429 Siege of Orléans by the English		
	1431 Joan of Arc burned as a heretic	
	1431–1449 Councils in Basle, Ferrara and Florence	
		c. 1450 invention of book printing by Johannes Gutenberg
1453 Turks conquer Constantinople		
1455–1485 English Civil War		
		1464 Academy of Florence founded by Cosimo Medici
1479 Union of Castile with Aragon		1473–1481 Sistine Chapel built
	1483 Martin Luther born	
1492 Conquest of Granada		
	1498 Girolamo Savonarola burned in Florence	

1500

General History	Religious and Ecclesiastical History	Cultural History
	1503–1513 Pope Julius II	1503 Leonardo da Vinci, "Mona Lisa"
	1512–1517 Fifth Lateran Council	
	1513–1521 Pope Leo X	
1515 Battle of Marignano		
		1516 Thomas More, *Utopia*
	1517 Luther's theses, Wittenberg	

General History		Religious and Ecclesiastical History		Cultural History	
1519	Charles V elected emperor			1520	Raphael died
		1523–1534	Pope Clement VII		
1524–1526	Great German Peasant War				
1526	Battle of Mohács				
1527	*Sacco di Roma*	1527	Reformation in Sweden		
		1530	*Confessio Augustana*	1530	Georgius Agricola, *De re metallica*
1531	Schmalkaldic League	1534–1549	Pope Paul III		
		1534	Reformation in England	1534	François Rabelais *Gargantua*
				1536–1541	Michelangelo, "The Last Judgment"
1538	Armistice of Nice	1540	Jesuit Order approved by the pope		
		1542	Re-establishment of the papal Inquisition		
		1545	Council of Trent opened	1543	Nicolaus Copernicus, *De revolutionibus orbium coelestium*
1546/47	Schmalkaldic War	1551–1553	Second session of the Council of Trent		
1553–1558	Mary Tudor, queen of England	1553	Miguel Servet executed as a heretic in Geneva		
		1555	Peace of Augsburg		
		1555–1559	Pope Paul IV		
1556–1598	Philip II, king of Spain				
		1559–1565	Pope Pius IV	1559–1574	Matthias Flacius *Magdeburger Centurion*
1562	Start of the Huguenot Wars in France	1562–1564	Third session of the Council of Trent		
1566	Iconoclasm in the Netherlands	1566–1572	Pope Pius V		
1572	St. Bartholomew's Day Massacre, Paris	1572–1585	Pope Gregory XIII	1568	Church Il Gesù started in Rome

General History		Religious and Ecclesiastical History		Cultural History	
1572	Start of the revolution in the Netherlands				
		1573	Collegium Germanicum founded		
1576–1611	Emperor Rudolph II				
1579	Union of Utrecht				
				1582	Gregorian calendar introduced
		1585–1590	Pope Sixtus V	1585	William Shakespeare in London
1588	Defeat of the Spanish Armada				
1589–1610	King Henry IV	1592–1605	Pope Clement VIII		
		1592	Definitive version of the *Vulgate*	1592	Michel de Montaigne died
1593	Huguenot Wars in France ended				
1598	Edict of Nantes	1597	Pater Canisius died		

1600

General History		Religious and Ecclesiastical History		Cultural History	
				1602	Tommaso Campanella, *Civitas Solis* (printed in 1620)
1603	Queen Elizabeth I of England died	1603	Jesuits recalled to France; Counter-Reformation in Lower Austria		
		1605–1621	Pope Paul V		
1608	Protestant Union founded			1608	Peter Paul Rubens founded workshop in Antwerp
1610	Henry IV murdered				
1618–1648	Thirty Years' War				
		1623–1644	Pope Urban VIII		
		1627	Collegium de Propaganda Fide founded		
				1632	Galileo Galilei, *Dialogo sopra i due massimi sistemi del mondo*
1640	Start of the bourgeois revolution in England				

General Literature

CHAUNU, P.: *Eglise, culture et société. Essais sur la Réforme et Contre-Réforme (1517–1620)*, Paris, 1981.

DELUMEAU, J.: *Le catholicisme entre Luther et Voltaire*, Paris, 1971.

DELUMEAU, J.: *Naissance et affirmation de la Réforme* (N.C. 30), 3rd edition, Paris, 1973.

DICKENS, A.G.: *The Counter-Reformation*, London, 1968.

DROYSEN, G.: *Geschichte der Gegenreformation*, Berlin, 1893.

EDER, K.: *Geschichte der Kirche im Zeitalter des konfessionellen Absolutismus (1555–1618)*, Vienna, 1949.

Enciclopedia cattolica, Vol. 12, Vatican City, 1948–1954.

EVENETT, H.O.: *The Spirit of the Counter-Reformation*, Cambridge, 1968.

GRIGULEVIČ, J.R.: *Ketzer—Hexen—Inquisitoren (13.–20. Jahrhundert)*, Vols. 1 and 2, Berlin, 1976.

Histoire de l'Eglise depuis les origines jusqu'à nos jours, Vol. XIV, 1, 2, 1962, 1964.

Lexikon für Theologie und Kirche, 11 Vols., Freiburg i. Br., 1957–1967.

LUTZ, H.: *Reformation und Gegenreformation*, Munich, 1979.

PASTOR, L.: *Allgemeine Dekrete der Römischen Inquisition aus den Jahren 1555–1597*, Freiburg i. Br., 1912.

PASTOR, L.: *Geschichte der Päpste seit dem Ausgang des Mittelalters*, Vols. II–XIII, Freiburg i. Br., 1889–1928.

SCHMIDT, K.D.: *Die katholische Reform und die Gegenreformation*, Göttingen, 1975.

SCHOONJANS, J.: *L'inquisition*, Brussels, 1932.

TREVOR-ROPER, H.R.: *De la Réforme aux Lumières*, Paris, 1972.

VACANDARD, E.: *L'inquisition. Etude historique et critique sur le pouvoir coercitif de l'église*, Paris, 1907.

VEKENÉ, E. VAN DER: *Bibliographie der Inquisition. Ein Versuch*, Hildesheim, 1963.

The Roots of the Medieval Inquisition

BALLESTEROS GAIBROIS, M.: *La obra de Isabel la Católica*, Segovia, 1953.

BENNASSAR, B.: *L'inquisition espagnole (XVe–XIXe siècle)*, Paris, 1979.

BORST, A.: *Die Katharer*, Stuttgart, 1953.

LE BRAS, G.: *Les institutions de la chrétienté médiévale*, Vol. 2, Paris, 1959.

CEDILLO VON: *El Cardenal Cisneros*, Vol. 3, Madrid, 1921.

FICKER, J.: *Die gesetzliche Einführung der Todesstrafe für Ketzerei*, MIÖG, 1, 1980.

GRUNDMANN, H.: *Ketzergeschichte des Mittelalters*, Göttingen, 1963.

GUENÉE, B.: *L'Occident aux XIVe et XVe siècles. Les Etats* (N.C. 22), Paris, 1971.

HAVET, J.: *L'Hérésie et le bras séculier au moyen age jusqu'au XIIIe siècle* (Bibliothèque de l'Ecole des Chartes), Paris, 1880.

HINSCHIUS, P.: *Das Kirchenrecht der Katholiken und Protestanten*, Vols. 5 and 6, Berlin, 1895–1897.

JEDIN, H.: *Kleine Konziliengeschichte*, Freiburg i. Br., 1959.

LEA, H.C.: *Geschichte der Inquisition im Mittelalter*, Vols. 1–3, Bonn, 1905–1913.

LEA, H.C.: *Geschichte der Spanischen Inquisition*, Vols. 1–3, Leipzig, 1911–1912.

LLORENTE, DON J.A.: *Kritische Geschichte der spanischen Inquisition*, Vol. 1, Gmünd, 1819.

LOGAN, D.F.: *Excommunication and the Secular Arm in Medieval England*, Toronto, 1968.

LUCKA, E.: *Torquemada und die spanische Inquisition*, Vienna and Leipzig, 1926.

MÂLE, E.: *L'art religieux de la fin du Moyen Age*, 4th edition, Paris, 1931.

PATSCHOVSKY, A.: "Die Anfänge einer ständigen Inquisition in Böhmen. Ein Prager Inquisitoren-Handburch aus der ersten Hälfte des 14. Jh." In: *Beiträge zur Geschichte und Quellenkunde des Mittelalters*, Berlin (West) and New York, 1975.

PATSCHOVSKY, A.: *Quellen zur böhmischen Inquisition im 14. Jh.*, Weimar, 1979.

PATSCHOVSKY, A.: "Zur Ketzerverfolgung Konrads von Marburg." In: *Deutsches Archiv für Erforschung des Mittelalters*, Annual Set 37, No. 2, 1981.

RAPP, F.: *L'église et la vie religieuse en Occident à la fin du Moyen Age* (N.C. 25), Paris, 1971.

The Papal Inquisition on the Threshold of a New Era

"Autobiografia di Monsignor G. Antonio Santori, Cardinale de St. Severino." Edited by G. Cugnoni, in: *Archivio della Reale Soc. Romana di Storia Patria* XII, 1889, pp. 327ff.

BERTOLOTTI, A.: Martiri del libero pensiero e vittime della santa Inquisizione nei secoli XVI, XVII e XVIII, Rome, 1891.

CANTIMORI, D.: *Italienische Häretiker der Spätrenaissance*, Basle, 1949.

CANTÙ, A.: *Gli eretici d'Italia*, Vols. 1–3, Turin, 1864–1866.

CAPASSO, C.: *Paolo III*, Messina, 1924.

CARROCCI, G.: *Lo stato della Chiesa nella seconda meta del secolo XVI*, Milane, 1961.

CONSTANT, G.: *La légation du cardinal Morone près l'Empereur et le concile de Trente*, Paris, 1922.

DOSTÁLOVÁ-JENIŠTOVÁ, R.: "Jakob Palaeologus." In: *Byzantinische Beiträge*, Berlin, 1964, pp. 153ff.

FEVRE, L.: *Au cœur religieux du XVIe siècle*, Paris, 1957.

JEDIN, H.: *Gerolamo Seripando. Sein Leben und Denken im Geisteskampf des 16. Jh.*, Vols. I and II, Würzburg, 1937.

JEDIN, H.: *Geschichte des Konzils von Trient*, Vols. 1–4, Freiburg i. Br., Basle and Vienna, 1949–1975.

JEDIN, H.: *Katholische Reformation oder Gegenreformation?* Lucerne, 1946.

JEDIN, H.: *Krisis und Abschluss des Trienter Konzils 1562/63*, Freiburg i. Br., 1964.

JEDIN, H.: *Krisis und Wendepunkt des Trienter Konzils 1562/63*, Würzburg, 1941.

KAVKA, F., and A. SKÝBOVÁ: *Husitský epilog na koncilu tridentském a původní koncepce habsburské rekatolizace Čech*, Prague, 1969.

LAPAYRE, H.: *Les monarchies européennes du XVIe siècle. Les relations internationales* (N. C. 31), Paris, 1973.

La riforma cattolica. Documenti e testimonianze. Edited by M. Marocchi, with an Introduction by M. Bendiscioli, Brescia, 1967.

L'eta della controriforma in Italia (a cura di Maria Antonucci), Rome, 1974.

Lettres de Pie V sur les affaires religieuses de son temps, Paris, 1826.

LUTZ, G.: *Kardinal Giovanni Francesco Guidi di Bagno. Politik und Religion im Zeitalter Richelieus und Urbans VIII*, Tübingen, 1971.

LUTZ, G.: "Rom und Europa während des Pontifikats Urbans VIII." In: *Rom in der Neuzeit*, Vienna 1976, pp. 72ff.

LUTZ, H.: "Italien vom Frieden von Lodi bis zum Spanischen Erbfolgekrieg (1454–1700)." In: *Handbuch der europäischen Geschichte*, Vol. 3, Stuttgart, 1971.

MECENSEFFY, G.: *Geschichte des Protestantismus in Österreich*, Graz and Cologne, 1956.

MERCATI, A.: "I costituti di Niccolò Franco (1568–1570) dinanzi l'Inquisizione di Roma essenti nel Archivo Segreto Vaticano." In: *Studi e testi*, 178, Vatican City, 1955.

MERCATI, A.: "Il sommario del processo di Giardano Bruno." In: *Studie e testi*, 101, Vatican City, 1942.

MOUSNIER, R.: *Le XVIe siècle. Les progrès de la civilisation européenne et le déclin de l'Orient*, 3rd edition, Paris, 1961.

PASTOR, L.: "Allgemeine Dekrete der römischen Inquisition 1555–1597." In: *Historisches Jahrbuch der Görres-Gesellschaft*, 3, 1912.

RANKE, L.: *Die römischen Päpste in den letzten vier Jahrhunderten*, Vol. 3, revised edition, Cologne, 1957.

Reformation, katholische Reform und Gegenreformation. Handbuch der Kirchengeschichte, Vol. 4, Freiburg i. Br., Basle and Vienna, 1967.

REPGEN, K.: *Die römische Kurie und der Westfälische Friede. Idee und Wirklichkeit des Papsttums im 16. und 17. Jahrhundert*, Vols. 1 and 2, Tübingen, 1962, 1965.

RILL, G.: "Jacobus Palaeologus (1520–1585). Ein Antitrinitarier als Schützling der Habsburger." In: *Mitteilungen des Österreichischen Staatsarchivs*, 16, 1963, pp. 28ff.

ROŽICYN, V. I.: "Protokoly processsa Džordano Bruno v venecianskoj inkvizicii." In: *Voprosy istorii religii i ateizma*, 1, 1950, pp. 325ff.

SIECKEL, T.: *Das Reformations-Libel des Kaisers Ferdinand I. vom Jahre 1562 bis zur Absendung nach Trient*, AÖG, XLV, 1971.

ŠUSTA, J.: *Pius IV. před pontifikátem a na počátku pontifikátu*, Prague, 1900.

SZCZUCKI, L.: *W kregu mýslicieli heretyckich*, Ossolineum, 1972.

ZEEDEN, E. W.: *Das Zeitalter der Gegenreformation*, Freiburg i. Br., Basle and Vienna, 1967.

The Inquisition as an Instrument of the Spanish State

BENNASSAR, B.: *L'inquisition espagnole aux XVIe–XVIIe siècles*, Paris, 1979.

CHAUNU, P.: "Inquisition et vie quotidienne dans l'Amérique espagnole au XVIIe siècle." In: *Annales ESC* XI, 1956, pp. 229ff.

FORT, E.: *Catalunya i la Inquisició*, Barcelona, 1973.

GARCÍA CARCEL, R.: *Herejia y sociedad en el siglo XVI: La Inquisición en Valencia 1530–1609*, Barcelona, 1980.

HINSCHIUS, P.: "Die Anweisungen für die spanische

Inquisition vom Jahre *1561.*" In: *Deutsche Zeitschrift für Kirchenrecht*, Series 3, Vol. VII, *1897*, pp. 76ff. and 203ff.

KAMEN, H.: *Die spanische Inquisition*, Munich, *1967*.

LEA, H.C.: *Geschichte der spanischen Inquisition*, Vols. *1–3*, Leipzig, *1911/12*.

LEA, H.C.: *The Inquisition in the Spanish Dependencies*, London, *1908*.

LLORCA, B.: *Die spanische Inquisition und die "Alumbrados" (1509–1667)*, no place, *1934*.

LLORENTE, J.A.: *Kritische Geschichte der spanischen Inquisition, von ihrer Einführung durch Ferdinand V.*

an bis zur Regierung Ferdinands VII., Vols. I–IV, Gmünd, *1820–1822*.

ROTH, C.: *A History of the Marranos*, Philadelphia, *1932*.

SCHÄFER, E.: *Beiträge zur Geschichte des spanischen Protestantismus und der Inquisition des 16. Jahrhunderts*, Vols. *1–3*, Gütersloh, *1902*.

TELLECHEA, I.: *Aspectos económicos del proceso de Carranza 1567/68)* Príncipe, Vienna, *1972*, Nos. 128, 129, pp. 193ff.

TURBEVILLE, A.S.: *The Spanish Inquisition*, London, *1932*.

The Move to a Denominationalized Society

BAUMER, J.: "Wallfahrt als Handlungsspiel." In: *Europäische Hochschulschriften*, Series 19, A, Vol. 12, Frankfurt/Main, *1977*.

BAUMGARTEN, P.M.: "Ordenszucht und Ordensstrafrecht." In: *Beiträge zur Geschichte der Gesellschaft Jesu, insbesondere in Spanien*, Munich *1932*.

BECKER-HUBERTI, M.: *Die tridentinische Reform im Bistum Münster unter Fürstbischof Christoph Bernhard von Galen 1650–1678*, Münster, *1978*.

BELLESHEIM, A.: *Geschichte der katholischen Kirche in Irland von der Einführung des Christenthums bis auf die Gegenwart*, Vol. 2, Mainz, *1890*.

BELLINGER, G.: *Der Catechismus Romanus und die Reformation*, Paderborn, *1970*.

BOSSY, J.A.: *The Counter-Reformation and the People of Catholic Europe. Past and Present*, *1970*, pp. 51–70.

BOSSY, J.A.: *The Social History of Confession in the Age of Reformation. Transactions of the Royal Historical Society*, 5th Series, XXV, pp. 21–38.

BRIZZI, G.P., A.D.'ALESSANDRO and A.DEL FANTE: *Università, Príncipe, Gesuiti*, Rome, *1980*.

BROU, L.: *Marie "destructrice de toutes les hérésies" et la belle légende du répons Gaude Maria Virgo. Ephemerides liturgicae*, 62, *1948*.

BUSCHBELL, G.: *Selbstbezeugungen des Kardinals Bellarmin*, no place, *1924*.

CLAESSENS, C.: *L'inquisition et le régime pénal pour la répression de l'hérésie dans les Pays-Bas du passé*, Turnhout, *1886*.

DEROO, A.: *Saint Charles Borromée*, Paris, *1963*.

FAUREY, J.: *L'Edit de Nantes et la question de la tolérance*, no place, *1929*.

GINNES, M.: "Preaching Ideal and Practice in Counter-Reformation Rome." In: *Sixteenth Century Journal*, 11, *1980*, pp. 109–127.

GOTHEIN, E.: *Staat und Gesellschaft im Zeitalter der Gegenreformation*, Berlin and Leipzig, *1908*.

HENGST, K.: *Jesuiten an Universitäten und Jesuitenuniversitäten*, Paderborn, Munich, Vienna and Zurich, *1981*.

HOFFINGER, J.: *Geschichte des Kathechismus in Öster-

reich von Canisius bis zur Gegenwart*, Innsbruck, *1937*.

JEDIN, H., and P.BROUTIN: *L'Eveque dans la tradition pastorale du XVIᵉ siècle*, Mechelen, *1953*.

Katholische Kontroverstheologen. Edited by W.Klaiber, Münster, *1978*.

KRASENBRINCK, J.: *Die Congregatio Germanica und die katholische Reform in Deutschland nach dem Tridentinum*, Münster, *1972*.

LEA, H.C.: *A History of Auricular Confession and Indulgences in the Latin Church*, Vols. *1–3*, Philadelphia and London, *1896*.

LÉONARD, E.G.: *Histoire générale du protestantisme*, Vol. II, Paris, *1958*.

LUTZ, H.: *Ragione di Stato und christliche Staatsethik im 16. Jahrhundert*, Münster, *1961*.

MILWARD, P.: *Religious Controversies of the Elizabethan Age. A Survey of Printed Sources*, Lincoln and London, *1977*.

MONTER, E.W.: "Crime and Punishment in Calvin's Geneva, *1562*." In: *Archiv für Reformationsgeschichte*, 64, *1973*, pp. 281ff.

Nuntiaturberichte und Nuntiaturforschung (Kritische Bestandsaufnahme und neue Perspektiven). Edited by G.Lutz and R.Elze, Rome, *1976*.

PRESS, V.: *Calvinismus und Territorialstaat*, Stuttgart, *1970*.

REINHARD, W.: "Gegenreformation als Modernisierung?" In: *Archiv für Reformationsgeschichte*, 68, *1977*, pp. 226ff.

RUSCONI, R.: *Predicazione e vita religiosa nella società italiana da Carlo Magno alla Controriforma*, Turin, *1981*.

SCHELLHASS, K.: "Akten über Reformtätigkeit Felician Ninguardas in Bayern und Österreich *1572–1577*." In: *Quellen und Forschungen aus den italienischen Archiven und Bibliotheken*, Vols. I–V, *1899–1903*.

VILLOSLA, G.R.: *Storia del Collegio Romano dal suo inizio alla soppressione della Compagnìa di Gesù (1773)*, Univers. Gregoriana, *1956*.

"Visitation im Dienst der kirchlichen Reform." In:

Katholisches Leben und Kirchenreform, edited by E. Zeeden and H. Molitor, Vols. 25 and 26, Münster, 1967.

WIEKI, J.: "Das heilige Jahr 1575 in den zeitgenössischen Berichten der Jesuiten." In: *Archivum histo-riae pontif.*, XIII, 1975, pp. 283–310.

WRIGHT, A.D.: *Federico Borromeo and Baronius: Turning Point in the Development of the Counter-Reformation Church*, Reading Univ. Occ. Paper 6, 1974.

Index Librorum Prohibitorum

LE FEBVRE-MARTIN, H.J.: *L'apparition du livre*, Paris, 1950.

GRUNDLER, F.: *The Roman Inquisition and the Venetian Press 1540–1605*, Princeton (New Jersey), 1977.

KADLEC, J.: "Die Bibel im mittelalterlichen Böhmen." In: *Archives d'histoire doctrinale et littéraire du Moyen Age*, no place, 1964.

REUSCH, H.: *Der Index der verbotenen Bücher*, Vol. 2, Bonn, 1883–1885.

SKÝBOVÁ, A.: "Knihovna arcibiskupa Antonína Bruse z Mohelnice." In: *Kniha a knihtisk v Českých zemích od husiství do Bilé Hory*, Prague, 1970.

STEINHERZ, S.: *Briefe des Prager Erzbischofs Anton Brus von Müglitz 1562/63*, Prague 1907.

Art as an Instrument of Catholic Renewal

Kunst und Reformation. Edited by E. Ullmann, Leipzig, 1982.

DE MAIO, R.: *Michelangelo e la controriforma*, Rome, 1981.

MÂLE, E.: *L'art religieux après le Concile de Trente*, Paris, 1932.

MANDROUX, R.: "Le baroque européen: mentalité pathétique et révolution sociale." In: *Annales*, XV, 1960, pp. 898–914.

SCHNÜRER, G.: *Katholische Kirche und Kultur in der Barockzeit*, Paderborn, 1937.

TAPIÉ, V.L.: *Baroque et classicisme*, Paris, 1957.

Trattati d'arte dell' Cinquecento. Edited by Barocchi, Vols. II and III, Bari, 1962.

WATERHOUSE, E.: *Some Painters and the Counter-Reformation before 1600.* Transaction of the Royal Historical Society, XXII, 1972, pp. 103–118.

WEISBACH, W.: *Der Barock als Kunst der Gegenreformation*, Berlin, 1921.

ZERI, F.: *Pittura e Controriforma*, Turin, 1957.

Sources of Illustrations

Alinari, Florence 5, 8, 9, 26, 34, 37, 39–41, 44, 72, 73, 75, 76, 88, 104, 105, 107, 110–112, 115–117

Archiv für Kunst und Geschichte, Berlin (West) pp. 46, 60 above, 146, 204 above, 207, 205 below

Beyer, Klaus G., Weimar 4, 113

Bibliographisches Institut, Leipzig p. 96

Bibliothèque Nationale, Paris 20, 21, 51–53, 97 / pp. 202, 214, 216, 226

British & Foreign Bible Society, London 99

Deutsche Fotothek, Dresden 1, 2, 6, 50, 54, 57, 66, 67, 79, 82, 92, 98, 120, 121 / pp. 44, 47, 58, 99, 101, 115, 127, 129, 135 below, 136, 147

Eulenspiegel Verlag, Berlin p. 53 below

Germanisches Nationalmuseum, Nuremberg pp. 195, 205 above

Giraudon, Paris 3

Istituto Centrale per il Catalogo e la Documentazione, Rome 42, 46, 69, 84, 85, 94, 100, 106, 109, 118 / pp. 53 above, 94

Koninklijke Musea voor Schone Kunsten van Belgie, Brussels 71

Kulturgeschichtliches Museum, Osnabrück p. 161

Kunsthistorisches Museum, Vienna 65, 70, 81, 87, 103

Malter, Barbara, Rome 78 / pp. 89, 92, 93, 194

MAS, Barcelona 7, 22, 24, 25, 30, 32, 58, 59, 61, 62, 108, 114, 122, 123 / pp. 48, 111

Metropolitan Museum of Art, New York 23

Musei Civici, Milan p. 92

Österreichische Nationalbibliothek, Vienna 29

Paul, Alexandr, Prague 10, 13, 16, 18, 19, 35, 47, 56, 60, 63, 64, 68, 74, 90, 101, 102 / pp. 41, 43 above, 45, 53 below, 54, 57 above, 57 below, 59, 60 below, 62, 90, 128 below, 130, 132, 133, 134, 135 above, 139, 140, 148, 150, 151, 152 right, 153, 159, 160, 162, 187, 188, 189, 190, 191 center, 191 left, 196, 197 above, 197 below, 198, 199, 200, 203, 204 below, 206 above, 206 below, 221, 228, 249, 250, 251

Petri, Joachim, Leipzig 17 / p. 193

Photo Meyer, Vienna 77

Savio, Oskar, Rome 28, 38, 43, 48, 80, 83, 86, 89 / pp. 55, 91, 97

Scala Antella, Florence 11, 12, 15, 27, 31, 33, 45, 119, 124

Service de documentation photographique de la Réunion des musées nationaux, Paris 36, 95, 96

Staatliche Museen zu Berlin 93

Stedelijk museum, Amsterdam p. 136 above

Ullstein Bildarchiv, Berlin (West) pp. 115, 128 below, 130

Verlagsarchiv 14, 49 / pp. 42, 43 below, 44, 51 above, 62, 98, 191 left, 212

Wagemüller, Regensburg 91